George Grant Francis

The Smelting of Copper in the Swansea District of South Wales

From the time of Elizabeth to the present day

George Grant Francis

The Smelting of Copper in the Swansea District of South Wales
From the time of Elizabeth to the present day

ISBN/EAN: 9783337322854

Printed in Europe, USA, Canada, Australia, Japan

Cover: Foto ©Andreas Hilbeck / pixelio.de

More available books at **www.hansebooks.com**

THE

SMELTING OF COPPER

IN THE

Swansea District

OF

SOUTH WALES,

FROM

THE TIME OF ELIZABETH

TO

THE PRESENT DAY:

BY

COL. GRANT-FRANCIS, F.S.A,

JUSTICE OF THE PEACE FOR THE COUNTY OF GLAMORGAN,
AND BOROUGH OF SWANSEA;

V. PRESIDENT OF THE ROYAL INSTITUTION OF SOUTH WALES,
CORRESPONDING MEMBER OF THE SOCIETY OF ANTIQUARIES OF SCOTLAND,
AND THE WELSH MSS. SOCIETY,

AUTHOR OF "SWANSEA CHARTERS;" "NEATH AND ITS ABBEY;"
"MEMOIR OF HENRY DE GOWER, BISHOP OF ST. DAVID'S,"
ETC., ETC.

"*Of the entire make of Copper in Great Britain, fully Nine-tenths appear to be smelted in the Swansea District.*"—PHILLIPS.

SECOND EDITION.

Illustrated.

HENRY SOTHERAN & CO.,
LONDON AND MANCHESTER.

1881.

TO

HIS ROYAL HIGHNESS

𝔄lbert 𝔈dward, 𝔓rince of 𝔚ales,

DUKE OF CORNWALL, K.G.,

THIS WORK

(𝔅y 𝔥is 𝔖pecial 𝔓ermission,)

IS HUMBLY DEDICATED

BY HIS OBLIGED AND GRATEFUL SERVANT,

GEORGE GRANT-FRANCIS.

NEW ATHENÆUM CLUB,

PALL MALL EAST,

LONDON, *October,* 1881.

Preface.
—:o:—

THE First Edition of this Work, issued in the year 1867, was limited to a very small impression. It was presented in its entirety to friends and Public Institutions, and was thus exhausted within a week or two of its publication.

The Author continues his History of the Industry through the earlier parts of the present century to our own day, sketching the establishment of individual works, describing their localities and furnishing the names of promoters, partners, and ground landlords, with other information of a like nature.

Here, too, will be found the names of those Nobles, Knights, and others, who joined in starting that grand old Company, the "Mines Royal," in 1580, as well as the strange powers granted by the Crown to those Associations from which such great results sprung and have continued to this time. In addition to those from Elizabeth's reign, charters of the like nature are quoted down to the period of Queen Anne, and most interesting extracts taken from the private day-books and ledgers of those eras are given in elucidation of the text.

An Appendix supplies much matter of cognate interest; *e.g.*, the Copper, brass, and silver coinage of the "Token" period, carefully registered from originals belonging to the Author, and by him presented to the Royal Institution Museum at Swansea.

INTRODUCTION.

The Author having commenced his search in the Public Record Office, found himself rewarded by a mass of evidences from which he has given *verbatim* transcripts of a most valuable character of what he may justly term proofs direct from Queen Elizabeth's Customer, Smythe, and the Founders of this important Industry, of their relations with their Employés, which, he believes, had not before been made public, embracing details of the most interesting nature in a social and mercantile sense, together with much that is extremely curious in reference to the manipulation of mines, furnaces, and the chemistry in practice, during the active reign of that Queen. In these days of disagreement between masters and men, much may be gathered of lively interest from these original letters, illustrative of the confidence with which the employers and workmen then co-operated—"in the trust that the Mynes may prosper, that good greement may exist to set the work forward, whereby they may all have profitt, and the commonwealth be maintained to God's honer."

Evidence is also produced, derived (amongst other sources) from the letters of Mr. Secretary Walsingham, showing how greatly the English of those early days of the trade were indebted to the "Germans," or "Dutch," from their then skilled knowledge in metallurgy.

PREFACE

To the First Edition.

For some years past the early history of the Metal manufactures of this country has received considerable attention from topographers, antiquaries, and metallurgists, and it cannot be denied but that the germ, growth, and final settlement of any great staple trade must be a subject of considerable interest to a numerous class of readers amongst "a nation of shopkeepers"; more especially so to the District in which the particular manufacture has proved a settled success.

When years ago compiling the materials for my "History of Neath and its Abbey," the manufacture of Copper in that locality naturally attracted my serious attention, and I gave to the public in that work such information as I had then obtained; the accounts however were meagre, the result unsatisfactory. Since that period I have never ceased my searching, and when Dr. Percy prepared the first volume of his admirable work on Metallurgy in 1861, I placed at his disposal all the materials I had up to that time accumulated, and much of which may be there perused (vide page 289 *et seq.*) Still the result was unsatisfactory. Carew, the Cornish historian, had left it as a fact that "copper ore was, in the early part of the 17th century, sent into Wales to be refined," and it has been inferred that the art had attained considerable development at or near Neath long prior to its introduction into Swansea. The learned Dr. concludes by saying "It must however be left to future *antiquarian* researches to elicit more precise evidence on this subject than we at present possess."

Little as was certain with respect to the topography of the matter, still less is known of the *modus operandi* by which the process of Copper Smelting was conducted at its first settlement on the great coal-field of the eastern margin of Swansea Bay in the reign of Queen Elizabeth.

The evidences which I have recently discovered in that great repertory of historical lore, the Record Office, will, I venture to submit, be entirely new and of very high interest, and though I have been urged to send them to other channels of general information, I have selected the *Cambrian* not only as the earliest organ of the Copper Trade in this locality, but because it always generously opened its columns to the public for this and other cognate subjects for more than sixty years.

I had long held an opinion that we were greatly indebted to the Germans for our success in Copper Smelting, and so expressed myself when writing on Copper Smoke in August, 1865. I find Dr. Percy has given the same opinion in his Preface.—The following original documents will prove the correctness of those surmises.

The Fifty Copies of the Original Work
WERE, BY THE AUTHOR, PRESENTED TO
THE FOLLOWING GENTLEMEN AND LIBRARIES:

BRITISH MUSEUM LIBRARY, London.
BODLEIAN LIBRARY, Oxford.
BISHOP GORE'S SCHOOL LIBRARY, Swansea.
CHEETHAM'S LIBRARY, Manchester.
ROYAL SOCIETY'S LIBRARY, London.
ROYAL INSTITUTION LIBRARY, Swansea.
THE MUSEUM OF PRACTICAL GEOLOGY, London.
SOCIETY OF ANTIQUARIES' LIBRARY, London.
THE AUTHOR'S LIBRARY, Cae Bailey, Swansea.
THE PUBLIC LIBRARY, Neath.
THE GENERAL LIBRARY, Truro.

BATH AND SON, Mining Office, Swansea.
BIDDULPH, J., Dderwenfawr, Swansea.
BIRD, G. E., Coleridge House, Swansea.
BRUCE, Rt. Hon. H. A., M.P., Duffryn, Aberdare.
BUDD, E., Portland Place, London.

CAMERON, N. P., Mayalls, Swansea.
CHRISTOE, W. H., Poltisko, Truro.

DILLWYN, L. Ll., F.L.S., M.P., Hendrefoilan, Swansea.

EDMOND W., Mines Royal Works, Neath.
ELFORD, T., Copper Ore Wharf, Swansea.

FRANCIS, J. R., Cae Bailey, Swansea.
FRANCIS, G. G., jun., Cae Bailey, Swansea.
FRANCIS, A. W., Kensington, London.
FALCONER, T., County Court Judge, Swansea.

GILBERTSON, W., Pontardawe, Swansea.
GRIFFITHS, T. D., M.D., Dynevor Place, Swansea.
GWYN, H., M.A., M.P., Duffryn House, Neath.

HILL, B., Clydach, Swansea.
HUNT, R., F.R.S., School of Mines, London.

JENKIN, J. T., Miranda, Swansea.
JOHNS, W., Water-street, Neath.
JOSEPH, J., F.S.A., The Bulwark, Brecon.

KEMPTHORNE, J., London Road, Neath.
KNIGHT, Rev. H. H., B.D., Rectory, Neath.

LOGAN, Sir W. E., F.R.S., F.G.S., Montreal, Canada.
LONG, W. H., Surgeon, Swansea.

MICHAEL, W. H., Harrowhill, London.
MINING JOURNAL, London.

NEWTON, KEATS AND CO., St. Helens, Liverpool.

PADDON, J., M.D., The Laurels, Swansea.
PERCY, J., M.D., F.R.S., School of Mines, London.
PHILLIPS, THOMAS, Mayor of Swansea.

REEKES, T., School of Mines, London.
RICHARDS, E. M., Brooklands, Swansea.
RICHARDSON AND Co., Copper Ore Wharves, Swansea.
RICHARDSON, JAMES, Swansea.
ROWLAND, D., Sydenham, London.
ROGERS, P. BURRS, Swansea.

VIVIAN, H. H., F.G.S., M.P., Parkwern, Swansea.

WALTER, JAMES, Uplands, Swansea.
WILLIAMS, H. W., *Cambrian* Office, Swansea.
WILLIAMS, J., Waterloo-street, Swansea.
WILLIAMS, JOSHUA, Aberdyllis, Neath.

Illustrations.

—:0:—

I.—*Swansea and Copper Works, from the Sea.*
  (*Exhibited in the Royal Academy, 1880.*) [*Facing Title Page.*

II.—*The Armorials of H.R.H. Albert Edward, Prince of Wales, on the Plate dedicatory.* iii.

III.—*Customer Smythe, temp. Eliz.* 1

IV.—*The Magnates of the Copper Trade in early part of 19th Century* 35

V.—*Works at Glasmount* 104
  (*By* J. W. M. TURNER, R.A.)

VI.—*The Llangavelach Copper Works*, 1745 .. 106

VII.—*The White-Rock Copper Works, Kilvey*, 1744. 116

VIII.—*View of the Hafod Works, Swansea*, 1881. *Established* 1810.. 136

IX.—*The English and Danish Arms, blended* .. 150

X.—*Tokens of Brass, Copper and Silver, between 1666 and 1813* 161

XI.—*An Autotype of " General Court of the Welch Copper Company, at the Sadlers' Hall, London, in 1722 "* 171

XII.—*The Armorials of H.R.H. Alexandra, Princess of Wales* 172

XIII.—*Swansea Town, Harbour and Bay* .. .. ib.
  (*In the Royal Academy Exhibition, 1880.*)

XIV.—*The Arms of the Port of Swansea* 173

XV.—*Plan of Swansea Port and Bay, with the Ports adjacent, including Docks and Railways, and the neighbouring parts useful by way of reference herein* 175

THO.^{S} SMYTH Esq.^{R}
CHIEF CUSTOMER OF LONDON TO QUEEN ELIZABETH,
AND FOUNDER OF THE COPPER TRADE IN THE SWANSEA DISTRICT,
A.D. 1584.

FROM THE ORIGINAL IN POSSESSION OF HIS DESCENDANT,
THE RIGHT HON. THE LATE VISCOUNT STRANGFORD, P.S.A.

On the Smelting of Copper in South Wales.

I.

Mr. WILLIAM CARNSEWE to Mr. SMYTH.
15 January, 1583.

In te d'nie   in te d'nie.   Emanuell   in   d'nio Confido speram' nos.

I thanke yow for yo'r good int'taynm't and the monyes yow delyveryd me trustynge that yow shall well conceyve that neyther of them is loste thoo it lye a wateign for a time.

Att my retorne from London to my homlye howse, w'ch was the laste of Nove'b, I mett Mr. Weston's lett'rs from Bewlaye the 17 of the same November, but for that I colde nott speke w'th that messenger nor convenyentlye retorne him answer, I have as yow heer see aft'r the steyll of my rude retheryk wryttyn to hym, w'ch I sende yow unsealyd herew'th becawse yow joyn together in suche maner of actyons that yow maye be p'vye to my delynge w'th him as the case dothe requyre, wherby he may the bett'r resolve hemsellfe what farther to doo in the matt'r, and soo sende me suche hys resolutyons as he shall thynke beste in convenye't tyme.

Carew, in this very year 1583, was compiling his "Survey of Cornwall," and he thus speaks of Mr. W. Carnsewe, * "A gentleman of good qualitie, discretion, and learning,

---

* In May 1582, Mr. Carnsewe wrote to Sir Edw. Stradling, then High Sheriff of Glamorgan, and a person of great influence, on behalf of one Richard Vyvyan, of Trenouitthe, Cornwall, who had been at Neath repairing his ship, but had been diversly molested, etc., etc. He also expresses a hope to see Sir Edward at St. Donatt's. It is quite reasonable to suppose that this had some connection with the new Copper works at Neath.—G. G. F., vide Stradling correspondence, p. 271.

and well experienced in those mynerall causes," p. 17. "He was Quarter-Master to the then Ld. Lt.-General of Cornwall, Sir Walter Raleigh, Knight," p. 83.

And at p. 127, he further says —

"Aside from Bodmyn, toward the North Sea, sundry gentlemen have there planted their seats, as in St. Kew, Master Carnsewe at Bo-Kelly," etc. " Carnsewe, rightly Carndeaw, purporteth in Cornish, a black rock ; and such a one the heire owneth, which gave name to his auncient possessed maunsion, as the maunsion of his ancestors. His house, Bo-Kelly, may be derived from *Both* in Cornish, a *Goate* and *Kelly* which is lost; and the Goate he giveth for his armes. This gent's father married the *d.* of Fitz of Devon, and left behind him three sons, Richard, Mathew and William, with two daughters," etc.—G. G. F.

In Vivian and Drake's edition of the "Visitation of Cornwall of 1620," published in 8vo., 1874, there is given at p. 35, a pedigree of Carnsewe, through four generations, beginning with Wm. Carnsewe of St. Kew, in Co. Cornwall, who *m.* Jane, *d.* of Edw. Stradling, of St. Donat's, in Wales. They had two sons, Wm. and Geo., both of St. Kew, from the latter of whom descended Francis Carnsewe, who was baptized the 10 Nov., 1572, and who was living at Thilly, in Cornwall, in 1620. The Carnsewe's bore *Sable*, a goat passant *Or.* p. 303.

Yo'r man my frynde Ulryke, folowyd not myn advyse in all poyntys, w'ch I gave hym beffore I rood towardys London, and therffor he is nott in suche a forwardnys in that worke as I thowghte to have founde hym at my retorne, but he knowythe howe to manage his busynys well ynoghe for all that.

* Memo.—Should another Edition come out, I think it would be better on the whole, that the letters and other information to Secretary Walshingham, dated in 1580-1581, should precede the Carnsewe correspondence. But, for the more easy understanding of the subject at large, it is perhaps *better as it is.*—G. G. F.

Mr. Weston's p'vydence in bryngynge hys * Dutche myners
‡ hether to aplye such busynys in this countrye y's more to be
comendyd then his ignorance of o'r countrymen's actyvytyes
in suche matters, who owte of all p'adventure be as skylfull
in mynyge, as harde and dylygent laborers and as good chepe
workmen in that kynde of travell as are to be founde in Europe ;
wherof to make yow good p'ffe lett the same Mr. Weston's
† Germans have some myn assignyd only to them, and lett
yo'r Ulryke take suche as he is nowe acquayntyd w'th of owr
countrymen, and the sam that wreoght in that worke at
Treworthye laste when it was by Burchardys frowardniss
gyvyn ov'r, w'che was abowte 23 yerys paste (1560), and let it
be consyderyd w'che of them for on hole somers space shall
put yow to moste chargys, and gayne yow moste, and soo of
them that doo lesse yow shall make yo'r estymacyon by p'ffe.

Yo'r Ulryke, as hys dutye ys, wyll advertyse yow what is to
be donne in these matters that nott wythstandynge yow shall
nott be displeasyd w'the me for shewynge yow that it weere
good for yow to ord'r yo'r matters soo, as att the begynny'ge
of M'che nexte suche mynys as yow wyll have to be wroghte
weere sett upon w'the men well orderyd under ther captaynys
and guyders that thaye myghte soo contynew untyll the ende
of Octob'r or Novemb'r at farthyste, and that ther wagys
maye be dulye p'd them att ev'ye monthys ende and such
other necessaryes as roopys, iron, talowe, tymb'r, etc' p'vydyd
in dewe tyme that theye lacke it nott att need, wherby ther
works shall be henderyd, as by Ulrykys experyence it hathe
latlye too well byn p'vyd ; soo shall yow by the exspencis of
one 1000 merks have good intelligence of the valewe both of
owr mynys & men : then maye yow make p'vysyen for
erectynge yo'r Meltynge howsys and woodys for cole & fewell
as the thynge shall requere to have the same in a redynys a
fore hande.

* † Dutch is here used *synonymously* with Germans.
‡ Hither, *i.e.*, Cornwall.

Mr. Smythe, yow muste not over charge yo'r Ulryke, he is subjecte to infyrmytes and disseasys, and verye carfful & dylygent in hys busynys; by ov'r charginge hym yow maye make hym synke under hys burden. I love the man's vertewe, w'che makythe me wryt thys myche unto yow of hym. I shall nev'r recov'r that w'che I have loste by suche ov'r chargynge, therffore I shewe yow that easye labor maye longe indure.

And thus w'th my humble & hartye reco'me'dacyons I doo co'mende bothe yow & yo'rs to the Grace of Allmyghtye Godd. Bokellye in Cornub', this 15 Januarye A'o 1583, an' computatur, by yo'r

WILLM. CARNSEWE.

[Endorsed.]—To my good frend Mr. Cornce.*

II.

MR. THOS. SMYTH TO MR. CARNSEWE.
22 NOVEMBER, 1583.

I am very glad that I have spoken w'th you And also † for the twoe sheets of paper † you delivered me, w'ch for yo'r good advise therein I wilbe readie to pleasure you any way I may or canne. I find that yo'r opinion carrieth knowledge and skill, w'th experience of the things you write of. I doe determine to followe the same for myn owne parte and will deale w'th my Company, to satisfye them accordingly. There is but myselfe and one more in the cittie and therefore I cannot resolve the entringe into those causes. I doe disburse all the money laid out in the meane while. These causes

---

* It is clear that the letter was written to Mr. Smythe; it was probably sent to Mr. Cornce afterwards for perusal. Indeed, he is personally indicated in the last paragraph but one.

† Mr. Carnsewe on the previous page says, he had ridden to London; but though I made diligent search for the "twoe sheets of paper" in the Record Office, I could not find them.—G. O. F.

begonne by Mr. Weston and so I entring into it and others by his cariage delivering us some reasonable reasons for th' entring into that acc'on. I will not forgett to putt him and the rest of owr Company in mynd to deale frendly and kindly with yo'r selfe, Mr. Mohun & Mr. Edgecome, whose company I desier as greatly, as the gaine that shall come thereof.

Mr. Weston writeth me of yo'r kinde dealinge w'th him and also desireth me to pay you xl*li*, or to such as you doe appoynt for the same. Now you beinge here, I will deliver the same unto yo'r selfe, w'th thanks for your pleasuring of him.

£40

I am also yeld you my hartie thanks for the greate favour and frendshipp you have shewed unto my frend and servaunte Ulricke, who I assure you is a verie honest and skilfull man, and one that I doe much credit for his honesty and his trusty and true dealings.

I doe send him by you xl*li*, w'ch I pray you deliver him. I am well assured that Mr. Weston will send him money, for that I have caused a frend of myne to send him twoe hundred pounds in Wales,* parte thereof I am suer he will send to Ulricke.

£40

£200

Thus I end with my hartie comendac'ons to yo'r selfe.
Written the xxijth of November, 1583.

Yo'r lovinge frend,
THOMAS SMYTH.

III.

MR. THOMAS SMYTH TO ULRICK FROSSE.

17 JUNE, 1584.

To my lovinge servante, Ulricke Frosse, overseer of ye mineral woorkes at Perin Sands, &c., in Cornwall.

(Receaved the 21th July, 1584.)

Ulrick, yow shall understande yt Mr. Weston is latelye com

* Probably at Neath.

hether, w'th whome I & ye rest of [my company] have sundry times co'ferred towchinge ye p'ceadings & hoped succes of o'r Cornish mynerals. He putteth us in hope of very greate benefite to arise unto us by ye same, havinge set doune a pamphlet ther'of accordinglye where [he trus]teth (God permittinge) to make better than an h'ndreth tonns waighte of p'fecte copper yerely & the same sett of charges not to stande us in xxv*li* the tonne w'ch is xxvs. the c. weight.

The Partners do greatly like of his [confidential] offers, albeit in very deede I muste stande somwhat doubtfull how the same will fall oute, & yt by sondrye resons, who [managed the] northern mynes* geve us experience at w'ch place I can not lerne was ev'r made in one yere above 1300 of copper . . . but lxv. tonn weighte and most yers far les, althoughe o'r copper mine there is reported to yelde plentith of owre. What the charges of o'r owre gettinge and makinge into copper will draw to, I muste suspende my judgmente untill I shall hereafter understande the same, by p'ces of time & accompt: yet it is not to be thoughte that o'r owers can be gotten alwaies after one rate, nether in price nor in quantetye, & no doubte many charges will grow about them extraordinary unlooked for.

Thus muche have I thoughte good to signifie unto yow w'ch I will yow keep to y'r selfe, onlye make my good frinde Mr. Carnsewe previe therunto desiringe his opinion & advice in the same; and (besids yo'r generall letter w'ch yow ar' to write to S'r W. Winter, † S'r Lionell Ducket & me, of ye state and p'ceadings of these mines, I praye yow fayle not to adv'tice me p'ticulerly & directely) what owrs yow have gotten in all to ye date of y'r next letter, at what mines w'th ye charges and so nier as yow can ges what

* Probably pointing to Keswick Cum.

† Winter and Duckett were orig. sharcholders in the Mines Royal, see list of them, *Post.*

standeth yow in ye gettinge of a tonn waight of copper owrs, what goodness yow do thinke ye owrs be in ther co'tent of mettall, also ye likelehode of o'r sev'all copp' mines & what the quantetyes of those owers may yerly be gotten, the same beinge supplied w'th sufficient nomber of miners & thinges thereto necessarye, & generally write me yo'r beste knoledge of ye p'ceadinges, with ye state & likely succes of all yo'r woorkes; w'ch like adv'ticements I thought to have receaved from yow ye laste terme, but had not one letter, wherof I mervailed, the rather co'sideringe Mr. Weston was appoynted then to be here, when it had bin well donn that ye Partners might have understoode the state of there mines for the better & open dealinge w'th him in those causes: nevertheles upon ye good co'fidence they repose in his honeste care & cunninge, we have made a new supply & assesment every parte aunsweringe I [100] w'ch w'th suche others as he and his frindes in ye contrye ar to aunswere for, dothe make ye supplye hetherto of those woorkes to amount to xxiiij c*li*, & this I thinke to be a sufficient stoke to maintayne those woorkes thoroughly w'thout farder charging us hereafter; but that we shall now looke after a while to renewer in o'r owre & reape a yerly p'fit, and thus muche ye said Mr. Weston hath firmly p'mised us.

Roberte Denham, this berer, is sent now doune to yow w'th ye Companies generall letter & instructions w'ch I shall se folowed with co'venient speede, furderinge the same, & let him se & fully surveigh ye mines, makinge him [acquainted] at large of yo'r p'ceadings therein to thende he maye bringe us up a p'fecte reporte therof accordinge to ye instructions delivered him in charge w'th suche lead owrs as he is appoynted to sende up well and surely packed, and to be directed to me at my house.

Mr. Weston himselfe purposeth to be w'th yow (God p'mittinge) aboute the ende of this moneth by whom yow shall understande furder, & so I do co'mit yow to God: fro' my house in Fannchurch Street in London, this xvij of June, 1584.

Your master and frinde,
THOMAS SMYTH.

I woulde yow shoulde not imparte the state of o'r Mines by yo'r letters into the north, hence forthe.

IV.

MR. THOMAS SMYTH TO ULRICK FROSSE.
7 JULY, 1584.

To my lovinge servaunt, Ulricke Frosse, ov'seer of ye minerall woorkes at Trewoorth, near unto Perin Sandes, in Cornwall.

(receaved the 21th of July, 1584.)

I wrat yow my laste let'r to have binn sent yow by R. Denham w'ch now yow shall receave herewith, because Denham goeth w'th Mr. Weston thorough Wales, & so will both of them be w'th you [soon] (God p'mittinge). I have wreeten yow in my said letters of o'r agreement heere w'th ye said Mr. [Denham] & yt we have furnished him accordinge to his requeste, havinge receaved his p'mise to be no farder charged hereafter, but hopinge shortly & from time to time to receave o'r [moneys] backe agayne & a dayly benifite, w'ch ye Lord God graunte to succede accordingelye. I told you in my laste y't he accompteth to make p'fecte roughe copper for xxv*li* the ton waighte, and he p'mised indeed to make it for xv*li*, hopinge (by H. Hering's former reports made) to get the owrs for xv*s* the tonne, whereof iiij. tonnes will make one tonne of copper but nevertheles if he can make it for xx*li* the tonne no faulte wilbe founde. The feare o'r Partners have is, that we shall not gett owrs in any great quantetye to raise worthy co'modityc, for by yo'r late let'r of ye 17 [of June see ante., p. 5.] receaved by this berer, Mr. Carnsew, it appereth y't yow have not above 50 tonns gotten in all, w'th ye w'ch yow have to gett 20 tonns more before Michelmas next.

Well now, y't Mr. Weston goeth doune to yow himselfe he will take farder order to have the mines well applied, w'ch is o'r desier & expectation at his own handes, thinkinge he will bringe H. Heringe w'th him once agayne into Cornwell, in hope y't he will better . . . lye his busines & w'th more quietnes & better agrement betweene yow & him then hath binn. In the w'ch causes Mr. Weston (w'th ye advice of Mr. Carnsew) will take order, and also for transportinge ye copper owres to o'r new Meltinge House at Neath in Wales, w'ch house I understande is ready; and we have taken order here yt agaynste he shalbe ready to make Copper he shall have from Keswike one of o'r cop'er makers, w'th an under melter, & ye Douch carpenter for a time to serve and ready him in these causes.

And in meane time till his cominge to yow, to ye end yo'r workinge of copper owers shoulde not fayle I have entreated Mr. Carnsew by my let'r to lend yow 20 li, w'ch mony, if Mr. Weston do not p'sently awenswere him at his now cominge into ye covntrye, I will then se him thankfully repayed my selfe, beinge loath at anye hande the woorke should fayle for want of reasonable supplye. Wherfore let them be well applied, & accordinge to my former let'r adv'tice me directly of the p'ceadinge of these workes & what quantities of owers yow get from time to time.

It is thought good that about Michelmas next Yow shall go lye at Neth, to take charge of o'r Melting House & things there, a place more for yo'r quietness then Cornwall is, as yow shall understande farder hereafter, and also by Mr. Weston.

I pray yow be more diligent in writinge to me then yow

haue binn of late time, for except yo' last let'r reced by Mr. Carnsew's brother*, I hearde nothinge from yow since Ester last :

Thus wisshing yow health & good succes, I co'mit yow to God : from my house in Fannchurch Street, this vijth of July, 1584.

Yo'r M'r & frinde,
THOMAS SMYTH.

V.
ULRICK FROSSE TO MR. THOMAS SMYTH.
22 JULY, 1584.

To his right worsh. Thomas Smith, esq., principall Customer of London, at his house Fanchurch Street, in London.

Right worshipfull and my very singuler good M'r 'after moste humble co'mendations, pleaseth it yow to be adv'tised that Mr. Carnsewe was here the xi. of July laste paste to se o'r woorkes, & o'rmyne here at Perin Sande, and wente downe w'th me into the bottom of the worke, and so up alongste the new audiet we made, w'ch is at this p'sente above 50 fadom longe, under all ye olde workes, but we do not lighte w'th any owre as yet ; w'th greate springs of water we lighte still in goinge up, w'ch will put us to great charge in the ende I feare me. We have yet above 17 or 20 fadom to the deepe shafte where the moste owre was lefte by reporte, to w'ch we thinke to com aboute the later ende of Auguste w'th God's helpe ; the Lord sende that we maye lighte w'th suche owre that will requite the former charges, and to helpe yo'r Worsh. parte to yo'r one agayne, w'th some p'fite.

Mr. Carnsewe did also ride w'th me to the Copper myne at St. Ann's, o'r Logan, to se that worke. I thinke he will adv'tise your worshipp how he do like the workinge bothe of

* *Vide* the Carnsewe brothers, as described at p. 2, ante.

Perin Sande and Logan. I measurde and receaved this laste weeke at Logan 10 tonne of goode & cleane sorted Copper owre, & truste to have as much more ready of sorted owre shortly: I caused it to be sorted very cleane & good, consideringe the far cariage, and better it wilbe when it shall com to the meltinge: for the clener it be sorted, the lese will the charges be in meltinge of it: the copper loade in Logan doth holde out resonable as yet, I pray God it may longe continewe.

I sente yo'r Woorshipp at Ester laste, by a poore laborer, the seconde quarter yer's racninge of o'r charges here, and sith that an other letter dated ye 15 of Maye, by Mr. Keligreis man, and one by S'r Frauncies * Godalphin' man, dated the 19 of June; in it I sent yo'r Worsh. a noth of certayne Copper mines, w'ch I thoughte we woulde have taken in hande this Somer if Mr. Weston had come hether before this time, or else [to] have had monye to set in hand w'th them, for the monye I hath did but serve me to mayntayn the worke w'ch I have in hand alreadye untill hetherto, and if I mighte have had better store of [money & things I] would have wroughte all Perin Sande longe before this time, as well by nighte as by day, and so mighte we have come to the principall place by St. James daye att the longe[st] woulde have set our copper myne a woorke by weste, and if there be suche store of owr gett in that myne as it is reported, we woulde have gotten good store of owr above the grounde by this time: where so for lacke of monye I could not take in hande, I . . . hande w'th Mr. Carnsewe of late for the 40li. he hath of yo'r Worsh: because I lacked money, & can not here of Mr. Weston's co'minge as yet; he awenswet me agayne, that he told Mr. . . . . . that he would receave the said 40li. of yo'r worship in co'sideration of suche stuffe he hath [now in] his hande that woulde do him pleasure for

* See some further account of him in Carew, p. 153.

meltinge of o'r owers, and so Mr. Weston was co'tent therewith, as Mr. Carnsewe told me: yet neverthe les he did speake to Mr. Recever for 20li. for me, untill Mr. Weston do com hether to mayntayn those woorkes w'ch I have in hande, for I tolde Mr. Carnsewe that I would take no monye up of Mr. Recever, before I hath letters from yo'r Worshipp so to do.

I do send yo'r Worshipp herein closed the third quarter yere racninge of o'r charges here, the Lorde send us some p'fitable mynes, wherby this charge maye be recovered agayne w'th some reasonable p'fitt, I shall do my diligence and be carefull aboute them so muche as lies in me to do by God's helpe: for I thanke my God I have my health agayne, and able to go into every woorke my selfe, to se the working thereof:

I receaved no letters from your Worsh. sith the 24th of Marche laste paste, I look dayly for Mr. Weston here, to take some order for settinge in hande of some more places to se what good may be donne, wherby we maye continew a woork w'th some in the . . . .

This I reste to troble yo'r worshipp, & so w'th my hartely desier to o' Lorde God for your Worsh. & all yo'rs longe & p'ssperis health.

Frome Perin Sande, the 22 of July, 1584.

Yo'r woorshipp's poore servante,
ULRICKE FROSSE.

VI.
ULRICKE FROSSE TO MR. WM. CARNSEWE.
3 AUGUST, 1584.

Right Worishipfull my dewtey remembret. S'r I have received the 21 of July from you by the hand of your man the som of 5li. starling, and sinch by the hand of John Ston the first of August, [instant] the sum 5*li*. mor, and if it wher not for your Woriship's healp, I should be dryven to give over our workes, and so I shall make my M'r to understand of it what herte and loose it would have been for the workes— spe'ially Treworthie, trusting your Worship will healp me as much as yow are able, to meantain it, and I shall then put my best healp into it. I thannke your Worship most hartyly for your freindly * letter, written unto my M'r in my behalff, and the Lord send me grace that I may desarved, trusting yow will, at Mr. Weston's coming first to your house, lett him understand likwysse, and as consarning your stuff you have to serve our toren for melting of our Copper ewre, I doe know, that it is good for that porpos and w'th out the sam, or such like wee shall have much to doe to make our ewre to ryne, for the most copper ewres her will be very strong to melte. It wher good to be knowne what quantytie ther is of yt, and how the same may be brought to the sea syd, whit what charges, and as for the goodnes of yt that can not be knowne, because, the first meltyd slackes, or sinder as yow caled the copper stone, and stone slackes be all mynglyd to gither, whereby it can not be knowne what quanttytie of either sorte ther is, neither can it be sorted, but through such as hath knowledge of it, to know the on from the other, for if either sorte hath ben by it selff, the better and more proffet it hath ben for yow, for then might wee have mad sayes of the Copper stone, and so might yow have knowne by the say, and the quanttytie of the sayd copper stone how much copper hath ben in it, and silver likewise, if it hold † silver.

I would yow did consyder upon all your stuff as neer as yow can what quanttytie ther is of it in all, one with an

---

* This is the first letter of this series, see page 1.

† It is clear by this that the early smelters were aware of *argentiferous* ores, the which some folk of the present day are prone to imagine to be a modern discovery.—G. G. F.

other, and how the same may be brought to the sea w'th what charge, and also what yow exstime it of your on consyderation to be worth betwist two brethern, and so to lett me understand of yt by your letter betwixt yow and me, be for Mr. Weston doe come to your howse.

Wee did light w'th a lyttle ewre at Treworth, the quanttytie of all most on C. waight in one nest by itself, but cut sunc out again, it is but of the co'mon Lead ewre.

I suppos wee ar w'thin 12 faddem to the deepe shaft wher the ewre was most left by report, w'ch I hop wee shall recover w'thin this moneth and leesse; in Logan the lode holds out reasonable well for it, the Lord bethank it.

This I rest, and so commit yow and all yours to the Almightie God. From Cut'bert P'ish the 3 of August, 1584.

Your Worship to command,

ULRICKE FROSSE, M.Mr.*

[Indorsed.]

To the right Worshipfull Mr. Wm. Carnsewe, esquier, at his howse at Bockelly.

receyvid 8 Aug., a'o., 1584, by R. C.†

VII.

ULRICKE FROSSE TO MR. WM. CARNSEWE.

9 JUNE, 1585.

Right Worshipfull my dewty surves co'mendacions to yow. S'r your letter sent to Mr. Weston I have receyved this 8 of June. Mr. Weston is now at London. I sent your Worship a letter by Mr. Weston's man, a weeke befor Whit Sunday,

---

* In the charter of James 1st to the Mineral and Battery Works Society, which may be perused subsequently, one Christopher Schutz an Almaigne born is, described as "Work Master." I suspect therefore these letters stand for "Mining Master."—G. G. F.

† R. C. was probably the brother Richard of Mr. Carnsewe, alluded to at p. 2.

and therw'thall som of our stone and Copper, also how wee doe speede in our melting, of w'ch I thanke God it doth goe reasonablye well forward, and lak but only good store of rich ewres.

I trust you have receyved my letter before this, therfor I stee at this p'sent. William Langfforde made hast away, because he could not see the melting, w'ch I mad stee of this very same day he did com hither, because I doe tary for som mor and richer ewres from your syd, and also because I have some thinge to mend at our water weere, and about our fornisses, but mean to begine again w'thin 8 or tene dayes, God willing.

At Mr. Weston's coming to your syd, your Worship shall understand mor, I hath writtne to yow after, but that I have ben a whil in the north parte of * England.

Thus I rest, and so commit yow and all yours into the hand of Almightie God. From Neethe this 9 of June, 1585, in hast.

Your Worship to comand to his poore
ULRICKE FROSSE, M.Mr.†

[Endorsed.]
To the Right Worshipfull Mr. Wm. Carnsewe, esquier, at his house, at Bokelly, in Cornwall.
rec' 19 Junii, a. 1585. Ulryke.

VIII.
ULRICKE FROSSE TO ROBERT DENHAM.
4 JULY, 1585.

To his lovinge frinde Robert Denha'.

Frinde Denha', I have me hartely co'mended unto yow; yow shall understande yt we did lacke ower more than 14 dayes ago, for we have founde out a waye to melte 24C of

---

* Probably visiting Keswick and Cumberland.
† See note at foot of the previous page on this.

owre everye daye w'th one furnas, the Lorde be thanked, and if we may have owre anoughe from yo'r side we maye with God's helpe melte w'th <u>tow furnases</u> in 40 weekes 560 tonnes of owre, having reasonable p'vision made for it; desiringe yow from hence forwarde to sende such owres as yow have w'th as much speed as maye be, not caring what owre it is. Yo'r owre of St. dives is very harte to melte it, hopinge we will over com it,* what St. Ust owrs will do, we longe to se it.* This I rest, the Lorde send yow good succes about yo'r mines.

And so I co'mit yow to God. Fro' Nethe, the 4th of July, 1585.

Yo'r frinde,
ULRICKE FROSSE.

When yow do send any more owre, if yow can, sende of all sorts, the better it will melte & w'th more p'fit.

[Endorsed.] The copys of U. to D. [Ulrick to Denham.]

IX.
JOHN OTES TO MR. WM. CARNSEWE.
27 OCT., 1585.

S'r, my dewtie remembred unto your Worshipp. The pyckman you spake of came to St. !∪ఒ S . . the 9 of October, and brought w'th hem 2 letters from yo'r Worshipp, th' one to Hance Hearing, th' other to myself. At the same tyme I had some [special] occatzon to be from St. Ives, but y'e Wensday I came to St. Ives agayne, and receaved the two letters of my host. So the Frydaye I went to St. Yeust, and carryed Hances l'ter with me, thinking yt the said Rodger Richard was thither to worke; soe we marvayled that he did not com, but brought the letters to St. Ives, and harde no more of hem att the present.

* Evidently those of St. Ives and St. Just, Cornwall.

The 14 of October came John Bwaple, one of Wales, w'h his bark for a frayght of the Copp' owre, and did delyver hem the 21 of October, 15 Tonn & 8 hundred of copp' owre for Wales. The 15 October came one Thom's Roberts from Wales, from the Company, w'h a fraight of tymber and necessaryes for the workes. I receaved his fraight at St. Ives, and for my lyffe I could not gett any * owre from St. Yeust to St. Ives, to fraight hem for Wales, but went awaye w'hout any, for Bwaple wold carry more owre yf I had it at St. Ives.

Mr. Denham must take y't order to have owre brought in the so'mer to St. Ives, for men will not deale nowe in the wynter tyme, unlesse it be very faire wether, whiche I pray God to send us and bless us, and to send us His grace, geving yo'r Worshipp thankes for yo'r good letter.

More to certyfye your W'rshipp for the western worke at St. Ives. There was 2 men of o'rs wroght one whole weeke, and wrought 2 feathem from the place. Mr. Denham did appoynt forth right in the load and found nothing, but at the place they began : more, the clyff is so lose that it falls, so y't the men wold not work but one week, soe it is gyven over tyll Mr. Denham's return.

And wheras Mr. Martyn and Mr. Denham did gyve me in charge to increase o'r workmen to the number of 30 in the whole, we should not have had monyes to certyfye them senight agon, but we have of workmen 20 some weeks at y'e most we have no more, but w'hin, and I am dryven to seeke for that I cannott gett or receave the monyes Mr. Denham did appoynte me. I paid £3 for the fraight of our tymber hither, as was wrytten in Arthur Rigbye's letter, and other charge we weare at about other busynes, I hoape as resonable as yf Mr. Denham were p'sent hemself, and by God's helpe what I maye doe I am willing, for y't Mr. Denham hath y't

* "Wales" in this paragraph doubtless means Neath.

confydence in me. And desyring the Almyghty to blesse me, and to send me His grace and goodness. I meane well, what I may to ev'y man, for as the scrypture sayth, better it is to have a poore lyving, w'h honesty and good creadytt, then all the world other wyse.

Thus far bold to trouble yo'r W'rshipp w'th my harty comendatyons to yo'r sonnes, I leave, committyng y'or W'rshipp to the tuityon of God, w'h increase of w'rshipp.

From St. Ives, the 27 of October, 1585,

Your W'rshipps to his power more wylling then able,

JOHN OTES.

I sent this letter by John Stone, to send it to your Worship, and the 30 October being Satterday, I came to St. Ives, and fynding the letter not sent, I thought it convenyent to com my self, to certyfy your W'rshipp in what state we [were in]. Mr. Denham wild me to receave with the money I had of him, first of Mr. Napyan iij*li*. xvij*s*., vi*d*. [and] of Harry Karwethers, iiij*li*. xvij*s*., the which I cannot receave it; more, I had a note to receve of Pascow Wynsor, xij*li*., y'e w'ch Mr. John Carnesew p'mysed to sent it before this.

Yf it maye be yo'r W'rship's pleasure to helpe us about a vj*li*. tyll Mr. Denham's return, it should do us great pleasure, for y't Mr. Denham p'mysed to be w'h us at this p'sent, and I thinke it wilbe a fortnight before his return. No more to yo'r W'rshipp.

[Indorsed.]

To the W'rshippfull Mr. Wyllyam Carnsewe, esquyer, at Bockelly, geve these w'h speed.

X.
JOHN OTES TO MR. CARNSEWE.
NOVEMBER, 1585.

I am sorry to trouble yo'r w'rshipp so oft, and do greatly

marvayll y't Mr. Denham do absent himself so long, desyring y'r w'rshipps' advyse:

I borrowed of Pascow Wynsor iij*li*. so y't the same & all the monyes y't was deliv'd me is gon aboute the mynerall worke, and we owe the workmen in p'te for the last weeke ending the 13 of November, besydes this weeke, so yf it were possyble to pay this same, which commeth to vj*li*. & upwarde, I would make the workmen stay one fornight longer, yet they do worke in such wetenes y't in paying there wage, it geves them a hart to worke. There is one hath p'mysed to lend me xl*s*., so yf I cold gett iiij*li*. more it wol do well, for I ame sure Mr. Denham will not be from us, not fornight more; I did think I should receave of Mr. John Carnsewe aboute vj*li*. as he p'mysed me, so he did what he might to gett som for me and cannot tyll it be a weeke or for'night hence, And then we shall surely have it, nowe yf yo'r w'rshipp might be a meane for a iiij*li*. at this p'sent for y't I wold begon west warde to morrowe betymes. For I did hoape I shold have some newes here of Mr. Denham.

[Indorsed.] 1585

Delyv'yd John Ottyes upon this byll, the 18 Nove'br, 40*s*.

XI.

ULRICKE FROSSE TO MR. W. CARNSEWE.

7 MARCH, 1586.

I have rec'd your Worshipps' letter dated the 27th January, w'ch letter I did rec' the 6th of March her at Neath.

Understanding therein that yow have noe letters from me sinch I departed out of Cornwall, I have advertissed your worshipp long befor this time in twoo sondry letters of our dowings her.

Wee looke dayly for the Copper Refiner from *Keswicke, and have in readines as much copper roste and blake copper as will mak a 20 tonne lotte of good fine copper.

Wee have done noting all this winter for lake of ewre. Wee are able to melt it w'th two fornises in the space of 40 weekes the quantitie of 560 tonne of ewre if wee might have it, and if the ewre be clean and well sorted the mor copper it will yeld. I doe not doubt but to bring out all that is in the ewre. I did befor Mr. Martin, melte 24 c. of our first melted sinder w'ch doth com of the ewre, and did not find in it the weight of halfe one onz of copper stone, w'ch is a saigne that we bring out all. I would glatly see your worshipp her to see our melting, no doubt you would liket well in nough, for I tare stand the tryall of it, who so ever will take in hand, to bring out as much as any other will doe, and w'th as little charges.

We will melt in the space of 7 houres the quanttitie of 24 C. of ewre, and spend not above 8 or 9 seks of chare coles, and thre horslod of sea coles, and if the ewre be well and clean sorted the mor copper stone will it yeld; melting many sorts of ewres to gither is the most proffet, and will melt a greattayll souner.

All my care is, and ever was, to have ewre enough, and then no doubt we will make copper good store, by the Grace of God, having good ewre and clean sorted, as is afor sayd, but hither to we have ben greatly hinderit for lack of ewre, w'ch the Parteners do finde. If lake of ewre hath not ben wee might have hath by this time above 40 tonne of copper, w'ch must be for seene hereafter, o'r els it wilbe long befor they Parteners will com to their owne againe.

This I reste to troble yow, and so, w'th my humble service comended to your Worshipp, unto good Mrs. Carnsewe, your

---

* The "Copper Refiner" would be a most important addition to the Staff at Neath.—G. G. F.

sonnes and doughters, w'th the rest of your houshold, beseech God to send yow and all yours long lyff and prossperius health, and so commit yow to God. From Neath, this 7th of March, 1586.

Your Worshipps to command,
ULRICKE FROSSE, M. Mr.

I hop to see your Worshipp this somer in Cornwall w'th God's healp, and then we shall hav som larger conference touching our melting of the severall ewres. Wee doe not doubt what ewre so ever do com to my hands, and it be never so strong to melt we will over com it, for a metchen* that wee have fond out by change, and if it hath not been for that, the rich copper ewre w'ch we call the plen ewre at † St. Youste would put us to harte shifte for melting of it, a very strong ewre to melte as ever I did see o'r did com to my hands, but I thank God wee are able to master it well in nough. God send us anough of it, for the metchen* we have for it doth not only healp to melt it easye but also to melt it speedelye, and w'th small fewle and bringes out all that is in it, this may your worshipp give me credit to be the trought. I thank the Lord for it; God send the mynes to prospere, and to mak good greement amongst the Parteners in setting this work forward, whereby they may have p'fitt, and the comone wealt may be maintained to God's honner.

Befor the insealing hereof I hath news out of Cornwall, how that Mr. Trevinian hath discharged all the workmen at ‡ St. Youit, and taken away all their tooles, and given charge to his officers that no ewre should be caried away, I must therefor desyre your worshipp to tak som orther, that our bark, being now at § St. Dyves, may have her lading of ewre, for this time, away with her. Understanding by a gentleman w'ch

* This word was probably *slang* amongst the workmen for ability to overcome, or matching, equal to.

† St. Just.   ‡ St. Just.   § St. Ives.

did com from London of late, that Mr. Martin, and Denham wilbe in Cornwall very shortly.

[Endorsed]

To the Right Worshippfull Mr. William Carnsewe, esquier. Delyver this at his house at Bockellye, in Cornwall.

XII.
ROBERT MARTYN TO MR. CARNSEWE.
8 APRIL, 1586.

[Headed.]

(Robert Martyn's retorne to my wrytynge, W. C.)

S'r,—By yo'r note in wrytynge I doo p'ceve yo'r travell hathe bene greate, and your chardge not a litle, beside those things delliv'd to Mr. Weston at Perin Sands for the furtherance of o'r woorke. I hope when the P'tners shalbe informed therof in such sorte, as I see good cause the should, thaye will use considerac'on accordingly.

I will cause R. D.* to waight uppon you withe all the co'venient sped he maye, beinge right sory that my busines will suffer me no longer to remayne, the cause therof I have mad knowne unto yo'u accomptinge my departuar to be a hinderaunce unto my self, not knowinge where to spend tyme to bett'r purpoze.

I praye God to send you health and strengthe to p'form yo'r i'tended journy into Walles, † no man shalbe more gladder to se you ther then myself.

I am right sory the wante of 100*li.* frome the P'tners should hinder so good a purpoze. I do not mystrust but at my next beinge in London they will bett'r consider of the same.

If it be not my chaunce to offer my dewtifull service to Mr. Edgcom befor my dep'ture, I beseche yo'u vouchsafe to

---

* No doubt Robert Denham.   † This of course was to the New Works at Neath, then busily occupied.—G. G. F.

remember the same. I hope his Wo. will thinke good we doo not want.

And so I pray God to contynue yo'r health, with increase of many happy dayes.

The foregoing Letters are not only extremely curious and interesting in themselves as shewing the manner of conducting important matters of business in the time of Queen Elizabeth; shewing too, that there was then, as there is now, a gentle feeling between master and servant, and that there was also the same difficulty of getting means to carry on the work, the same generous trust and advance between friends in a common cause—and as if to prove that "there is nothing new under the sun"—there was thus early, an appreciation of practical knowledge tending to a commercial success such as cannot be surpassed in the present day, for Dr. Percy, in his "Metallurgy" of 1861, says—

> "The smelter, by having at command a *variety* of ores, may render an ore profitable which otherwise would have no value. Frequently copper can be extracted at a less cost by smelting several ores in a mixture, than by smelting one ore by itself."

Ulrick Frosse, writing more than 250 years ago, had ascertained the same economic law, for he told his friend Denham to

> "Send such ores as you have, not caring what ore it is; when you do send, if you can, send of *all sorts*; the better it will melt and with more profits."

I trust that I have at length definitively settled the Origin of Copper Smelting at Neath, in what is now known as "The Swansea District." It is clear that to "the right worshipful Thomas Smyth, esquire, principal Customer of London, and his friend and loving servant Ulrick Frosse, that very honest and skilfull man," *we* are indebted for the "great Staple" which, founded in the days of Elizabeth, has grown to such gigantic proportions in the reign of * Victoria. IN JULY, 1584, it was announced that the ores would be transported out of Cornwall to "the new Melting House at NEATH IN WALES, then ready," and it was "thought good that about the Michaelmas following, Ulrick should live at Neath to take charge of it and the things there." See p. 9 and elsewhere, *ante*, as to these facts.

It is further proved that whatever was the metallurgic talent of native workmen, the Germans (or, as they were often in those days called, the Dutch)† were the skilled workmen who forced on the art to a higher perfection than it had hitherto attained in this country; for not only Ulrick, in July of the very next year, 1585, writing as to melting 24 cwt. of ore every day with one furnace, the Lord be thanked," but we shall just now have further incontestable evidence of the rapid strides made by Jochim Gaunse and Stembarger, of whose *German* origin there can be no question.

From Keswick, in Cumberland, came those pioneers of the trade—"the Copper Refiner, the Copper maker, the under Melter, and the Dutch carpenter† to serve and ready Ulrick in these causes;" and I purpose now to show *how* they conducted their work, and what were the difficulties they had to overcome in "the corrupt humors" with which they contended in converting the Cornish ores into marketable Copper. Probably few Trades can shew such a clear and concise description of their *modus operandi* as will be found in the following confidential communications to the then Secretary of State (Walsingham, one of Elizabeth's most astute councillors,) who not only was probably interested in the concern himself, but had to look after the good Queen's

* Vide page 13, *ante*.

† At page 3, *ante*, it will be seen that Mr. Carnsewe describes "Dutche myners" as Germans, and at page 23, is a like description, "the Dutch workmen which have been sent from Germany."

proportion of the profit reserved by the Patent which she had granted to Thurland & Hoechstetter in 1564.

On the 18 July 159 , a very interesting letter was written to Mr. Secretary Cecil, then Governor of the Mines Royal Co. from Keswick, by Marcus Stembergerus, Ric. Ledes, and Emanuel Hechstetter, about their Copper works there, the last paragraph of which is as follows:—" We certify this, lest we " might be supected of fraudulend dealing, and refer ourselves " and our causes to you and the Company, and beseech you " to consider our hindrances and losses (as Germans) of our " own stock laid down in these mines."—G. G. F.

XIII.
GEORGE NEDHAM* TO SIR FRANCIS WALSINGHAM, KNT.
[Headed.]
MARCH, 1582, COVERING ONE OF A.D. 1581.

Offers made by Jochim Gaunse for makeing of Copper, vitriall, and coppris, and Smeltinge of Copper and Leade ures.

1. Wheras Mr. Stembarger, at his laste beinge in London, made his propos'tion to the Company that for everie quintall of rough copper he made (being cxij *li.*), he must have vij. kebulls† of copper ure gotten in Gode's gifte myne,‡ everie kebull whereof is in waite clv. *li.* at the least, w'ch after a cxij *li.* to the hundreth, amounts to xc iiij xx v *li.*§ of ure, and for all manner of charges of fireworke and smeltars' wages to bring the same xc iiij xx v *li.* of ure into rough copper, he offreth to do it for xiiij *s.* iiij *d.*

* I find that he was one of the original Partners of the M. R., in 1580, as will be shewn a few pages further on.

† The buckets in which the ore was raised from the mines.

‡ Again specially named at p. 28, para. ix., and which was one of the chief pits of Calbeck.

§ This is as though we should say, Ten hundred-weight, four score and five pounds.—G. G. F.

2. Mr. Jochim doeth offer to bringe fully so much copper out of the like quantity of ure, and to beare all manner of fireworke, smelters' wages, and the Queene's parte likewyse therin comprehended, for ix *s.* iiij *d.*, w'ch is lesse then Mr. Stembarger's offer, by v *s.* in a quintall: so as by his order of rosteinge and smelting, putting to, the charges of gettinge, shawdring and carrieing the ure, the quintall of rough shall not stande v *s.* in above xxvj *s.*: and by his order of workeinge he will make as much copper or more then Mr. Stembarger doeth.

3. And further, the said Jochim doubteth not but after he hath rosted and smolton iij. or iiij. saies of o'r Copp' ure, in the great works,* after such manner as he hath devised since his comeing from Keswick, to attaine to such farther knowledg of the nature of all o'r copper ures in Cumberlande and Westmoreland that he shalbe able to kill all the corrupt humors that be in them, and therby to bringe out more copper then heretofore hath byn: and w'th lesser charge then is above written.

4. And further, he will take out of the ure either vitriall or coppris, as the tyme and occasion of sale therof shall serve, w'ch will not onely be soulde to the great benniftt of the Companie, but also by takeinge the said vitriall of coppris from the ure before it come in to the first smeltinge, it doeth in the first smeltinge very much helpe and save the Copper from wasting and causeth the ure sooner to smelt: in w'ch rostes both of vitriall, copper, and coppris makeinge he will use nothing but peate, whereas Mr. Stembarger and his Father have used much woode.

5. After copper ure be rosted and redie to smelting (w'ch roste is done in one fire,) then must the vitrall or coppris, or w'ch of them shalbe thought moste mete, be taken from the ure, before it come to the smeltinge, first w'ch is done by letting water passe through the ures: of w'ch water

* Doubtless pointing to those just completed and at work at Neath.

the coppris or vitriall must be made; and that water doth not onely drawe the vitriall and coppris from the ure, but also divers other hurtfull humors, being by nature enemyes to the Copper; as arsenick, sulpher, antimony, allome, and ironn; w'ch, being taken away as aforesaid, maketh the ure w'thin iiij dayes, by once rosting and once smelting to yeeld black copper and copper-stone,* w'ch Mr. Stembarger nor his Father coulde do under xvj. rostings and xvj. weekes' time.

6. And wheras, in o'r first vitriall that was made he drew xx li. of Copper out of the ure to make a C. of vitriall; he can nowe make the vitriall in as great quantity as we can utter it, and as good as his first vitriall was, and will take but x li. of copper to the cxij li. of vitriall: and as for ye charge of makeing therof w'th other circumstance, is to be declared by word and not by writing.†

7. And yf we cannot have utteraunce of so much vitriall as we can make, then may we make of that substaunce coppris, w'thout takeing any copper from the ure, and the same copperris w'ch we shall make for dyeing of cloth will excell in goodness both that w'ch is made here in England by the ‡ Lord Mountjoye his preveledg, or any other coppris comeinge from beyonde the seas, the chardges of makinge therof is also to be declared by mouth.†

8. For vent of this coppris ther wilbe great quantitie used in Cumberland, Westmorelande, Yorkshire, Cheshire, and Lancanshire onely for dying, who are constrained to transeporte it from London thether. And likewise ther wilbe much soulde into the North parte of Scotlande, who have often

* Copper-stone is the *German* version for what in England is called Regulus.

† Copper Manufacturers of the present day are often said to keep close the secrets of the Trade; if so, it appears to be an old practice amongst them, being often repeated as a request for attention.

‡ Lord Mountjoy was one of the original partners of the Mines Royal, see p. further on; but this refers also to his Grant from the Queen.

tymes both come and sent to Keswick to buye coppris; and, makeing more quantitie then we can utter there, we may send to London and other parts of England, or into Fraunce, Spaine, and other Countryes, who have it brought them from Lubeck, Dandzick, & Andwerpe, being a longer viadge and greater charges.

9. And wheras, the riche Copper ure gotten in the mynes of Calbeck* being enfected w'th such corruptions, that hetherto Mr. Danyell or his Sonn coulde never smelt them alone as they came from the myne, but were forced to myngle them w'th rosted stone of the first smelting of Gode's gifte ure.† Mr. Jochim at his being at Keswick, in ij fires, that is with once rostinge and once smeltinge it, as it came from the myne, w'thout myngling, did bring it into black copper and copperstone.

10. And in like manner, the rich leade myne at Calbeck, w'ch houldeth good quantity of silver, and hath cost the Company great sommes of mony, lieth now unwrought, being a myne whereout great proffitt myght be yearely gotten by the silver and the leade; w'ch ures neither Mr. Danniell nor his ‡ Sonn, Mr. Stembarger, hitherto could smelt to preserve the leade and bring the silver from it, but by such wast of the ure and silver that their doeinges were rather to losse than proffitt. Mr. Jochim hath made divers smale sayes therof, whereby he doubted not to smelt it in such sort as the most part of the leade shalbe preserved, and the silver brought out to great gaynes.

And Further, GEORGE NEDHAM declareth his knowledg and opineon to the Right Honorable S'r Fraunces Walsingham, cons'ninge these Articles of Jochim Gaunse, for makeing of Copper, vitriall, and coppris; and the smelting of Copper and Leade ures in form following:—

* In Cumberland, which has of late years fallen from this richness to almost *nil*. † See this also mentioned at p. 25, *ante*.
‡ This evidently means Son-in-law.

For his offer made in the seconde Article I knowe it to be trewe, and in my notes geven your Honnor vij monthes paste, I did offer to make the great C. of rough Copper for 27s. 8d.

For his offer in the iij Articles, by such experience as I have gotten by conference w'th him* in the knowledg in the nature of our ures, that I dare assure my self he is able to performe his p'mise & especially by bringing more copper out of the ure then Mr. Stemberger nowe doth.

For the iiij Article, I can my self make vitriall in such order as we made at o'r being at Keswick; but not so good cheape as Mr. Jochim can now do it, nor to save the x*li* of copper in the C. of vitriall as Mr. Jochim can do.

For coppris makeing, I have no p'fect skill, but must learne it of Mr. Jochim, which I am verie desirous to do, being a comoditie w'ch I knowe will yelde us great p'fitt for the Co.

For his offer made in the ixth Article, I knowe he can do it, for I myself at my laste being at Keswick, did smelt the Copper ure gotten in * Calbeck myne alone, w'thout putting any thinge to it, and in v fires & viij dayes did make good rough copper therof.

Your Honor's most Humble to comaund,
GEORGE NEDHAM.

[Endorsed.] XIV.

A description of the Doeinges of Jochim Ganse and George Nedham, at the Copper Mynes by Keswicke, in Cumberland, A.D. 1581.

Right Honourable,—As soone as Mr. Jochim & I came to Keswicke, the firste thinge we did take in hande, was to searche out both the nature and the number of the hurtfull humors that were naturally bred in oure Copper ures gotten

* This tends to shew that Needham was an *English* copper smelter, who was getting all he could out of the *German* Jochim.—O. G. F.

in that countrie, wherein after sundrie trialls, we attained to some perfection, and found that in our Copper ures, were tenn severall substance's, whereof iiij ar visible, w'ch ar iron, copper, a kinde of black stone, (wherein the copper groweth) and a kinde of white stone named sparr: the other vj humors, w'ch ar in the said ures, and invisible, ar sulpher, arsenique, antimony, vitriall, calcator, and allom; so as in ten substances w'ch ar in our Copper ures, the copper is one, and the other substances by their naturall operation ar all hurtfull and venemous humors to the copper; for some of them by wasteings the copper in smeltinge, and by their drynes make it bretle and black; the other by theire toughe and moiste nature, be a great let to the speedie smeltinge and bringeinge the ure into rough copper. The number, nature, and propertie of w'ch ix hurtfull humors being wholly unknowne to Mr. Daniell [qy. Hockstetter] and his Sonne, or to any other of the Duch workemen w'ch have bin sente from Germany* to the mynes, that have borne our copper ures, had bin the onely cause of the unreasonable charge, and long tyme spent before they could make of those ures perfect rough copper: w'ch copper after the order used in tymes past by Mr. Daniell and his Son, thei never coulde, nether yet can make under xxij tymes passinge thro the fire, and xxij weekes doeing therof ane sometyme more. But now the nature of these ix hurtfull humors abovesaid being discovered and opened by Jochim's way of doeing, we can, by his order of workeinge, so correct theim, that parte of theim beinge by nature hurtfull to the copper in wasteinge of it, ar by arte maide freindes, and be not onely an encrease to the Copper, but further it in smeltinge: and the rest of the other evill humors shalbe so corrected, and their humors so taken from them, that by once rosteinge and once smeltinge the ure (w'ch shalbe done in the space of three dayes),

* Which is again evidence that Daniel and Stembarger were "Germans."

the same copper ure shall yeeld us black copper and
copper-stone, w'ch nether Mr. Daniell nor his Sonne coulde
or yet can do under xvj tymes passinge through the fire, and
xvj weeks in doeing thereof: and further, in once rosteinge
and once smeltinge the same black copper and copper-stone
again, w'ch shalbe done in ij days, after Mr. Jochim's order
of workeinge, I will bringe the black copper and copper-stone
into perfect rough copper, w'ch Mr. Stembarger cannot
make under xxij tymes passing through the fire and xxij
weekes in doeinge therof and sometymes more !

I have therfore thought necessarie to sett it downe in write-
inge, that y'r Honnor might see the several names of the ix
infections w'ch ar in our copper ures, w'th the nature and
operation of every of them, by what meanes thei do hurt
unto the Copper, before thei be corrected, and being
corrected, by what meanes thei be helpfull to the copper.

The Names of the ix infectyve and evill Humors:—

1. The first is Sulphur, being a mynerall substance w'ch
verie quickly taketh fire, and wilbe consumed in smoke by
blast, whereby it goeth away very violently, and in goeing
away will not onlly carry w'th it some of the copper or any
other mettall it is joyned with, but also maketh the copper
black and bretle so that it wilbe broken w'th the hammar, in
manner like glasse.

2. The ij corrupt humor is Arsineque, by nature a kinde
of poyson, being in like manner a minerall substance, wilbe
consumed w'th fire in to Smoke, w'ch is a vere daungerous
ayer or savor, and by his force maketh the copper white
and brether then the sulpher doeth. This Arsenieque is not
onely in great quantitie in our copper ures, but is by nature
so forceable of it self, that it is Lorde and Ruller over all the
rest, and consumes both ye sulpher, and antimony, so y't thei
ar not to be seene: and in my opinion, by his drynese doth
so dry and take away the force of the other iij liquid and

tough humors, that thei have no force to let them from speedy smeltinge and departinge from his drosse.

3. The iij corruption is Antimony, w'ch is in like manner a mynerall substance, and by rosteing wilbe consumed into smoke. Itt is in nature much like to sulpher and arsenieque in makinge the copper black and brether; besides it is great let and hinderer to the copper in smeltinge; and by the opinion of some that in refineing, it doeth consume part either of golde, silver, or copper w'ch ar smolten w'th it.

4. The iiij corrupt humor is Vitriall, in like manner a mynerall substance, and if the force therof be not corrected by rosteinge before the ure wherin it groweth be smolten, it fretteth the Copper and maketh it bretle and black coulered; but by stampeinge the copper ure into powder and by rostinge the same powder after Mr. Jochim's rule before it be smolten, and then letting water passe through the same rosted powder, the water doth not onllie carry the vitriall from the powder or ure, but also carrieth w'th it the burnt powder or sinder of the sulphur, arsenicque, and antimony, whereby it so clenseth the ure that when it cometh to the smeltinge the copper cometh forth easelie, w'thout such quantitie of slagges or drosse, as otherwise would be, if the ure were not rosted and the vitriall in this manner taken from it; thus is the vitriall, of an enimye made a freinde.

5. The v*th* corruption is * Calcator, beinge the mother or corpus of vitriall, and a mynerall substance; this will not be consumed w'th smoke, but gathereth into a body and substance, and very forceablie abideth the fire, although in nature it be not fullie so hurtfull to the Copper as vitriall is, but carrieth away corrupt humors w'th it as vitriall doth.

* I have not yet come across the modern term for "Calcator," nor can I find the word itself in any of our old books; but my friend, Mr. R. Hunt, F.R.S., at Jermyn Street, has since drawn my attention to his 6th Edn. of Ure's Dicy. p. 854, where he has stated that "Calcother" (Calc-okre) is an antiquated name for oxide of iron, doubtless another form of the same word.—G. G. F.

6. Allom is the vj*th* corrupt humor, a mynerall substance, and by nature a let to ye smeltinge of the Copper; it also hindreth ye vitriall, and of all the rest of the ix infections is least hurtfull to ye copper.

7. The vij*th* humor is Iron, beinge one of the vij mettalls but no mynerall, w'ch being engendered and bred up in the earth w'th the copper ure, will not lightlie be gotten from it, and especiallie when the copper ure is smolten greene as it cometh from the myne, w'thout rosteinge, then the iron doth joyne and incorporat himself w'th the copper, by reason of the other ij moist humors hereunder written as shall plainely apeire unto yo'r Honnor by samples that I have to shewe, w'ch is onely the greatest cause of so many chargable fires and longe tyme w'ch Mr. Daniell and his Sonne do spende before thei can make rough copper. And accordinge to Mr. Jochim's order of workeinge the nature and substance of the iron yt is our copper ure being beaten into powder, and rosted as aforesaide, the drosse and corruption that is in the iron is so dryed up, that when it cometh to smeltinge it is not able to runne or gether itselfe together like a slagge as it doeth being smolten greene before the ure be rosted: and the best substance w'ch is the right iron ure, beinge by rosteinge brought into the perfection of iron, is, by the water and strength of vitriall, converted into copper, as I have proved sundrie tymes: so as this cheefe of the hurtfull humors beinge thus corrected, it is made of an enemye a freinde and helper of the copper.

8. The viij*th* hurtfull humor that is in our copper ure, is a kinde of Black Stone, * wherin the copper is bred and doth growe, and is incorporated w'th the copper, as shall plainely be shewed unto yo'r Honnor, w'ch stone beinge a liquide and tough substance, and smolten before it be rosted, doth

* Evidently alluding to the native matrix in which the ore was found in Cumberland.—G. G. F.

so joine itselfe w'th the iron and copper, being bred up together, that thei will hardly be parted but by great charges and long tyme; but as is before declared, beinge rosted before it come to smeltinge (what by force of the fire and of the venemous arsenicque) this hurtfull stone is so dryed up, that when the ure cometh to smelteinge, it cannot incorporat itself to any substance to become a slagge or drosse, but is like a sinder consumed w'th the force of the fire, wherby it can no way hinder or lett the copper.

9. The ix*th* and the last corrupt humor is a kinde of White Stone, named Sparr, w'ch in all respects is like to the black stone, and if in the same sorte it be not corrected, it is no lesse prejudiciall to the smeltinge then the other

Thus, Right Honnorable, I have so breefly as I coulde, rudely sett forth the nombre, nature, and operation of the hurtfull Humors that be in our Copper ures, and how by arte thei may be so corrected that such of them as be moste hurtfull enemyes, shalbe made freindes; and the hurtfull force of the rest so overcome and taken away that thei shall not hurt or hinder the copper makeinge. Moste humblie beseecheinge yo'r Honnor to pardone my boldnes in troubleing you, and to accept my goodwill herein: and hearafter (as occasion and tyme shall serve) I do purpose by Godde's Grace to sett forth a more ample discourse, and by the help of Mr Jochim not onely to dissipher ye hurtfull Humors that be in any ure (groweing in this realme) be it copper or lead, but also a remedie so to correct or kill the same, as the same ures ither of copper or leade shalbe smolten to benefitt without the hurt of those humors.

[Endorsed.]

NOTES touching that which was don at ye Copper Mynes by Mr. Nedham and Joachim Gaunse, with offers of Joachim Gans for the Melting of Copper and making of Vitryol.

Having so far (I hope) interested the reader in the general

MAGNATES OF THE COPPER MANUFACTURE

IN THE SWANSEA DISTRICT,
DURING THE EARLIER PORTION OF THE 19TH CENTURY.
TAKEN FROM THE LIFE & REPRODUCED BY THE AUTOTYPE CO.

1. J. H. VIVIAN ESQ. M.P. F.R.S. &c.
2. M. WILLIAMS ESQ. M.P. J.P. &c.
3. HUSSEY, LORD VIVIAN, G.C.B. &c.
4. R. J. NEVILL ESQ. J.P. &c.
5. P. L. GRENFELL ESQ. J.P. COL &c.

subject, I now proceed to give the names of the Shareholders in this, to us, most interesting concern "The Mines Royal Society," from an original list supplied to Mr. Secretary Walsingham,—it is true, that we only get a moiety of them, viz., the English proprietors, but the names of the foreign holders may again turn up or be known to some of my readers—in which case I trust we may some day see a complete List of the Co. published.

XV.
SHAREHOLDERS IN THE MINES ROYAL SOCIETY.
A.D. 1580.

The hole mass of the Minez Royall waz divided intoo xxiiij*ti* equall parts, whearof Thurland, for the English, had xij parts, and Daniel, for the Straungerz, had the other xij. The English parts again divided too partnerz and intoo porcionz as foll'weth:—

```
The Lorde Treazorer [Burleigh]  ....ij parts.
The Earl of Pembrook* ..........ij parts.
The Earl of Leicester  ..........j part.
The Lord Montjoy*  ............a quarter of a part.
Alderman Ducket*  ..............j part.
Spinola .......................ij parts.
——— Tamwoorth  ..............d'mi. part.
Thom's Revet  .................d'mi. part.
W. Patten*  ...................d'mi. part.
——— Culverwell  ..............d'mi. part.
W. Wynter* ....................j q'rter of a pt.
John Dudley ...................j q'ter.
W. Burd  .....................j quarter.
Customer Smyth*  ..............j q'ter.
Geffray Ducket ................j q'ter.
Allderm. Gamage  ..............j q'ter.
——— Barnz. in Cheap..........j q'ter & q'mi. q'ter.
——— Springham  ..............j q'ter.
George Needham* ...............j q'ter.
Matthu Feeld  .................q'mi. q'ter.
Anthony Ducket ................j q'ter.
```

S'ma..xiiij parts.

* Referred to in some of the letters printed in several of these pages.

The rezidu of the parts whearof most be at the dispozicion of Daniel, hoow he hath bestowed them, or what remayneth w'th him, not yet certeinly known.—W.P. [Patten.]

[Indorsed]—The distribution of the parts of the Mynes Royall. 1580.

This return is initialled W. P., most probably the "W. Patten" of the List, who is down for a half-part. I understand this name of 'Patten' has long remained connected with the Copper Trade*—Is it possible that the 'Daniels' so respected in the days of good Queen Bess were the stock of the † Daniels no less trusted in this our time by their employers in Mining and Smelting operations at Swansea. Have they, I wonder, any *tradition* of their origin and whereabouts?

It is time now to come to the Royal license under which these "English and Straungers" derived their authority for seeking ores and erecting works for the smelting thereof. Before giving details of the Patents or Charters of Elizabeth, James, etc., it may perhaps be well to premise that the metalliferous ores in this country were reserved to the Crown, and that it was therefore necessary to have a Grant for the searching for and the working of them, and further that it was also requisite to have a Patent or Crown Grant for the constitution of a Company or aggregation of persons, such as is *now* effected more generally by an Act of Parliament or a "Limited Liability Company registration."

* *Vide* Percy's "Metallurgy," Vol. I., p. 291, where it is stated that an ancestor of the present Col. Patten first introduced Copper Smelting into Lancashire in 1717 or 18, and Mr. Keates informs me "they for long "time remained heads of the Firm of the Cheadle Copper and Brass Co., "for I recollect more than 60 years ago, Col. Patten (the Father of Lord "Winmarleigh) saying, his ancestors had been connected with Mining and "Smelting for generations."

† After all, I strongly suspect that "Daniel" was but the Christian name of Hochstetter the German, see next page, *post*. Indeed, on reading more carefully the paragraphs before and after the List of the Mines Royal Shareholders, I have no doubt about it.—G. G. F.

On the 6th Sept., 1595, Lord Burghley made a note or order that "The Royal Company of Miners should certify what "Copper they have and how much they owe to the Queen and "Customer Smyth's Exors. to answer for Copper delivered." Records, Domestic papers, 8vo., p. 99, while in the following 14 Novr., Lord B. desires that "Mr. Smyth be spoken to, for "Copper for the Ordnance for the two new ships."—G. G. F.

XVI.
W. PATTEN, Esq., TO SIR F. WALSINGHAM, KNT.
19TH Nov., 1581.

May it pleas yoor Honor somwhat to the purpose of that whearin ye voouchsafed yesternight too gyve me heering, and too the content ye may be a littl instructed in the state of oour severall graunts, as well of the Mines Royall as of the oother.* I dru oout this *brevet* again too day for yoo, but being gon before my cumyng, the same noow send I, reddy further in thees matters too signify my knulege (that cost me deer) untoo yoor Honor at the good pleasure of the same which in prosperetee & health with encreas of mooch dignitee God's majesty long preserve. From Alldermanbery this xixth of November, 1581.

Yoor Honors allweis right humbly at comaundment,

W. PATTEN.

It may have been observed that hitherto we have adopted the usual mode of dates in succession, but now it becomes necessary to invert that order, consequent on Mr. Patten's information touching the Letter's Pat. given at the commencement of the "Mines Royal" establishment in 1564, when he wrote his letter of explanation to Sir F. Walshingham from

* This "other" was, doubtless, the Mineral and Battery Company: as, indeed, is shewn in the fifth paragraph of this letter.

Aldermanbury, in Nov., 1581, a period of 17 years, during which they had, as we have shewn, been most actively employed as a Company in promoting the interests they had acquired, and were about to extend them still further as will be perceived on perusing the following confirmation and extension by King James of the

> Graunts from the Q. Ma'ti.
> By Charter dated *xmo*. Octob'r Anno R'e *vjmo*.
> A.D. 1564.

MADE TO Thomas Thurland M'r of the Savoy & Daniell Hogstetter a Germain, and too their heyrs & assignees.

Of poour & authoritee too search dig try rost & mellt allman' of mines & ures of Golld Sylver Copper & Quicksilver, And too take up woorkmen, tymb'r, wood, cole & such lyke at reasonable wages and prises and allso too purchas bonds in ony estate of enheritauns w'hin the Coountees of York Lancast'r Cumb'land Westmerlond Cornwall Devon Glouce'ter & Worce'ter and the Principalitee of Wales as well w't'in her Ma'te oun grounds as oothers.

Her Highness too have of all golld & sylver that shall be foound neat w't'oout help of fyer or melltyng the *xth* part, And of all golld ure & sylver hollding viij*li* weight in the C. weight the lyke *xth*, and of every C. of copper *ij*"*s*. or the *xxth* p't at her Highnes' chois, during the fyrst *v*. yeers next then and after those *v*. yeers *ijs*. *vjd*. upon the C. of copper or the *xvth* part or just valu thearof at her lyke chois.

And too have the preferment in bying of all Pretioous stones or pearl too be foound in the woorkyng of those mines. And of Tynn too have in name of coynage, as in Cornwail her highnes hath. And of Lead as in oother places used, &c.

The oother L'res Patents dated the *xvijth* of Septemb'r then next viz., Anno R'e *vijmo*. 1564 supradic'o.

Made too Will'm Humfrey & Chr'ofer Shutes a Germain and too their heyrs & assignees of poour & authoritee too dig search & try (as aforesayd) w't'in Englond & the English pale in Irelond (excepting the places aforegraunted)

All ures simpl or mixt of Golld Silver Copper Quicksilver & of all oothers. And allso for Tynn & Lead as hath been used in oother places. And for the Calamine stone,* And for makyng Lattyn thearw't', & all kynde of batry waer of lattyn, iern, steel & of all maner of plates.

Her Hyghnes too have for the fyrst vj yeers then next, the x*th* part of all the pure mettalls or ures of Golld, Sylver & Quicksylver. And of every C. weight of mixt ure hollding viij *li* or aboove of those rich mettalls too have all the x*th* part. And of Tynn in name of coynage, as her Ma'ti hath in Devon and Cornwoll. And of Lead as in oother places of the Realm. And of the calamine* the xx*th* part or just valu thearof. And of every C. of Copper for the said fyrst vj yeers ij*s*. or the xx*th* part at her lykyng, and after those vj yeers ij*s*. vj*d*. or the xv*th* part or valu at chois aforesayd, &c.

[Endorsed]

Untoo the right honorabl' Sir Frauncis Wallsingham, Knight, One of the twoo Principall Secretaries unto the Q. Ma'ti.

I am indebted, and so is my reader, to the liberality of Mr. Jno. Thomas, colliery proprietor, of Court Herbert, near Neath, for copies of these two Charters of † King James, of which I shall now give the material points only, as the entire would occupy too much space, being greatly overlaid in the originals with legal repetition and verbosity.

* *Lapis Calaminaris*, this is an ore of Zinc, used for the making of brass, or "Lattyn," as it is here termed; frequently found in England.

† These copies were lithographed and on parchment, and Mr. Thomas assured me that the transcribing and a few copies only cost him 50£, and by the pains taken with them I can quite believe him.—G. G. F.

XVII.
CHARTER CONFIRMATORY TO THE MINES ROYAL SOCIETY,
[A.D. 1604.]*

Granted at Windsor, the Twenty-eighth day of January, in the Second Year of King James the First.

JAMES, by the Grace of God, King of England, Scotland, France and Ireland, Defender of the Faith, &c. To all to whom these Presents shall come, Greeting.

WHEREAS, our late dear sister, ELIZABETH, late Queen of England, by Her Letters Patent, bearing date at Westminster, the tenth day of October, in the Sixth year of Her reign, [1564] for the considerations therein mentioned, did give and grant full power, license, and authority to Thomas Thurland, Clerk, deceased, late one of the Chaplains and Master of the Hospital of the Savoy, and to Daniel Houghsetter, a German born, and to their heirs and assigns and every of them, for ever, by themselves, their servants, labourers or workmen, or any of them, to search, dig, open, roast, melt, stamp, wash, drain, or convey waters, or otherwise work for all manner of mines or ewers of gold, silver, copper and quicksilver, within Her Counties of York, Lancaster, Cumberland and Westmoreland, Cornwall, Devon, Gloucester and Worcester, and within Her Principality of Wales, or in any of them, and the same to try out, convert, and use to their most profit and commodity, and the commodity of every of them for ever, as well within Her own lands, grounds and possessions, as also within the lands, grounds and possessions of any of Her subjects, set, lying, and being within Her said Counties and Principality, or in any of them, without any let or

* The original Charter to the Mineral and Battery Wks. Co. was dated 6 days sooner, and should therefore be printed *before* that to the Mines Royal; but I desire to follow the sequence given them by 'W. P.,' doubtless for some good cause sufficiently well known to him.—G. G. F.

perturbation of Her, Her heirs or successors, or of any other person or persons whatsoever, together with divers other powers, authorities, licenses, privileges, benefits and immunities specified in the said Letters Patent for and concerning the effectual obtaining and enjoying of the premises as by the same Letters Patent, among divers other clauses and articles therein contained, more plainly and at large it may and doth appear.

And whereas, HER pleasure, intent and meaning in Her said Letters Patent was, that for the better help and more commodity of the said Thomas Thurland and Daniel Houghsetter and their several assigns, they and every of them might from time to time, and at their pleasure, grant, convey, and assign parts and portions in the said licenses, privileges, powers, authorities, benefits and immunities, and thereupon they and their several assigns have, since the making of the said Letters Patent, for divers good considerations, granted, assigned and conveyed unto divers other persons, their heirs and assigns, divers parts and portions of the licenses, powers, authorities, privileges, benefits and immunities aforesaid, with such profit and commodities as should or might arise by the use of the same.

And WHEREAS, the said Thomas Thurland and Daniel Houghsetter, and most of their grantees and assigns be since deceased, [*i. e.*, between 1564 and 1604] and all or the greatest part of the said licenses, powers, authorities, privileges, benefits and immunities, together with all or the greatest part of the profits and commodities by the use of the said licenses, powers, authorities, privileges, benefits and immunities arising and growing are now, by divers descents, devises, conveyances, or other lawful means, descended, devised, conveyed, or come unto the persons hereafter named (that is to say) to our right well-beloved Cousin, William Earl of Pembroke,* and to our right trusty and right well-beloved Councillor, Robert, Viscount Cranborne, our principal Secretary; and to our trusty and well-beloved Henry Lord Windsor, and to our right trusty and right well-beloved Councillor, Thomas Lord Burghley, and to our right trusty and well-beloved Thomas Lord Gerrard, and to our trusty and right well-beloved Counsellor, Sir John Popham, Knight, Chief Justice of the Pleas before us to be holden, assigned, and to our trusty and well-beloved Sir Edward Wynter, Knight, Sir Francis Popham, Knight, Sir John Smith, Knight, Roger Owen, Knight: Francis Needham, Arnold Oldsworth, Christopher Toldervey, William Gamage, Francis Beale, Otes Nicholson, Esquires: Richard Darnford, Gentleman; Edward Barnes, Mercer; Emanuel Demetrius, Merchant Stranger; Abraham Van Deldon, Merchant Stranger; Emanuel Hochstetter,† and Daniel Hochstetter.

And WHEREAS, the said Thomas Thurland and Daniel Hochsetter, in their lifetimes, and the said persons so as aforesaid interested in the said licenses, powers, authorities,

---

* Of these names it may be worthy of note, that this Earl of Pembroke was a Court favorite of the Tudors, and received many Grants of Manors, &c., in Glamorgan; amongst others, those of *Neath* and the adjoining districts: That Francis Needham was the writer of the letters at pp. 25, 34, in this Vol., who also appears in the list of original shareholders: Gamage, was the name of a well-known Glamorganshire family: Demetrius, the stranger, was, possibly, a Greek merchant, of London; while Van Deldon and the Hochstetters were evidently Dutch or Germans, the latter, in all probability, two sons† of the original Grantee:—On the foregoing Note I desire further to remark, that Lord Pembroke from *his Manors at and near Neath*, was well aware of the Coal to be thence obtained at reasonable cost, of suitable quality, and in any quantity; all very important matters in relation to smelting operations; the which it may be observed has ruled the retention of *Sites* for such furnaces ever since.— G. G. F.

† *Vide* p. 38.

privileges, benefits and immunities, and in the profits thereof arising, their ancestors, and those whose Estate they have by virtue of our said Letters Patent and by the skilful directions of the said Daniel Houghstetter have travelled in the search, works, and the experiments of the mines and ewers aforesaid, to their very great charge and expenses, and have brought these Works to very good effect, whereby great benefit hath ensued and is like more and more to ensue to Us and this our Realm of England, if the persons now and hereafter having interests in the licenses, powers, authorities, privileges, benefits and immunities aforesaid, and the profits thereby arising, might, by our Grant, be incorporate and made a perpetual Body Politic, thereby to avoid divers and sundry inconveniences which, by the several deaths of the persons abovesaid or their assigns, should also from time to time ensue.

Know ye, therefore, that We, minding and carefully intending the furtherance and advancement of the said Mineral Works so prosperously attempted, and with great charges begun and continued to the benefit and commodity of this our Realm of England and the subjects of the same, are not only well pleased and contented that the said William, Earl of Pembroke (and the others before-named), their heirs and assigns of every of them, together with such other persons and person as now have any lawful interest of or in the said licenses, powers, authorities, privileges, benefits and immunities, or any of them, shall enjoy, have, and use all the authorities, privileges, grants, liberties and licenses contained and specified in the said Letters Patent above remembered, according to the articles, clauses, grants and covenants in the same contained, which WE, for Us, our heirs and successors, do by these presents ratify and confirm, and do will the same in all respects to be construed and taken beneficially in favour of the said William, Earl of Pembroke [and the others before-named], their heirs and assigns, and of the heirs and assigns of them and every of them, but also for the better and more advancement of the said Mineral Works, and also to prevent such inconvenience as might hereafter be a let or hindrance to the same of our especial grace, certain knowledge, and mere motion have given and granted, and by these Presents for Us our heirs and successors, do give and grant to the aforenamed William, Earl of Pembroke, [and others aforenamed], that they, by the name of Governors, Assistants, and Society of the City of London of and for the MINES ROYAL, shall be from henceforth for ever one Body Politic in itself, incorporate and a perpetual Society of themselves, both in deed and name, and them by the name of Governors, Assistants and Society of the City of London, of and for the Mines Royal, WE for Us, our heirs and successors do constitute, make, ordain, incorporate, name and declare to be a Body Politic, corporate and perpetual, and by that name to have succession and continuance for ever by these Presents, and that they and their successors shall and may from time to time for ever, have a Common Seal to serve for the affairs and business of the said Governors, Assistants and Society, and of their successors, and that they and their successors shall and may be for ever able persons in the law as well to purchase, obtain, get, have and enjoy to them and their successors for ever, by the name aforesaid, of all and every person and persons now having or which hereafter shall have any lawful interest of, in, or to the said liberties, licenses, powers, authorities, profits, commodities, and other things whatsoever by the said late Queen granted by Her said Letters Patent or of, in, or to any part or parts thereof, all such right, title and interest as they or any of them have of, in, or to the same, or any of them, or of, in, or to any profit, benefit, or advantage arising of or by the same, or any of them, or of or by any parts or portions of the same, or any of them, as also to purchase, obtain, get, or have, to them and their successors, of whatsoever person or persons, bodies politic or corporate, in fee and perpetuity, or for term of life, lives, or years, or otherwise, at their wills and pleasures, lands, tenements, rents, reversions, and hereditaments, whatsoever they be, by the name of Governors, Assistants, and Society of the City of London, of and for the Mines Royal, and by the same name shall and may lawfully alien, grant, let, or set the same lands, tenements, rents, reversions, and hereditaments, or any part thereof, to any person or persons able in the law to receive and take the same, and that they and their successors, by the name of Governors, Assistants, and Society of the City of London, of and for the MINES ROYAL, shall and may be able in the law to sue and be sued, [&c.]

And furthermore, WE, for Us, our heirs, and successors, do by these presents, grant unto the said Governors, Assistants, and Society, and their successors, that they shall and may have one Governor, or two Governors of the said Society, and one Deputy or more Deputies to the said Governor or Governors, at their will and pleasure, and six more Assistants, at their will and pleasure, to assist and be joined with the Governor or Governors of the said Society, for the time being, or his or their Deputy or Deputies, for the better government of the said Society, and the matters, things, and causes of the said Governors, Assistants, and Society of the City of London, or of, or for the Mines Royal, from time to time, as need shall require.

And further, WE do make, ordain, and constitute, by these Presents, the before-named Robert Viscount Cranborne and Sir John Popham, Knight, to be the first and present Governors of the said Society, until the first Monday in the month of May, which shall be in the year of our Lord God Sixteen Hundred and Five, and further if need shall so require, until one other Governor, or two other Governors shall be chosen in their place.

And We do likewise make, ordain and constitute, by these Presents, the aforesaid Sir John Smith, Knight,* and Arnold Oldsworthy, Esquire, to be the first and present Deputies to the said Governors, until the said first Monday in the said month of May, in the said year of our Lord God Sixteen Hundred and Five.

And We do likewise make, ordain, and constitute, by these Presents, the above-named Sir Roger Owen, Knt., Francis Needham, Christopher Toldervey, William Gamage, Francis Beale, and Otes Nicholson, to be the first and present Assistants to the said Governors and to their said Deputies, to have and enjoy the said offices of Assistants [until the time aforesaid].

And further, We for Us, our heirs and successors do by these Presents grant to the said Governors, Assistants and Society of the City of London, of and for the Mines Royal, and to their successors, that they the said Governors, Assistants and Society, and their successors and every of them, shall and may from henceforth, until by rules and ordinances hereafter to be made as hereafter is declared, it shall be otherwise appointed, in places convenient and honest, as well within our City of London as elsewhere, within our Realm of England, where the Governors of the said Society, or his or their Deputy or Deputies for the time being, shall from time to time appoint, and after for ever, at such other place or places within our said Realm of England, as by rules and ordinances hereafter from time to time to be made, from time to time shall be appointed, assemble, and meet together in good and decent order, as well for the keeping of their Courts and for ordering of their affairs, business and things, as also for

* Had this Sir Jno. Smith, appointed Deputy in 1604, anything to do with either Sir Thos. Smith or Thomas Smyth the Customer?—G. G. F.

elections from time to time to be made of their Governor or Governors, and of his or their Deputy or Deputies, and of the Assistants aforesaid, or of any of them, and for the doing and executing of all and singular the powers, authorities, and things by these our Letters Patent in anywise granted, according to the purport and true intent hereof shall and may at such times and in such places as by ordinances, laws or rules, according to the tenor of these presents to be made, shall be from time to time therefor limited or appointed, name, elect, and choose one sage and discreet person, or two sage and discreet persons of the said Society, at their liberty and pleasures, to be the Governor or Governors of the said Society for one year ensuing, and so long after the same one year until one other Governor or two other Governors (as the case shall require) shall be duly elected and take upon him or them the room or rooms of the Governor or Governors of the same Society and one or so many more sage and discreet persons of the said Society as by the like ordinances, laws, or rules shall be limited or appointed to be the Deputy or Deputies of the said Governor or Governors, for so long a time as by the said laws, ordinances, or rules shall be limited or appointed, and six or so many more discreet persons of the said Society, as by the like ordinances, laws, or rules shall be limited or appointed to be the Assistants of the said Governor or Governors, and of his or their Deputy or Deputies, for so long a time as by like ordinances, laws, or rules hereafter shall be limited or appointed.

And that if it shall fortune the said Governor or Governors, Deputy or Deputies and Assistants, or any of them before by these presents appointed, or which shall hereafter be elected or chosen as is aforesaid do die or decease out of this transitory life before the end of the time for which they shall be so elected and chosen as is aforesaid, that then and so often it shall and may be lawful to or for the said Governor or Governors, Assistants and Society for the time being, or the most part of them, or so many of them as by ordinances, laws, or rules hereafter to be therefore devised, in form aforesaid, shall be limited and appointed to name, elect, and choose other discreet person or persons of the said Society, at their liberty and pleasure, to have and use the office, room and place, offices, rooms and places, of the same person or persons so deceased.

Moreover, WE for Us, our heirs and successors, have given and granted, and by these presents do give and grant unto the said Governors, Assistants, and Society of the City of London of and for the Mines Royal and to their successors, that the said Governors and Assistants that now be by these presents nominated and appointed, and the Society aforesaid, or the most part of them, and the Governor or Governors Assistants and Society of the City of London of and for The Mines Royal that hereafter shall be, or the most part of them, or so many of them as by ordinance, laws, or rules hereafter to be devised in form aforesaid shall be thought meet and convenient, shall have full power and authority from time to time at all times hereafter to keep assemblies and courts for the good rule and government of all causes, matters, and things belonging to the said Governors, Assistants, and Society of the City of London of and for the Mines Royal, and at such of the same assemblies and courts which, by laws, rules, or ordinances in that behalf, shall be made according to the purport of these presents shall be limited or appointed, to make, ordain, establish, and enact all such statutes, acts, ordinances, and rules for admitting of more persons which have or shall be appointed to have, for term of their life or lives at least, the benefit of such part of the said licenses, powers, authorities, privileges, benefits, and immunities as in these presents is hereinafter expressed, and in manner and form hereafter in these presents expressed, to be members of the said body public, and for the expelling or dismembering of such as shall be deemed unworthy to continue members of the said body corporate, and for the good and laudable demeanour and order of the Governor and Governors of the said Society, from time to time, for ever, and of his and their Deputy or Deputies, and of the Assistants of the Society that now be, or hereafter shall be, and also for the good government and order of the said Society, and of every person of the said Corporation, and of all and singular their causes, affairs, things, and business, from time to time, for ever, and for every other thing and matter whatsoever in these Letters Patent specified, or by the same referred to be ordered or directed by laws, rules, or ordinances hereafter to be made as to them shall be thought good, meet, convenient, and necessary, and the statutes, acts, ordinances, and rules, or any of them at their will and pleasure, at any such their assemblies and courts, as by their rules, ordinances, and laws in form aforesaid, to be devised shall be limited, to alter, change, revoke, and make void in part, or in all, from time to time.

And further We do for us, our heirs and successors, as much as in us is will and grant, by these presents unto the said Governors, Assistants, and Society of the City of London of and for The Mines Royal, and to their successors, that the said Governors, Assistants, and Society that now be, by these presents, nominated and appointed, and the Governor, Assistants, and Society that hereafter shall be, or the more part of them, or so many of them as by the ordinances or rules hereafter to be therefor devised as is aforesaid, shall be limited or appointed at such of their said courts and assemblies as in form aforesaid—shall and may not only admit into the said Corporation and Society such and as many persons whether they be English or denizens, aliens or Strangers, as by the statutes, acts, ordinances, and rules aforesaid, or any

E

of them, shall be prescribed or appointed, so that every such
person so hereafter to be admitted shall either according
to the tenor and true meaning of the statutes, acts, and
ordinances, and rules in that behalf hereafter to be made
as is aforesaid, be appointed at or before time of his
admission to have for the term of his life at least the benefit
of a quarter of one four-and-twentieth part of the licenses,
powers, authorities, privileges, benefits, and immunities
aforesaid, or else being admitted within one year now next
ensuing, shall be appointed, as is aforesaid, at or before the
time of his said admission to have, for the term of life at
least, the benefit of half-a-quarter of one four-and-twentieth
part of the licenses, powers, authorities, benefits, and immunities aforesaid, or else, being a Gentleman and a
Freeholder of an estate of inheritance to his own use, without
condition, in deed of lands and tenements within the counties
of Lancaster, Cumberland, and Westmoreland, or any of
them, to the clear yearly value of forty marks of lawful
English money, over and above all charges, shall, according
to the tenor and true meaning of the statutes, [&c.,] and
shall be admitted within the space of three years now next
ensuing, and not at any time after, but also shall and may
minister to such person so to be admitted an oath, tending to
the due performing and keeping of rules, statutes, and
ordinances, in form aforesaid to be made, and a note of such
admittance shall deliver in writing, under their Common Seal,
to the person so admitted, which person or persons that shall
fortune hereafter to be, in manner and form aforesaid,
admitted into the said Society and Corporation, shall from
the time of his or their admittance and oath, taken in manner
and form aforesaid be free of the same; and that no person
or persons who shall hereafter be admitted into the said
Society in any other manner or form than is before expressed
or contrary to the purport or true meaning of these presents,

shall, in anywise, be or be accounted any member of the said Society or Corporation; and that no person or persons which now be or hereafter shall be admitted into the said Society, in manner and form before expressed, and according to the purport and true meaning of these presents, and which, at the time of his admittance, hath or shall have, or is, or shall be appointed to have the benefit of one quarter of one four-and-twentieth part of the licenses, powers, authorities, privileges, benefits, or immunities aforesaid, or more, shall alien, renounce or depart with, or be otherwise according to rules, acts, and ordinances, in that behalf hereafter to be made as is aforesaid, amoved, avoided or excluded of or from his whole benefit or interest of and in the said licenses or other the premises, or of or from so much of the same as the residue of the said benefit or interest of or in the said licenses and other the premises which shall remain to him during his life at the least, shall not amount and extend to the benefit of one whole quarter of one four-and-twentieth part of the said licenses and other the premises shall anywise at any time after be, or be accounted to be any member of the said society or Corporation, and that no person or persons which now be or hereafter shall be admitted into the said Society in manner or form before expressed, and according to the purport and true meaning of these presents, and which, at the time of his admittance, hath or shall have, or is or shall be appointed to have the benefit but of one half-quarter of one fourth-and-twentieth part of the licenses, [&c.,] shall in anywise or at any time after be or be accounted to be any member of the same Society or Corporation, anything before in these presents contained, or any act, rules, or ordinance hereafter to be made to the contrary in anywise notwithstanding.

And also that the said Governors, Assistants, and Society that now be by these presents nominated and appointed, and the Governors, Assistants, and Society that hereafter shall be, or the more part of them or so many of them as by ordinances hereafter to be therefore devised as is aforesaid, shall be limited or appointed at such of their said Courts and Assemblies, as in form aforesaid shall be limited may dismember and put out of the said Society and Corporation such person or persons as they shall determine unworthy to be continued a member of the said Corporation: And also that the Governors, Assistants, and Society of the City of London, of and for the Mines Royal, and their successors or as many of them as by the ordinances, laws, or rules, in form aforesaid shall be made shall be authorised, shall and may from time to time, at their pleasure, keep ordinary Courts and Assemblies for to put the statutes, acts, and rules so to be made, and remaining in force and not repugnant to anything contained in these presents in due execution, and to rule and govern according to the said statutes, acts, ordinances, or rules, every person or persons being a member or members of the body politic or Corporation aforesaid, and all the ministers, officers, laborers, and workmen of the said Governors, Assistants, and Society, and of their successors, and to execute and do full and speedy justice to them, and every of them, in all their causes, differences, variances, controversies, and complaints within any our realms, dominions, or jurisdictions among themselves to be had or moved in anywise.

And also We for Us, our heirs and successors, have granted, and by these presents of our special grace, certain knowledge and mere motion, do grant unto the said Governors, Assistants, and Society of the City of London of and for The Mines Royal, and to their successors, that they and their successors shall and may lawfully purchase, obtain, take, have, and enjoy to them and their successors for ever, lands, tenements and hereditaments whatsoever, which be not or shall not be holden of Us, our heirs and successors, immediately in capite or in chief, so that the said lands, tenements or hereditaments exceed not in the whole the clear yearly value of one hundred pounds of lawful money of England.

And also We will, and by these presents do grant for Us, our heirs and successors, to the said Governors, Assistants, and Society, that they or the more part of them, or so many of them as for the time, by statutes, acts, ordinances and rules in form aforesaid to be made, or any of them, shall be thereto appointed or authorised, shall and may have full power and authority by these presents from time to time, as to them it shall seem good, to limit, set, ordain, and put reasonable pains and penalties, by fines, forfeitures, and imprisonments, or any of them, upon any being a member or members of the body politic, Society or Corporation aforesaid, or a minister, officer, or servant, labourer or workman of the same, for any offence touching the said Governors, Assistants and Society, or their works, affairs, or other things contrary to the statutes, acts, ordinances and rules so to be devised and made as aforesaid, or any of them.

And further, We will by these presents, that if any of the Body Politic, Society or Corporation, at any time hereafter shall be found contrarious, rebelling, or disobedient to the said Governor or Governors and Assistants for the time being, or to any, the statutes, acts, ordinances, or rules to be made as is aforesaid and then remaining in force, and not repugnant to anything in these presents, that then the said Governors and Assistants of the said Society and Corporation for the time being, or the more part of them, or such and so many of them as by statutes, acts, ordinances, or rules aforesaid shall be therefore authorised, shall and may, by virtue of these presents, correct and punish all and every such offender or offenders, as well by fines, pains and penalties, as by imprisonment within any of the gaols or prisons of Us, our heirs or successors, as the quality of the fault shall require, according to their good discretions. And further, We will that none of the said offender or offenders shall decline from or refuse the justice, order, direction, power, or authority of the said Governor or Governors and Assistants, or the more part of them for the time being, or of the persons so to be authorised as is aforesaid.

Moreover, We, for us, our heirs and successors will, and by these presents grant unto the said Governors, Assistants, and Society, and to their successors, that the said Governor or Governors, and Assistants of the Society aforesaid for the time being, or the more part of them, shall have full power and authority to assign, constitute, and ordain one officer or divers officers as well within our said City of London as also in any other places of this our realm of England, which officer or officers we will to be called by the name or names of Serjeant or Serjeants of the City of London, of and for the Mines Royal; and that the said serjeants shall and may have full power and authority, by these presents, to take, receive, levy, and gather all manner of fines, forfeitures, penalties or pains of every person or persons of the said Body politic or Society that shall be convicted upon or for breaking of any statutes, acts, ordinances, or rules, to be made as is aforesaid.

And further, We will and also grant for us, our heirs and successors, that the said officer or officers shall have further power and authority for default of payment or for disobedience in that behalf, if need be to set hands, take, and arrest, as well the body and bodies, as also the goods and chattels of such offender or offenders and transgressors in all and every place and places being no town and city corporate: And if it shall fortune any such offender or offenders, their goods or chattels, or any part thereof to be in any city or town corporate where the said officer or officers may not lawfully intromit or intermeddle, that then the mayors, sheriffs, bailiffs, or other head officers or ministers within any such city or town corporate, upon a precept to them or any of them, to be directed under the common seal of the said Governors, Assistants, and Society for the time being, shall and may attach and arrest the body and bodies, goods and chattels, of such offender or offenders there being: and the said body or bodies, goods and chattels, and every part, and every part so attached and seized shall, according to the tenor and purport of the said precept. And further, We will and grant for us, our heirs and successors, by these presents, that all and every such mayor, sheriff, bailiff, and other head officers and ministers of such city or town corporate shall not be impeached, molested, vexed, or sued in any court or courts of us, our heirs or successors, for executing or putting into execution any of the said precept or precepts, [&c.]

Nevertheless, Our will and pleasure is, that in all assemblies hereafter to be had for the making or devising of any of the laws, rules, orders, or ordinances aforesaid, or for the making of the elections aforesaid, or for the doing of any other thing aforesaid, by these presents referred to be done, or which by any laws, rules, or ordinances to be made as is aforesaid, shall be referred to be done by the most part of the said Society, or by any other number by these presents appointed, or hereafter to be appointed in manner and form aforesaid, every person that shall be a member of the said body politic, and that shall be appointed in manner and form therefore before limited, to have the benefit of half-a-quarter or more of one four-and-twentieth part of the said licenses, powers, authorities, privileges, benefits and immunities, shall be admitted to have a voice and suffrage and to be accounted to be of the said numbers and none other in any manner of wise, the same account to be made and every such voice and suffrage to be reckoned, esteemed, and allowed, of in manner and form ensuing and not otherwise (that is to say), that the voice and suffrage of every person that shall be appointed in manner and form therefore before limited, to have the benefit of one four-and-twentieth part of the said licenses, powers, authorities, privileges, benefits, and immunities, shall be accounted, esteemed, and reckoned of as great account, force, and validity, and for so many voices and suffrages as the voices and suffrages of any two other persons of the said Society, whereof each one shall be appointed to have the benefit in manner and form therefore before limited, but of half-a-quarter of one four-and-twentieth part of the said licenses, powers, authorities, privileges, benefits, and immunities, be, or shall be, and so after that rate and proportion, the voice and suffrage of every singular person that shall be in manner and form therefore before limited, appointed to have the benefit of any greater part or proportion of the said licenses, powers, authorities, privileges, benefits, and immunities than one quarter of one four-and-twentieth part thereof shall be accounted, reckoned, or esteemed to be of as great account, force, and validity, and for so many voices and suffrages of so many other divers several persons whereof every one shall be appointed in manner and form therefore limited, to have but the benefit of half-a-quarter of one four-and-twentieth part of the said licenses, powers, authorities, privileges, benefits, and immunities, and whose said several portions shall not exceed in quantity the said part or portion of the said singular person be or shall be willing therefore, and straitly charging and commanding all and singular our officers, mayors, sheriffs, justices, escheators, constables, bailiffs, and all and singular other our ministers, liege men, and subjects whatsoever to be aiding, favoring, helping, and assisting to the said Governors, Assistants, and Society, and to their successors, and to their officers, ministers, serjeants, factors, deputies, and assigns, and to the deputies, factors, and assigns of every of them in executing and enjoying the premises and every of them from time to time, and at all times when they or any of them shall be thereto required, although express mention, &c.

In witness whereof, &c.

We shall now proceed with the other confirmatory Charter of King James the First, granted to "The Mineral and Battery* Works Society" six days previous to the one we have just been perusing. These two Companies were, in the time of Charles the Second, practically amalgamated, for in the year 1670, they had *the same* Governor, Deputy Governors, and Assistants, and were generally known by the name of "The Mines Royal"; and they so remained under one management until their dissolution in 1852, when, by the combined action of several of the Copper Companies of that day purchasing up the Shares and then not carrying out the executive clauses in the Charters, the powers were allowed to lapse, and so the charters lost their old vitality and legal force.

As in the former Grant we found a German joined to an Englishman, so here again we have the then Master of the English Mint partner with another German, "a workmaster of St. Annenburg in Saxony," skilful in the finding of Calamine or Zinc, and in the mixing of it with Copper for the making of Latten or Brass. The preamble of the Grant is, however, so explicit that I shall not further amplify but request its careful perusal for the very interesting details which it gives of the Originators and of their manufactures.

---

* This word might appear puzzling were it not remembered that it means hammered or beaten, which is peculiarly the practice with Copper and Brass manufacturers—the word remains in common use in the law, people being constantly before the Justices for assault and *battery*.

XVIII.
CONFIRMATORY CHARTER TO THE MINERAL AND BATTERY* WORKS SOCIETY.

Granted by Qn. Elizabeth, and

Confirmed at Westminster Abbey, the Twenty-second day of January, in the First Year of the Reign King James the First (1604) as follows:—

JAMES, by the Grace of God, King of England, Scotland, France and Ireland, Defender of the Faith, &c. To all to whom these our Letters Patent shall come, Greeting,

WHEREAS our dear late Sister Elizabeth, late Queen of England, having received credible information that her faithful and well beloved subjects, William Humphrey, then Say master of her Mint within her Tower of London, by his great endeavour, labour, and charges, have brought into her realm of England one Christopher Shutz, now deceased, an Almaigne, born at St. Annenberg, under the obedience of the Elector of Saxony, a Work-Master, as it was reported, of great cunning, knowledge, and experience, as well in the finding of the Calamine stone called in Latin "Lapis Calaminaris" and in the right and proper use of the commodity thereof for the composition of the mixed metal commonly called Laten, and in reducing it to be soft and malleable, and also in apting, mannering, and working the same for and into all sorts of battery wares, cast work, and wire, and also in the mollifying and mannering of iron and steel, and drawing and forging of the same into wire and plates, as well

---

* This should have preceded xvii, being dated 6 days earlier, see note at foot of p. 40.

But again, query as to this, for James's were but *confirmatory* Charters to those granted by Elizabeth, and in these the dates are the other way, giving the Mines Royal the precedence.—G. G. F.

convenient and necessary for the making of Armour, and also
for divers other needful and profitable uses. The said late
Queen Elizabeth thereupon, through the good hope she had
received of the information aforesaid, and certainty of the
same, of her special grace, certain knowledge, mere motion,
and prerogative royal, by her Letters Patents under the Great
Seal of England, bearing date at Westminster, the seventeenth
day of September, in the seventh year of her reign [1565],
for her, her heirs and successors, did give and grant full
power, commission, license, and authority to the said William
Humphrey and Christopher Shutz, their heirs and assigns,
and every of them for ever, by themselves, their servants,
labourers, workmen, deputies, and assignees, to search,'dig,
and mine for the said Calamine Stone, in all places of her
realm and kingdom of England, and within the parts of
Ireland known at the time of the making of her said Letters
Patents by the usual name of the English Pale, and all the
dominions and territories of the same, or either of them, and
the same stone, and the only use employing and commodity
thereof for the making and compounding of laten and
all other mixed metal to take, have, use, enjoy and employ,
and also all kinds and sorts of battery wares, cast works, and
wire of laten, iron, steel and battery, to make, manner, and
work into, and for all manner of plate and wire or otherwise,
needful and convenient for all manner, uses and purposes, to
their most benefit and profit, and to the benefit and profit
of every of them for ever: and any house or houses by their
or any of their discretion meet, necessary, and convenient for
the melting, mannering, casting, working and compounding
of the said metals, battery plate and wire, at their pleasure,
and at their own proper costs and charges to erect, build, set
up and use, as well in and upon any her own lands, grounds
and possessions, as also in and upon the lands, grounds and
possessions of any of her subjects within her said Kingdom

and Realms of England, and parts of Ireland, as is above said or either of them, or within any of her dominions, territories, borders or confines of the same, or of any of them, without any manner of let, perturbance or molestation of her, her heirs or successor, or of any other person or persons, together with divers other powers, authorities, licenses, privileges, benefits and immunities specified in the said Letters Patents, as by the same amongst divers other clauses and articles therein contained more plainly and at large it doth and may appear.

WHEREAS ALSO, the said late Queen Elizabeth, by her other Letters Patents, bearing date at Westminster the said seventeenth day of September, in the said seventh year of her reign, [1565] reciting by the same that where theretofore she had granted privilege to Cornelius de Vos for the mining and digging in her Realm of England for alum and copperas, and for divers ewers of metal that were to be found in digging for the said alum and copperas, incidentally or consequently, without fraud or guile, as by the same her privilege might appear. And further, reciting by the same her Letters Patent last mentioned, That whereas she, moved by the credible report to her made by one Daniel Houghsetter, a German born, and of skill and knowledge of and in all manner of mines of metals and minerals, had given and granted privilege to Thomas Thurland, Clerk, one of Her Chaplains, and Master of Her Hospital of Savoy, and to the same Daniel for digging and mining of all manner of ewers of gold, silver, copper, and quicksilver, within her Counties of York, Lancaster, Cumberland, Westmoreland, Cornwall, Devon, and Worcester, and within her Principality of Wales, and with the same further to deal as by her said privilege thereof, granted and made to the said Thomas Thurland and Daniel Houghsetter may appear, and where she then being minded that the said commodities and all other treasures of the earth in all other places of her realm of England, and also in the parts called the English pale, within her realm of Ireland, should be searched out for the benefit and profit of her, her said realms, and subjects of the same, and having then received credible information as well of the great industry, travel, and expense that her faithful and well-beloved subject, William Humphry, then Say Master of her Mint within the Tower of London, had about mines, mineral ewers, and matters metalline, of long time bestowed and borne, and then did whereby they were found out in divers and sundry the said other places of said realms, not only divers ewers of metals likely to prove right rich and profitable, but also as and by his diligence, procurement, and charges, there were then *brought and worne [sic] into her said realms of England Work-Masters of great cunning, perfectness, knowledge, and experience in all kinds of mineral works and water works for the draining of all manner of mines, therefore the said late Queen Elizabeth, of her special grace, certain knowledge, mere motion and prerogative royal, by the same her last recited letters patents for her, her heirs and successors, did give and grant full power, license, and authority to the said William Humphry and to Christopher Shutz, their heirs and assigns, and every of them for ever, by them, their servants, labourers, workmen, deputies, and assignees, to search, open, dig, mine, and try all earths, grounds, soils, and places of and in her kingdom and realm of England, and of and in all the dominions, territories, borders, and confines of the same, together with all and singular so much of her realm of Ireland, territories and dominions thereof, as then were within the limits and bounds of all which was or before had been known, called, or taken to be of the English pale, except only the Principality and Counties expressed in the

* Worne, possibly here means settled or used.—O. G. F.

said privilege to the said Thomas Thurland and *David
Houghsetter, as is aforesaid granted: and to convey, carry,
and work in waters and water works belonging to the said
mines, in all places and territories of and in her said realms,
and either of them, as afore is mentioned, except before
excepted for all manner of ewers, simple and pure, or mixed
and compound, of the metals of gold, silver, copper,
quicksilver, and for all other minerals and treasure likely to
be found in the said earth, grounds, places, and soils, or any
of them, and for tin and lead in such sorts as by the laws and
customs of her said realm thence was and before had been
lawfully, copperas and lead in her said realm of England,
as before is said only excepted: and the same ewers, simple
or mixed minerals, metals, and treasures, to drain, break,
stamp, wash, boil, roast, and melt, or otherwise to fine and
bring to best perfection of metal, and them and every of them,
to convert, take, enjoy, and use, to their most commodity
and profit, and to the profit of them and every of them for
ever, and any house or houses by their discretion, meet,
necessary, and convenient, for the working and mannering of
the said ewers, minerals, and matters metalline, at their
pleasure, at their own proper costs and charges, to erect,
build, set up, and use, as well in and upon any her own
lands, grounds, and possessions, as also in and upon the
lands, grounds, and possessions of any of her said subjects,
within her said realm or kingdom of England, and
within the parts of her said realm of Ireland aforesaid, or
either of them, or within any dominions, territories,
borders, or confines of the same, or of either of them,
without any manner of let, perturbance, or molestation
of her, her heirs or successors, or any other person or persons,
together with divers other powers, authorities, licenses,
privileges, benefits, immunities, and exemptions specified in

* Apparently a clerical error of David for Daniel.

the said last recited Letters Patents, as by the same amongst divers other Clauses and Articles therein mentioned, and plainly and at large it doth and may appear.

And whereas for the better execution of the said grants, powers, authorities, licenses, privileges, benefits and immunities, and for the raising a convenient stock to be employed in the building of water-works, erecting of houses, provision of wood, mine and coal, buying of tools and payment of wages, and supply of divers other things in and about the execution of the said grants, powers, authorities, licenses, privileges, benefits and immunities, they the said William Humphry and Christopher Shutz have heretofore granted to divers other persons, their heirs and assigns, divers parts and portions of the said grants, powers, authorities, licenses, privileges, benefits and immunities, to them, their heirs and assigns as aforesaid, made and granted together, with all such profits and commodities as should and might arise from the same.

And whereas the said William Humphrey and Christopher Shutz, and most of their grantees be since deceased, and all or the greatest part of the said powers, authorities, licenses, privileges, benefits and immunities to the said William Humphrey and Christopher Shutz, their heirs and assigns, by the said two several letters patent granted as aforesaid, together with all or the greater part of the profits and commodities by the use of the same powers, authorities, licenses, privileges, benefits and immunities arising and growing, are now by divers descents, devises, conveyances, or other lawful means descended, devised, conveyed, or come unto the persons hereinafter named, that is to say, to our right well-beloved Cousin, William Earl of Pembroke; and to our right trusty and right well-beloved Chancellor, Robert Lord Cecil, our principal Secretary; and to our trusty and well-beloved Sir Julius Cesar, Knight, one of our Masters of Requests;

Sir James Pemberton, Knight, Alderman of our City of London; Sir William Bond and Sir James Lancaster, Knights; John Osborn, Thomas Cesar, Francis Bartye the elder, Arnold Oldsworth, *Christopher Toldervey, William Gamage, Charles Chute, Henry Tamworth, and William Bond the elder, Esquires; Henry Palmer, Francis Bartye the younger, Richard Danford and George Browne, Gentlemen, and to Richard Martin the younger, and Nathaniel Martin, of our City of London, Goldsmiths, and to Richard Collins, of our said City of London, Stationer, and to Alexander Found, of our said City of London, Embroiderer.

And whereas the said William Humphry and Christopher Shutz in their lifetimes, and the said persons so as aforesaid interested in the said power, authorities, licenses, privileges, benefits and immunities, and in the profits thereof arising, their ancestors, and those whose estates they have by virtue of the said several Letters Patent, have travelled in the search, right use, working and experiment of the said Calamine Stone, and of other the said Battery Works, Ewers, Minerals, and matters metaline to their very great charge and expenses, and have brought the same to very good effect, whereby great benefit and profit have ensued, and is likely more and more to ensue to us and our said Realms, if the persons now and hereafter having interest in the powers, authorities, licenses, privileges, benefits and immunities aforesaid, and the profits thereby arising might by our grant be incorporated and made a perpetual body politic, thereby to avoid divers and sundry inconveniences, which by the several debts of the persons above said or their assigns should else from time to time ensue.

Know ye therefore that We, earnestly minding and intending the furtherance and advancement of the right use and working of the Calamine Stone, and other the premises, are not only

* Some of these may be found in the other Charter of a previous page.

well contented and pleased that the said [names before
mentioned] together with such other person and persons as
now have any lawful interest of or in the said grants, powers,
authorities, licenses, privileges, benefits and immunities contained and specified in the said several letters patent above
remembered, according to the clauses, articles, grants and
covenants in the same contained, which we for us, our heirs
and successors, do by these presents ratify and confirm, and
do will the same in all respects to be construed and taken
beneficially in favour of the same [names before mentioned]
and every other person and persons now have, or which
hereafter shall have any lawful interest of or in the said
grants, powers, authorities, licenses, privileges, benefits and
immunities, or any of them, by or under the persons aforesaid,
which have now the present interest in the same; but also
for the better and more advancement of the said working of
the said Calamine Stone at Battery Works and other the
premises, and to prevent such inconveniences as might hereafter be a let or hindrance to the same of our especial grace,
certain knowledge and mere motion have given and granted,
and by these presents for us our heirs and successors do give
and grant to the afore-named that they shall be from henceforth for ever one body politic and corporate in itself, and a
perpetual society of themselves, both in deed and in name by
the name of Governors, Assistants and Society of the City of
London of and for the Mineral and Battery Works, and them
by the name of Governors, Assistants, and Society of the City
of London of and for The Mineral and Battery Works, We
for Us, our heirs and successors, do by these Presents constitute, ordain, incorporate, name and declare to be one body
corporate and perpetual, and that by that name they shall and
may have succession and continuance for ever by these
Presents, and that they and their successors shall and may
from time to time for ever have a Common Seal.

The remainder of the Charter I shall give in the most abbreviated form, both for the comfort of the reader and the saving of space.

May by their name, &c., purchase lands.

May by the same name sue and be sued.

May have two Governors, two or more Deputies, and eight or more Assistants.

Names of the present Governors [before stated].

Names of the first Deputies [before stated].

Names of the first eight Assistants [before stated]

May hold Courts in London or elsewhere in England, until otherwise appointed.

To elect two Governors, two Deputies, and eight or more Assistants, who are to continue until others are chosen, and

If any die, power to choose others in their stead.

To have power to make laws, admit and increase members, and to fine and disfranchise the disobedients.

May alter and change bye-laws and make new.

Officers, &c., of the Company exempted from serving on juries.*

May admit aliens and strangers to be members.

May dismember those whom the Court shall deem unworthy to continue Members.

To keep Courts for hearing all causes arising between members, &c.

May purchase and hold lands, &c., not held *in capite*, to the clear yearly value of £100.

Power to inflict fines on offending members, and sue for same.

May imprison any offending members in gaols, &c.

May appoint one or more officers, called Serjeants, to levy fines.

* A few years ago I was present when this privilege was asserted and allowed by the Judges in the Assize Court at Swansea, to the then Manager, Mr. W. Edmond.—G. G. F.

The serjeants may arrest. But if in a city or town, Mayor or officer, upon a precept from the Court, to arrest.

The intent of this Charter to reform and supply some defects in former Patents.

Power to dig for Calamine Stone in England and Ireland, and make therewith mixed metals, &c.

Not to dig under any house, &c., without consent of owner, &c. Nor under any castle or other place belonging to the Crown without consent, and shall make satisfaction for all damages.

Four persons to arbitrate damages. If they cannot agree, the matter to be brought before His Majesty's Council, there to be decided.

All other persons forbid to use the Calamine Stone, or to dig or search for it. Forbids all persons to dig, get or mine any of the aforesaid ores, metals, &c., without license from the Company.

All other persons forbid to stop or hinder the Company or their servants, and also to use or occupy any the like engines without license, upon forfeiture of £100 for every offence, half to the Company and half to the Crown.

May hire artificers, and buy all manner of instruments, and may buy all timber except oak, elm and ash, and may chark* and use the same in and about the said works.

If the Crown thinks fit to have the other part of Ireland tried besides the English Pale, the Company to have the same prerogative as in English Pale.

The privileges granted to this Company are declared valid against all future grants, &c.

But if the Crown should think fit to resume this Grant, it may, first paying the proprietors the charges they have been at, provided it be kept for the use of the Crown, and not let to any person or persons.

* Evidence of the extent to which the use of Charcoal was applied in this manufacture, prior to the general use of native Coal.

And for the better execution of the premises, we will and command to all and singular our Justices, Barons of our Exchequer, and to our Serjeants-at-Law, Attorney and Solicitors-General, and to all other our ministers and officers whatsoever, that the said Governors, Assistants and Society, and all and every person and persons being of the same Society, or being any factor or agent of their or any of their business, shall have and enjoy all the benefit of these Presents from and after the said seventeenth day of September, in the said seventh year of the reign of the said late Queen, and that our said Justices, Barons, Serjeants, Attorney, Solicitor and other our Officers or Ministers aforesaid, or any of them, do not receive, allow, or suffer to be prosecuted in any of our Courts, any action, information, suit or process against the said Governors, Assistants or Society, or any other the person or persons aforesaid, and their factors or agents aforesaid, or any of them, for or touching any matter or thing in or by these Presents granted, any act or law, statutes or ordinances aforesaid whatsoever, to the contrary hereof notwithstanding, and as they tender the performance of our good pleasure in this behalf, and will answer for the contrary at their peril, although express mention, &c.

In witness whereof, &c.

*Tradition gives *the Site* of these important Works to the banks of the River Neath, and after much enquiry and local examination I have come to the conclusion that the premises east and near the present Neath Abbey Railway Station, now occupied by the Mines Royal Works, are on the identical spot

* In Lord Dynevor's private Act, 1st Vict., cap. xxvi., "The Mines Royal" taking is thus described in the schedule:—" Cadoxtan j. Neath, Mines Royal Copper Works and Lands, comprising several parcels of arable, pasture, and wood lands and gardens and cottages, together with sundry lands, part of which are in the hamlet of Duffryn, Clydach. 82a. 0r. 30p.—£300, in Duffryn, Clydach, 16. 3. 16."—G. G. F.

where those works were first planted by Customer Smyth and partners, and to which his loving servant Ulrick Frosse wended his way in the autumn of the year 1584.

On examining the premises under the kind auspices of Mr. William Edmond, the manager, he pointed out to me where, during some alterations of the works, he discovered the foundations of small ancient furnaces full three feet under the floor of the present works; further he pointed out the old House of the Managers still standing in the very centre of the smoke and exhalations from the works; though but a poor small residence as it would *now* be thought, it was evidently pretentious in its day, the jambs of the door and windows being enriched with "blockings" in the plaster work. This residence is reported to have been built for the first of the Places (who were for three generations its resident managers) about 17? In various walls of the works are dates cast in slagg or cut in native stone slabs, and I quote the following from sketches taken from the originals when examining the premises in 1865.—M.R. 1759 — M.R.Co. 1799 — M.R.C. 1800—M.R.C. 1805.

These important Companies were from the first patronized by Royalty and the nobility; William and the two Phillips (Father and Son) Earls of Pembroke, having been Governors; they were followed by Prince Rupert[*] and the Lord Ashley Cooper, who were succeeded by the Marquis of Halifax, who died in the year 1700. The Deputy Governors appear to have been chiefly taken from the rank of Knights, amongst whom many celebrated names appear, but few more interesting can be selected than that of Sir John Pettus, Kt.,

[*] It was this Governor who presented the interesting Portrait of the Foundress (Queen Elizabeth) by Zucchero, which so long adorned the board-room. It has recently been given to the National Portrait Gallery, in South Kensington Museum, where I have myself seen it.— G. G. F.

who distinguished himself by several important metallurgical works, and particularly by his translation of that of the German Metallurgist, Erckern, of whose character the following excerpts will give a fair impression and some knowledge.

In 1683, Sir John Pettus, of Suffolk, Knight, and for 30 years previous, a Deputy Governor of the Mines Royal Company, in his translation of the Assays of Lazarus Erckern, Chief Prover, or Assay Master of the Empire of Germany, dedicates his book to the Right Honourable George Marquess, Earl, Viscount Halifax, Baron of Eland, Lord Privy Seal, and Governor of the Society of the Mines Royal and Battery Works, and writes, "That the Government of Mines was a trust of great concern; for, from antient records, I find that Edward the IV. made Richard Earl of Warwick, and John Earl of Northumberland; and King Henry the VII. made Jasper, Duke of Bedford, and other Lords, Guardians and Governors jointly, of all His Mines in England, adding Wales; and Queen Elizabeth, in the 10th of Her reign, did form the Government thereof into Societies by the names of Governors, Deputy Governors and Assistants for the Mines Royal and Battery Works, and made Sir Nicholas Bacon Lord Keeper, and other eminent persons her Governors for England and Wales (adding those within the English Pale in Ireland), which Government did continue successfully to the Earls of Pembroke, and others for some years, and after His late Highness Prince Rupert was made a Governor, and your Lordship to our contentment doth succeed."

Sir John gave as one reason for publishing Erckern's work, "That we may not punish ourselves by fixing and disputing on the views of antient writers, and thereby making things to be diabolical which are only Divine favours shown us by natural agents, so as, for want of knowing the true practicks and experiments, they are divulged either by umbraging sophistications, or concealed under the name of philosophical secrets, which, no doubt but God intends for publick and common good, and therefore it shall be my study to unfold the metaphysical notions of this science by practicks, especially about the Philosopher's Stone, which study I value only for its fine pursuits and products of experiments."

He unhappily was at this time confined in the Fleet prison and dedicates his work—

"To my worthy friend Richard Manlove, Esq., Warden of the Fleet, in which I am here a confined person, for my being too good to others and too unjust to myself; those that think themselves prisoners to you are much mistaken, for they are prisoners to the Law, a guardianship very needfull for the people as a completion of Justice in point of restraints, for they are good for cooling the animosity between creditors and debtors, and between the Laws and contemnors of them; and for curing the sullen and contemptuous disposition of them to their superiors, for I can truly say that by my patient submission to them, and my misfortunes (being prepared by my 14 months' imprisonment in Windsor Castle under the late usurped power,) I do now, with more satisfaction to myself, undergo this under a legal power, and hereby affirm that no gentleman hath received greater receipts from you than myself, and therefore take the occasion to make my publick acknowledgments that I must acknowledge to my honoured subscribers and others, that had it not been for your incouragement and particular assistance with your purse, I could not have published this book."

It has generally been understood that the operation of the powers granted to these two Companies so far from promoting National interests, as was the declared object in their preambles, had an exactly opposite effect by crippling the free right of searching for and extracting ores from the various mining districts; and moreover, introducing a series of expensive lawsuits, which produced decisions sometimes in favour, and sometimes against the Company, until in the reign of William and Mary two Acts* were passed to settle the doubts and questions which had arisen consequent on the previous grants of Elizabeth and James.

The translation of Lazarus Erckern's book explains the art and nature in knowing, judging, assaying, firing, refining, and inlarging the bodies of confined Metals, and gives the various ways of extracting gold, silver, copper, lead, tin, antimony, and quicksilver from their ores, proving iron from steel, the making of saltpetre and allum from allum ore—and gives essays explaining † metallick words, and describes where the various mines are situated, and that the 'Mines-Royal' and 'Battery-Works' Societies held Royal mines in the various counties of England and Wales, in Bedfordshire, Cheshire, Cornwall, Cumberland, Derbyshire, Durham, Essex, Gloucestershire, Herefordshire, Kent, Lancanshire. Monmouthshire, Nottinghamshire, Northumberland, Rutlandshire, Shropshire, Somersetshire, Staffordshire, Surrey, Warwickshire, Westmorland, Worcestershire, Yorkshire, and in all the twelve Counties of Wales. We have government of them all both in England and Wales and part of Ireland, except the Lead Mines of Donegany, in Derbyshire, and at Mendyp, in Somersetshire. Of copper, Keswick Copper Mine, in Cumberland, caused a great suit between Queen Elizabeth and the Earl of Northumberland, concerning her right to it on account of "Royal Mines," which case is reported by Ploudon, whereby the Society for the Mines Royal have had, and still have the care

---

* In the 1st and 5th years of those monarchs.

† Query is "Calcator" given in it, I wonder—*no.*—G. G. F.

over it, but for want of fuel and skilful Miners it is of no use at present.

To work for Gold the Mines Royal Society granted two leases on Mines, one at Pullox-hill, in Bedfordshire, the other at Little Taunton, in Gloucestershire, but they were not eventually successful.

Of Silver we have none but intermixed with other metals, especially in Lead, and in the time of the late war Mr. Bushel set up mills at the Mines in Cardiganshire, and made out of these Lead Mines £20 of Silver out of every ton of Lead, and at the late usurpation his Majesty caused a Mint to be erected at Shrewsbury to * coyn the Silver from Wales; and the Lessees of the Mines Royal Society Work the Mines of Corisumlock and Talibont, in Cardiganshire in Wales (two Roman Mines); every year there were sent from hence (London) at least 800 tons of Bone Ashes by sea; our merchants for every 1000 Bones they send abroad pay 6s. 8d., and we pay for their bringing them unto us £1 5s. for every barrel of their Ashes.

Iron is not in our Patent, only from *Wire*, for the making of which we have Mills at † Tintern, in Monmouthshire.‡

Of Lead we have the government both in England and Wales, and the Society of Mines Royal have Lead Mines in Wales. Of Black Lead I know but of one Mine in Cumberland, and of late, it is curiously formed in cases of deal and cedar, and so sold as dry pencils, something more useful than pen and ink.§

* Smiles in his "Hugenots," says that in 1565, a Christopher Schutz first started the Wire Works near Tintern Abbey, while Godfrey Box of Leige, began the like business at Esher, in Surrey, where it was afterwards continued by two other Germans named Monineca and Demetrius. Was this last any connection of him named at p. 42, *ante ?*

† As may be seen in most collections of English coins.

‡ Which Works are still in operation, I believe.—1880.

§ An interesting fact as to the period when Black-lead Pencils were first brought into use, and made practically valuable.—G. G. F.

We have *mountains* of Lapis Calaminaris, especially in Gloucestershire, Somersetshire, and Nottinghamshire, but we let the Calaminaris go as ballast into foreign parts in very great quantities. The best Brass beyond seas is made of *our* Stone rather than their own, which deserves further consideration.

I remember about 30 years ago that one Demetrius, a German,* did set up a Brass Work in Surrey, and with the expense of £6000 (so he told me), made it compleat and to good profit, but the Foreign Merchants, joyning with ours, found ways to bring him into suits. He was at last necessitated to abandon the work, to his own ruin and the unspeakable loss to the Kingdom in the destruction of so beneficial a work.

The above concludes all I took out of Pettus's work as connected with the Mines Royal Company, and interesting to our purpose herein.

Robert Place (son of Isaac Place, Vicar of Haslingden, in Lancashire) was married to Catherine Swaine, daughter of Sampson Swaine, gentleman, Refiner of Copper, at Newlyn, in Cornwall, 4th March, 1754. His son John was born at Poole, in Cornwall, 15th June, 1756, and Edward his son was born at Neath Abbey, 29th August, 1758. Robert Place may have acquired the knowledge of Copper Smelting from his father-in-law, and between 1756 and 1758 came over to start and manage the smelting of Copper at the Mines Royal Works. There is some tradition that the Mines Royal Company had previously smelted Copper Ores at Redbrook, in Monmouthshire.† Their Lease expired in 1862, and 5 terms of 21 years

* This is conclusive against my suggestion in page 42 that he was a *Greek*. He must be added to the many *Germans* to whom we are so manifestly indebted for our present position in metallurgy.

† Feby. 19, 1869. To-day, referring to the Original of Grose's Tour in 1775, in B. Museum, I observed in his Diary, that "after passing Troy "House belonging to the Duke of Beaufort, I ascended a very steep hill "and passed some Copper and Iron Works, the walls of which were coped "with the scoriæ of the metal cast into cubes or bricklike forms, (so "common near Swansea) and could see at a distance the village of "Redbrook."—G. G. F.

would date 1757 as the starting of the Works under Place's management for the Mines Royal, and there is the date 1759 impressed in a cast slag in one of the old buildings.

Price, in his "Minerologica Cornubiensis," pub. 1778, mentions that the above-named Sampson Swaine, with some gentlemen of Camborne, in Cornwall, erected in 1754, Copper Furnaces at Entral, in that Parish, but afterwards removed them to Hayle, and that the then existing Copper Companies did all they could to "traduce the credit and stab the vitals of the undertaking." One of the Swaines came to Wales with Robert Place as an assayer, and his office is still at Mines Royal Works, Neath: but is now converted into a carpenter's shop.

I know nothing further of the Mines Royal Company till the 21st Sept., 1794, when they had 1277 tons of ore in stock; 230 tons of Copper Ore smelted weekly; about 130 tons produce from 7 to 8 per cent.; make of copper about 18 tons per week.

The following extracts from the orig. Books at the Mines Royal Works show the progress of events, and those relating to the old roof from the Copper Works at Melincrethyn, near Gnoll, at Neath, make a curious coupling of the two oldest works in existence in this county, and it is further interesting to note that a serious fear of the *Nuisances created by the Smoke** *existed, so far back as* 1796†—a nuisance only now [1865] about to be diminished, if not terminated, by Gerstenhöfer's patent, recently purchased and put into practice at great cost by Messrs. Vivian, in their Swansea and Taibach Works.‡

* That "Copper Smoke" is a doomed nuisance is pretty clear, for Messrs. Nevill and Co., at Llanelly, are adopting similar Calciners to those at Hafod, while Messrs. Grenfell and Son, White Rock, Swansea, and the Governor and Company of Copper Miners in Cwmavon, are about to patronise the plans of another *German*, Gurlt, for the utilization of the sulphur now thrown out as damaging Smoke on the lands near, and far from their respective Works. All other like Works should soon follow such unanswerable evidences.

† *Vide* p. 77, *post.*

‡ I am sorry to learn from Mr. Hussey Vivian, that as yet (Sept., 1868) the other Smelters have done *nothing* towards improving their works in this respect, neither have they down to 1881!—G. G. F.

EX MINES ROYAL BOOKS.

SIR ROBERT MACKWORTH.

Dr.							Cr.
	T. Q. lbs.		£ s. d.				£ s. d.
1793.—					1795.—		
April 16.—To	2 0 14 Copper, c. 18 m. 20...		10 9 1		September 29.—By Cash per Lady Mackworth ...		57 15 8
October 29.—,,	1 1 8 ,, c. ditto		5 17 10				
June 19.—,,	3 0 0 ,, c. ditto		13 8 9				
1794.—							
Decmbr 20.—,,	2 l Lady M.		9 10 0				
August 29,—,,	4 1 26 ,, ditto		18 10 0				
1795.			————				————
			£57 15 8				£57 15 8

LADY MACKWORTH.

Novmbr.17—,,	2 0 7 Coarse Copper	8 13 8		1796.—		
March 5.—,,	Cash	67 12 10		January.—By 736ft. of Roofing and Pantiles from Gnoll Wks.		76 6 6
1796.		————				————
		£76 6 6				£76 6 6
Decmbr.15.—,,	1 2 0	6 7 7		October 21.—By concave plate, to 15 cwt. at 8s.	5 4 0	
February 4.—,,	1 0 0	4 10 1		Balance	5 13 8	
		————				————
		£10 17 8				£10 17 8

CAPEL LEIGH, Esq.

1797.—				1797.—		
,,	Balance	5 15 8		August 30.—By Cash		21 10 7
August 13.—,,	3 2 20 Coarse Copper	15 14 11				
		————				————
		£21 10 7				£21 10 7

EXTRACTS.

From Mr. John Place, Manager to the Mines Royal Company.

1795.
30 March.—Sent 38 tons Copper to Rose Copper Co. Birmingham, and 17 tons to the East India Co.

28th Dec.—The Ores smelted for the Rose Copper Co.* are kept separate.

1796.
11 Jan. —By a Stack falling an arch gave way, bringing down seven others and the roof also.

18 ,, —Bought the old roof at Gnoll Works to replace our fallen one.†

25 ,, —Bought Barley for the workmen, but it is now selling at 5s. per bushel, or sixpence under what the Company paid for theirs.

14 March.—Barley too high in price for our consumption, so caused some of it to be sold in Neath market.

18 ,, —35 furnaces working.

16 May. —Coal so bad men left the works for two days.

23 ,, —Made 20 tons Copper this week.

27 June. —The Branch of the Neath Canal will not be ready before next June, it appears.

10 Oct. —Ores smelted this week, 136 tons; Copper made, 17 tons; Furnaces working, 38; Coals burnt, 315 tons.

31 ,, —I applied to Mr. Miers, who acts for his sister (Lady Mackworth) during her minority, as to a Lease of the Gnoll Works, with Rent and price of Coals. He is to consult with Mr. Hanbury, of Pontypool, to whom Lady Mackworth is to be married next March, when she will be of age.

14 Nov. —Mr. Miers, for Lady Mackworth, is ready to treat for a Lease of the Gnoll Copper Works. Coal 42s. per wey, as supplied to the late Gnoll Company.

26 Dec. —Lady Mackworth objects to sign the Lease, as she thinks *the Copper Smoke will waste the Gnoll House.*‡

1797.
2 Jan. —The accident that happened by the Stack falling, in January last, was more fortunate than otherwise, as the Roof that fell required to be made entirely new, and buying the materials at Gnoll Works for one third of what they would

---

* Mr. Keates writes "this proves that the Mines Royal Co. were at this time Smelting Ores for hire on account of the Rose Copper Co."

† *Vide* Account therefor on the previous page.

‡ The word "Waste" must be read here in its *legal* sense of injury, or mischief.

have cost new, and equally good—and this roof being of one span makes this part of the Works more airy and commodious.*

1797.
13 Feb. —Men began working 24 hours at a stretch. Mr. Parsons complains of them stealing much of his coal.

6 March. —'Tis not true that the French had landed at Swansea.

8 May —Mr. R. Parsons should send us better coals and better measure. Mr. Weaver, a Partner of Roe & Co. (of Macclesfield and Neath Abbey) is here and makes the same complaint.

Mr. Keates remarks upon this—" Roe & Co. had nothing to do with the Cheadle Works. Roe & Co. were Brass manufacturers at Macclesfield, in Cheshire, making their Copper at Neath Abbey, probably at the Works, afterwards occupied by the Cheadle Co. They later on built Copper Works close to Liverpool, and finally went out of the Copper and Brass trade about 1800."

12 June —Carmac and Co., of Ireland, have sent 32 tons of Copper to Swansea for sale. Produce, 18½ cwts. fine Copper per ton.

18 Dec. —The Furnacemen, on account of bad Coals, left their work this morning.

25 ,, —By reason of the Mail not arriving, my letter would, I fear, be too late for the meeting of our Company. The "Mines Royal"† is still at the Mumbles, with convoy, weather bound.

1798.
11 Jan. —All the men have left their work. They complain they do now work for less money than Roe & Co.'s men.

18 ,, —Our men have returned to their work, and I have promised them 6d. per day more, in all 16s. per week.

27 Aug. —Men are scarce on account of the harvest and Militia work. By our books,

The Companies then Smelting were the :—

Mines Royal Co.,	English Copper Co.,
Roe and Co.,	Chambers and Co.,
Freeman and Co.,	Anglesey Copper Co.,
Rose Copper Co.,	Yorkshire Copper Co.,
Lockwood Morris & Co.	Harford and Co.

For the above extracts from the original books, I am indebted to Mr. Wm. Edmond, of Clase, the late Manager of the Mines-Royal Works, Neath.

* This roof is still sound and on the works, 1866 and in 1881.

† The "Mines Royal" Sailing Vessel was afterwards captured by the French.

Though so many individuals and Companies issued Copper Tokens for the use of their workmen and the public, at the latter end of the 17th and the beginning of the 19th centuries, I cannot find that the Mines Royal struck any; a singular fact, when we reflect on its metallic and mechanical ability for such a monetary necessity. A friend has informed me that he has seen a Token issued by the *Brass Battery Company, but I have not been so fortunate.

That the dignity of these Companies should be fully sustained, they each received regular Grants of Arms from the Herald's College, and from amongst the armorial bearings of the Great Companies of the City of London given by Edmondson in his "Complete Body of Heraldry," from which I quote as follows :—

MINES-ROYAL, OR MINE ADVENTURERS' COMPANY. †

Incorporated 22 May, 1568.

"ARMS.—Argent a mine open of Earth colour, the upper part variegated with various shrubs *vert.*; within the mine a miner *proper*, vested *sable* on his head a cap *argent*, round his body a belt of the *last*, and in the attitude of working the dexter side of the mine, with two hammers: on the sinister side a candle *argent*, lighted *proper* in a candlestick *azure* fixed in the mine; on a chief *brown*, a square plate *or*, between a bezant on the dexter, and a plate on the sinister.

CREST.—On a wreath, a demi miner *proper* vested and capped as in the arms, holding in his dexter hand a pointed spade, erect *argent*, and his sinister hand a compass.

SUPPORTERS.—The dexter a miner, his face, legs and arms of a brownish colour, vested in a frock *argent*, tied about his knees as at work, cap and shoes of the *last*, holding in his dexter hand a hammer *azure* handled *proper*, the sinister supporter another miner *proper*, the cap, frock, and shoes *argent*, the frock loose and down to the ancles, in his sinister hand a fork *azure*, handled *proper*."

* See No. 29 Token, in APPENDIX. I suspect that the initials "B. B. Co." misled my friend.—G. G. F.

† *Sic* in Edmondson, but evidently a mistake, the correct name is to be found in the Charter itself, at page 45, *ante*.

MINERAL AND BATTERY WORKS SOCIETY.
Incorporated 28 May, 1568.

"ARMS.—Argent on a mount *vert*, a square Brazen pillar, supported on the dexter by a Lion rampant regardant; and on the sinister by a Dragon segreant, both *or*; in chief, on the top of the pillar a bundle of wire tied and bound together of the *last*, between a bezant on the dexter side and a plate on the sinister.

CREST.—On a wreath two arms embowed *proper*, both hands holding a Calamine Stone *argent*, spotted with red, yellow, and blue.

SUPPORTERS.—Two emblematic figures, viz.: the dexter, a Female *proper* representing *Science*, vested in a short bodice, coat, ruff, &c. *argent* (being the dress of the ladies in the reign of Queen Elizabeth). In her dexter hand a pair of compasses, and on her head a crescent, both *or*; crined of the *last*; the sinister figure an old Man *proper*, representing *Labour*, vested in a long frock turned up over his elbows, *argent*, in his sinister hand a hammer, *or*."

Elaboration could scarcely farther go, and the attempt to compel ordinary matters of routine life to fall under the technology of Heraldry is truly unfortunate, but the Companies being authorized to have "Common Seals;" that the devices must be supplied, was, I suppose, the argument used.

I have already stated how and when these Great Companies came to an end so far as respects their *Chartered* rights:[*] the old Works on the Neath River are now held by Messrs. Williams, Foster and Co., and are conducted under the ordinary commercial arrangements of the day.

Having at length exhausted my materials connected with the history of *The First Copper Works* established in Glamorgan by the Mines-Royal Society, I shall proceed with the next; but here a difficulty meets us at the very threshold. Did the "Mine Adventurers" or "The Governor and Company of Copper Miners in England" first light their furnaces, and if so, where, in *this County?* I am disposed to give the priority to Sir Humphrey Mackworth's

COMPANY OF "MINE ADVENTURERS,"[*]

at Melincrethyn, about one mile from the Town of Neath,

[*] The Mine Adventurers also had a Charter from William and Mary, dated 7 Sept., 1693. *Vide* a "familiar discourse," &c., 1700—p. 104.

on the London Road, where great heaps of Copper Slag remain to this day. Of the latter, or "The English Copper Company" as it is generally called for brevity, I know that its Charter is dated 1691, while Sir Humphrey himself tells us that he began in 1695, and the Company, as a Joint-stock, was not in possession of* a Crown Grant until the year 1704; still, there is no evidence that I am aware of for giving the Governor and Company a position in *Glamorganshire* before the 18th century. It is said they had works at Redbrook, in Gloucestershire, so far back as their first Charter, but I can find no testimony of their working in Wales before 1720. I shall therefore proceed to give Notes extracted from original documents and papers in the British Museum relating to the Mine Adventurers, under the title of

XIX.
MACKWORTH (SIR HUMPHREY) v. BREWER.

The Mine Adventure, fol. London, 1698—

Press-mark 522-6 M.—Old Catalogue.

It appears from these papers that Sir Humphrey Mackworth became engaged in Collieries and Copper Smelting Works at Neath, Anno 1695—that he was at first engaged on his own account, and that afterwards he transferred his Mines and Works to a Company called "The Corporation of the Governor and Company of the Mine Adventurers of England,"† of which the Duke of Leeds was Governor, and Sir Humphrey was Deputy-Governor and Resident Manager

---

* Here it is, however, shown that "the Co." held *its first meeting* in May, 1699.

† Chadwick in his life of De Foe 1859, p. 296, says that "De Foe being consulted on this scheme, and its probable chances of rubbing off the borrowed capital by the profits, referred to their own printed work entitled an 'Account of the clear profits of extracting Silver out of Lead, by the Governor and Commissioners of the Mine Adventurers of England, taken from their original accounts, and signed Thomas Horn, Accountant to the Co.'"—G. G. F.

of the Works *at Neath*. The Company consisted of a great number of members, many of them of aristocratic rank. The papers contain a list of the members.*

This Company must not be confounded with the better known and existing Company called

"THE GOVERNOR AND COMPANY OF COPPER MINERS IN ENGLAND,"

which afterwards erected Copper Works at Taibach. Amongst the papers is a printed copy of Articles of Agreement, dated 20 July, 1720, by which the latter Company acquired by purchase from Thomas Chambers, of the Transfer Office in the East India House, London, Gentleman, a lease of Copper Works, Furnaces, Forge, and Mill, at Lower Redbrook, in the County of Gloucester, for 30 years, at a rent of £100 per annum.

The most consecutive account of Sir H. Mackworth's Mines and Works is contained in a pamphlet, which seems to have been prepared by himself for local circulation, in 1705, with the following title:—

XX.

"THE CASE OF SIR HUMPHREY MACKWORTH AND OF THE MINE ADVENTURERS

WITH RESPECT TO THE ILLEGAL PROCEEDINGS OF SEVERAL JUSTICES OF THE PEACE,

For the County of Glamorgan, their Agents and Dependants."

From this case, in which it may be assumed Sir Humphrey *loquitur*, the following are abridged extracts:—

"The Coal Trade had been totally lost at Neath for 30 years and upwards for want of carrying on the Coal-works there—until Sir Humphrey Mackworth, in 1695, began to adventure great sums of money in finding and recovering the Coal in that neighbourhood; since which time the town of Neath, which was grown very poor for want of trade, was then become one of the best towns of trade in South Wales.

* The Rules, Orders, and Bye-laws of the Company, under date of 1706, and an engraving of its Corporate Seal, are also amongst these papers.

"The convenience and cheapness of Coal hath occasioned the building of great Work-houses, or Manufactories by Sir Humphrey Mackworth in Neath, at the expense of several thousand pounds; for smelting of Lead and Copper Ore, for extracting Silver out of the Lead, and for making Lytharge and Red Lead for the use of the Mine Adventurers."

These two paragraphs correctly state the case as it had often occurred in Wales, N. and S., with reference to the creation or suspension of trade and manufacture—discord, want of enterprize, absence of capital, general prostration and depression, which even in our time naturally follow like proceedings with similar consequences.

"These Coal Works and Work-houses employ a great number of men, women, and children, to whom several thousand pounds are paid every year, which circulates in this neighbourhood, and other trades are thereby increased, the market much improved, and the rents better paid, as has been acknowledged by Sir Edward Mansel and others; the country receiving money for provisions.

"The Coal Works wrought at that time lay chiefly under the common lands belonging to the town of Neath, and the Coals were in ancient times wrought by the Burgesses, each Burgess sinking a pit for himself. The Burgesses, at last, came to cross each other's works, which caused great differences and several law-suits; and these led to an arrangement by which the Burgesses granted a lease of the Coal-works to Daniel Evans, of Neath, Esq., a Burgess, yielding the Burgesses sufficient coal for their firing at the rate of twopence for each barrow of Coal, and also a rent or duty of one shilling to the Town for each weigh* of Coal sent to sea.

"The Burgesses granted leases in succession to David Evans, Esq., eldest son of their former lessee; to Frances, the relict of Edward Evans, and to Sir Herbert Evans, whose daughter and heir, Mary, became the wife of Sir Humphrey Mackworth.†

"During the last mentioned lease, Sir Humphrey Mackworth, being desirous to promote the good of the Town of Neath, gave liberty to the Burgesses to endeavour the recovery of the Coal in that Liberty for their own use, which they attempted at some expense, but, failing of success, all the Burgesses, in September 1697, did unanimously grant a lease to Sir Humphrey Mackworth for the term of 31 years, whereof about 23 years are yet unexpired.

* A "weigh" of Coal in Wales is calculated at 10 tons.

† This is the Eaglesbush family, I suppose—I think it likely that Sir Herbert was knighted by Charles I., in 1630—compulsorily as one of the tenants *in Capite* of the Crown. I recollect seeing his name as one of the persons in Glamorganshire who were likely to be called upon to accept knighthood. The date is, however, rather distant for such a supposition.—D. R.

"Sir Humphrey Mackworth attempted the recovery of the Coal-works by the assistance of the Colliers of that neighbourhood, but failed of success; whereupon he travelled into other counties to find skilful miners to assist him therein, and after great expense, and by carrying on a Level or Wind-way, commonly called a Foot-rid or Waggon-way, after the manner used in Shropshire and Newcastle, he recovered the said Coal-works; and at great expense continued the said waggon-way on wooden rails from the face of each wall of Coal, 1200 yards under ground, down to the water-side, three quarters of a mile.

"From the Coal-works carried on by these means, great quantities of Coal are brought forth and sold to use, whereby Her Majesty [Queen Anne] and the public receive annually, for the duty of these Coals, the sum of £1000 or upwards.

"It appears that the Coals were shipped to the port of Bridgewater, and other parts.

"The Mine-Adventurers had, however, much larger works than the Coal-works. They were lessees of extensive Lead Mines in Cardiganshire, from Sir Carbery Pryse, and the largest portion of their capital was employed in the manufacture of Lead, the ore having been brought from Cardiganshire to Neath to be made into metal. There are numerous printed accounts of the expense of refining Lead at Neath, and the names and wages of the workmen and boys employed are given. The highest number being 26, and the wages ranging from 3s. up to 26s. per week.

"The buildings consisted of the following Work premises, which are said to have been erected by Sir Humphrey Mackworth, at his own cost and charge, (before ever the Company was established or thought of) in order to set up a manufacture there for Copper and Lead on his own account, viz. :—

    An Old Smelting-house,
    A Copper-house,
    A Cleaning-Room,
    A Brick-Room, and
    A Stamping-Room.

"A Report of a Committee in the year 1708 states that they had erected several large Work-houses in the Counties of Glamorgan and Cardigan, consisting of 17 furnaces for smelting Lead, 2 for Copper, 8 for refining, and 2 for making Red Lead, and that there was room for 15 more.

"An account of Sir H. Mackworth's expenditure, by his agent, for ten years, under date of 15 April, 1710, gives a good notion of the extent of the Works.

"Disbursed in ten years, at the Copper-house at Neath, for wages, charges of smelting, refining, and making Red Lead, freight of Ore from Dovey, and of Lead from Bristol, and other charges—£16,689 15s. 4d.

"The Company allowed £30 per annum to Mr. Wm. Williams, a schoolmaster at Neath, for the education of the poor workmen's children—a similar allowance having been made in Cardiganshire.

"The origin of Sir H. Mackworth's connection with *Neath* seems to have been his marriage with the daughter of Sir Herbert Evans, of Eaglebush. He seems to have retained a residence at Bently, in the parish of Tardely, Worcestershire, and he had also property in Shropshire; the family originally came from Derbyshire.* The legal proceedings shew, by the proof of his own agent, that he acquired estates in the Counties of Glamorgan and Monmouth by his intermarriage with Mary, the daughter of Sir Herbert Evans, of Neath, that the rent of these estates amounted to £1200 per annum and upwards, and that his Coal-works produced him several hundred pounds more. It further appears that he bought estates in Monmouth and Glamorgan, and sold an estate in Salop to pay for them, at £5000. These disclosures were made on the part of Sir Humphrey to show that he had sufficient property to defray the expenditure (moderate it is asserted to be) of his household, so as to disprove the inference that he had paid the expenses of his private establishment by peculation as Deputy Governor of the Mine Adventurers.

"The complaints against the Justices referred to in the Case shew, if true, that Sir Humphrey experienced much local opposition in his Works. Attempts (he says) were made by interested persons concerned in other Coal-works to ruin and destroy his Works by disparaging the Coals at Bridgewater and other ports, and also the Port of Neath—and by threatening to press the seamen that came to his Coal-works. Attempts were also made to draw away the chief workmen. The case shows a great deal of anger and violence between the parties. The particulars are of but little importance now."

The foregoing extracts were made for me at the British Museum, by Mr. David Rowland, Solicitor, of London, who kindly adds in an accompanying letter,—"The Company appears to have been unsuccessful, and Sir Humphrey's management was impugned by some of the shareholders, who took legal proceedings against him and others similarly charged. The papers contain several elaborate defences drawn up by Sir Humphrey, and finally they show the

* There have been two Baronetcies in this family, the elder one created 1619, expired 1803; and the present, created in 1776, and now represented by Sir Arthur W. Mackworth, the sixth Baronet.—G.G.F.

failure of the legal proceedings, and an acquittal of Sir H. from all dishonesty by a majority of the Company.

A very large mass of original documents relating to these matters are still extant amongst the Gnoll Castle papers at Neath, to which ready access has been afforded me; the difficulty in such a case is not, the quantity but the quality of the extracts to be taken, pertinent to the special matter in hand; I select the following as historically interesting:—

XXI.

Att the First Select Committee of
THE FORTUNATE ADVENTURERS,
Held at Durham Court, in Great Trinity Lane, London, on Wednesday, the 10th day of May, A.D. 1669,
Present, Sir Humphrey Mackworth, Deputy Governor; Sir Thomas Mackworth, and ten Others.

"The Twenty Thousand Pounds Stock lockt up in the iron chest, was taken out, viewed, and told by the gentlemen present att this committee, and then laid again into the Chest."

[At length we are drawing on to the period when business had settled itself more into the shape it has assumed in our times, so that I have thought it prudent as far as possible to adopt the form and matter where practicable of the determinations of Boards and Directors, so as to make them mirrors of the times, and exhibit themselves and their doings in the words recorded and preserved in their own minutes.]

1699.
15 May—

    Sir Humphrey Mackworth offered now or at any other time when requested, voluntarily to make affidavit that he had *bond fide* disbursed in the management of the Mine Adventures the full and just sum of £14,840 and upwards, and thereupon the committee unanimously decided that he had dealt very justly and honourably by the Adventurers Co.

1699.
13 July—
Committee informed that the men in their employ at the Black Raven,* in Southwark, who had been brought from Cardiganshire, are ready to be employed by Sir Humphrey Mackworth, at Neath, and willing to be bound as should be directed. Ordered—That the men be sent forthwith to Neath. That they have a week's wages, and a bounty of 10s. each man. That Sir Humphrey be desired to enter into proper agreements with them at Neath, and take "an oath from every person employed at the refining furnaces for their fidelity under the trust reposed in them."

1699.
20 July—
Mr. Chauncey presumed it would not be amiss to have some person appointed at Neath to keep the accounts and act as Day Steward. Sir Humphrey desired time to consider the suggestion and select a fit and proper person at Neath. (Mr. Thomas Hawkins was eventually appointed.)

28 July—
Committee informed that the implements, utensils, and working tools belonging to the refining furnace in * Southwark had been sent by vessel for Neath.

1700.
4 January—
Any quantity of Lytharge not exceeding 1000 tunns may be disposed of by Sir Humphrey Mackworth, but not under £12 per tunn.

12 February—
The iron chest with the cash and writings ordered to be taken to the Bank of England.

1 July—
"Whereas Thomas Mansell, of Britton-ferry, Esq., has conferred several favours on this Company. *Ordered*—That a letter of thanks be sent to the said Thomas Mansell for his civility, and that it be referred to Sir Humphrey Mackworth, if he see fitt, to make a present of a † piece of plate of £10 in vallue.

18 July—
Application to Judges on the Norfolk Circuit [Holt and Hotsell] to allow the Jaylors to convey condemned criminals to the Mines [in Cardiganshire.]

* Gabriel Powell alludes to this, in his letter for perusal by the Duke of Beaufort, written in 1720, to Mr. J. Burgh, his agent, at Troy, near Monmouth, see *post*, p. 96.

† Is this "piece of plate" still in Lord Jersey's possession, I wonder? It seems not, but may be at Margam.

1700.

24 July—
Copy of a special letter of thanks to Sir Humphrey Mackworth, and also "we are likewise to acknowledge your generous favour in your consenting to have furnaces built in [? near to] Gnoll House, att Neath."

6th September—
Letter to be written to Sir Herbert Mackworth and other gentlemen of the committee now at Neath, to enquire why the proportion of Silver was so small from the Refinery there.

Also—
An account received that 17 condemned criminals had been pardoned by the King, provided they would, within two months, apprentice themselves to Sir H. Mackworth and partners for five years, to work at the mines. If they refused, or departed the mines, the pardon to be void. The jaylors would not undertake the charge of the criminals brought to London (from Bedford and Aylesbury); the Company having a vessel under charter, which they were obliged to freight to Neath, ten were sent down to that Town by it.

16th October—
Reported that two of the criminals sent to Neath hath run away.

27th November—
Secretary of State writes to ask whether the Company would take any and what number of Pyrates condemned, to work in the mines; reply "that they could not undertake to keep them without the power of an Act, fearing to incur the censure of Parliament," and then, "The possibility that the gentry and commonalty of Wales would be alarmed and dissatisfyed at it." The Duke of Leeds, the then Governor, concurring in this view of the matter, was asked to explain it to his Majesty [William the Third.]

23 December—
An offer to the Company by several Great Landowners to offer their interest for Sir Humphry Mackworth to be Knight of the Shire for Cardigan—thanks ordered therefor, and the Secretary ordered to attend Sir Hy. in his canvass.

1701.

6 May—
Ordered that the Agreement with Sir H. M. touching the Smelting Mills at Neath be taken into consideration at next meeting, and on the 29th May, referred to the Committee at Neath to report upon. Also, ordered that Mr. Waller do send for what number of men he shall require before the harvest, and that he raise what quantity of ore he can, both out of the Copper and Lead veins in Cardiganshire.

1701.
7 July—
An order to prepare a draft of proposed Charter.

22 July—
Opinion of the Committee that Sir Humphrey and his heirs male should be Perpetual Governors of the Company after death of the Duke of Leeds.

6 October—
Sir H. M. to give directions for the sayling of the ship 'Mine Adventure' now att Neath.

4 November—
Upwards of 800 partners in the Company.

1702.
16 January—
Attendance on Attorney Gen. for settling the Charter, ordered.

8 September—
Secretary reported that he had carried the (silver) bullion to the Tower, but could not get a dye made for the Coyning of the same with the Prince's Armes of Wales without a renewal of a former order.

That Mr. Francis Gwyn have 6 tunns of lead at £9 a tun delivered to him at Neath.

15 December—
Secretary reported that he had obtained a Warrant from the King for the coining our bullion with the Arms of Wales; the Secretary to carry Warrant to the Tower, get a Dye made and the bullion coined, in accordance with the said Warrant.*

1703.
18 February—
One Nicholas Newton, with other men, to be sent for from Cardiganshire to Neath to build as many furnaces for the smelting of lead ore as he conveniently can and the place will allow, on that side of the Smelting-house which lies next the hill.

12 March—
Mr. Waller to agree as cheap as he can with Robinson, the builder, to go to Neath to erect furnaces there.

---

* Hawkins, in his "Silver Coins of England," says, "The Plumes indicate that the Silver was derived from the Welsh Mines of Sir Carbury Price and Sir Humphrey Mackworth; the Rose occurs sometimes with the Plumes, because Silver from the West of England was combined with the Welsh Silver. The Coins with the Plumes were frequently called Quakers' money, because the Company by whom the Mines were worked comprised many persons of that denomination."

1703.

19 March—

Mr. Waller agreed to send Newton or Robinson speedily to Neath to build the furnaces for smelting there; and further it was

Ordered—

"That the £3 12s. 0d.* in new Silver, presented to the Queen [Anne] by Sir H. Mackworth,† be repaid him.

The rent for the Smelting Mills, Silver Mills, and Red Lead Mills at Neath, were debated, and it appearing that it was usual to allow rent for a place convenient for building manufactories with all the advantages that those at Neath have, from a great fall of water, and two large wheels one under the other, and especially so near a navigable river as these are, and that the said works were erected in a place where a Tucking Mill once stood, and was taken down to the great loss of Sir H. Mackworth, and whereas other houses, barnes, outhouses, and gardens lye convenient thereto and on view and estimate thereof, the Committee contracted with Sir H. Mackworth for the same at £200 per annum.

2 April—

Reported a new Slagg furnace had been erected at the end of the Smelting House next the Town of Neath.

Ordered, that Potters ore be delivered at Neath at £6 a tunn, and

1,200 tunns of Lead to be sold at Bristol at £8 a tunn.

23 April—

Secretary to settle the Charter with a Councillor-at-Law, and give such fees as Sir H. Mackworth shall direct.

5 May—

What Silver Bullion is already extracted at Neath to be sent to London by the Monmouth carrier.

10 May—

Letter writt to Neath to expedite those Furnaces, and spare no charge, but set all hands on that can be gott to worke in the building of same, &c.

25 May—

Ordered that Mr. Williams send some Stourbridge bricks ready made, and some Abbey Coal to Mr. Waller, in Cardiganshire, by the next vessel; and that the Test Furnace in the garrett be taken down and fixed in the house at Angel Court, on Snow Hill.

---

* As £3 12s. 0d. seems a small value to present to a Queen, it was probably the Silver value of a set of "proofs" of the coins struck for the Co.

† Doubtless as a compliment on her accession to the throne.—G. G. F.

1073.
15 June—
Oares to be carried from Neath to Cardiganshire for the smelting in the winter.

That the workmen at Neath go on refining when the smelting is out, and the new furnaces finished.

Sir H. Mackworth empowered to buy one great trough or two small ones proper for the river of Neath, and fit for loading or unloading vessels that can't come up that river.

9 July—
Committee reports That there ought to be six new Smelting and two new Refining Furnaces at Neath. That refining Lead with so small a produce of Silver as hath lately been, is not to be advantage of the Company. That the men's wages at Neath be the same as at Garrick, and no pay allowed for holidays, when they don't work.

That the Silver and Copper now there be sent up by land immediately. That the Lead now there be sent to Bristol, Glo'ster, and Worcester markets.

September—
Mr. Waller ordered to supply himself with Mostyn Coal for the winter.

21 November—
Refining processes to be kept private,* and no persons to be admitted into the Works but such as are bound to serve the Company in that art.

28 December—
Secretary ordered to get the Charter passed by the Queen [Anne] with all the expedition he can.

1 February, 1703-4—
Ordered that the memorandum given by Mr. Breton (one of the Committee) touching the smelting and refining at Neath, be sent thither by post for the Officers there to answer the same.

12 February—
Solicitor-General had inserted the names of the three sons of Sir Humphrey Mackworth in the Charter (viz.; Herbert, Kingsmille, and William), instead of " heirs male," as perpetual Chairmen or Governors of the Company.

16 March—
No more than one furnace begun at Neath, but others be finished.

1 March—
Eleven furnaces to be finished at Neath. Complaint to General Post-office as to the carrying of Letters to Neath.

* About which practice see my notes on prior pages,—G. G. F.

4 May, 1703-4:—
The new Charter of Q. Anne incorporating the Company produced.

18 May—
Oaths of allegiance and supremacy and for due execution of office, administered.

July, 1704—
That Vessels be procured with all expedition to bring metals from Neath to London at 45s. a tunn, if they cannot be procured cheaper.

25 October—
Sir H. Mackworth acquainting the Court that the Burgesses of the Town of Neath having endeavoured to impose on this Company some duties on the goods of the Company contrary to law, it is therefore

Resolved—
That the Officers belonging to this Company be countenanced and protected against any encroachments or impositions whatsoever, that shall or may happen on that account.

30 October—
Complaints about the Post to Neath, that five pounds to be allowed for fixing same and settling a bag to go direct to Neath.

23 May, 1705—
The pressing of the servants of the Company belonging to the Works at Neath again taken into consideration, and a determined resistance to such illegal practice determined upon.

4 July—
Sub committee report that they had prevailed on Col. Soames, at Bury, to procure the discharge of the men prest at Neath,* and further, that they had prevailed on one Edward Conway, Esq., barrister-at-law, to go to Neath and attend at the Quarter Sessions with *Certioraries* to remove all such orders as shall be made by the Justices to the prejudice of this Company.

11 July—
Stores wanted at Neath :—
1,000 tuns of Oare.
300 bushels of Oats.
100 tuns of Stourbridge Clay.
1,000 Lytharge Casks.

9 August—
Ordered that Mr. Ward be Counsell retained to goe down with Sir Humphrey and Sir Thomas Mackworth to Cardiff Great Sessions, on account of the pressing of the men at Neath.*

* Full particulars relative to these irregular proceedings will be found in my "Neath and its Abbey," 8vo., 1845. G. G. F.

27 February, 1706—
  Mr. Street, the engraver, laying before this Court the Bill for making the Maces, and a Seale for the Corporation of Neath, and engraving a plate for the special bills at 4¼ per cent., amount in the whole to £36 6s.,—Ordered that £36 be paid to said Mr. Street in full of his said bill. Then this Court presented the Seale to Mr. John Davies, Portreeve, and to Mr. Leyson Hopkins, Alderman of the said Town, for the use of the Corporation.

I imagine these facts as to the Maces and Seal* of the Corporation of Neath, from Silver doubtless made in their own Borough, is quite unknown to the existing Town Council. It is interesting to see that the Goldsmith's mark on the Maces answers accurately to the above date, but strangely enough I was unable to find any minutes whatever in the Corporation Minute Books touching this handsome addition to their official paraphernalia.

1706—2nd October,—
  Ordered That a letter be writt to Thomas Hawkins, to direct him to pay the Tax on the Work houses at Neath, without putting them to the trouble of distrayning.
  That Mr. Waller do buy such soft oar as is raised at the adjacent mines, in order to fflux our hard oares.

14 December—
  Ordered That when the Members of this Company meet by appointment att any Tavern for the service of this Company, That twelve pence each man be allowed towards their expences.

23 December—
  Further, That two Smelters and one Builder of Furnaces be sent from Neath to Cardiganshire, as soon as Mr. Waller shall desire to have them.

1706-7—26 March—
  And, That the note given by Mr. Jno. Davies, Portreeve of Neath, for the money laid out for the † Maces, be sent downe to Sr Humfry Mackworth.

28 May—
  Ordered, That Mr. Waller employ all the hands he can in raising oar, without respect to the charge it may cost for raising the same, and

* The entry below of 1706-7, 26 March, should be read with this.

† These Maces are of handsome Silver gilt, and inscribed "ANTIQUA VILLA ET BURGUS DE NEATH, COM. GLAMORGAN, ANO. DOM. 1706." They are stamped with [DM / NH] and the London Hall marks, a Lion, Pard's Head, and letter T.

G. G. F.

that he immediately imploy Carriers to carry such oar to the waterside, to the end that the Works at Neath may be fully supplyed therewith.

1707—12 November—
Confirmation of an Agreement between Sir H. Mackworth and the Borough of Neath for liberty of loading and unloading the Company's goods at the Bank or Quay of the Corporation of Neath.

We know that much contention between the Corporation and the Companies had not unnaturally arisen respecting the rates and tolls to be paid under the imports and exports, which the latter had so extensively promoted on the banks of Neath River, but which not being lodged on the Borough Quay itself, may have been considered untaxable elsewhere by the merchants who had provided their own works and wharf-like accommodation without Corporation aid. After much local contention and squabbling over some five and twenty years, it appears to have been harmoniously settled through the instrumentality of the ever ready and universal "Mackworth;" but whether the Schedule of 1733, made against foreigners or unfree persons and printed in my Neath Vol., was what was thus accomplished or is what is now charged at this Town and Port I do not know, for reliable information at the Corporation offices has been made in vain over several years. Referring to the same volume, it may be observed I note as amongst the Town papers, that in 1703, Sir H. M. had made "a MS. agreement with the Brass-melters;" that in 1709, "Liberty had been obtained by him from one Thomas Forest, a Patentee, to make Iron with Pit Coal," and that in 1713, "a Certificate about the Germans" had been lodged with the Corporation, probably for due and safe custody in the same town. Complications or necessities, the details of which might have been very interesting, if the originals instead of a mere list of them had been preserved in their muniment chest; it further shews us the commercial activity which had been introduced and practised at this period, through the recovery of the "lost Coal" with which Sir Sir H. M. has been credited in this work.

[EXTRACTS CONTINUED.]

1707-8—28 January—
Ordered, That the plumber at Neath proceed in makeing Flower potts, and that T. Hawkins send up by way of Glo'ster all such fflower potts as are ready made.

4 February—
Ordered That the Bullion be carried to the Tower, in order to be coyned, and that Mr. Skeate do attend the coynage and take care of the same.

10 February—
Ordered, that Mr. Gabb, the Copper Worker at Neath,* be taken into the Company's Works, and that Mr. Hawkins make the best bargaine he can for his services.

23 June—
Ordered, That the 279 oz. 18 dwts. of Bullion, and also 349 oz. 12 dwts. and 12 grains of bullion received from Hawkins (at Neath) be sent and pledged to Mr. Cartlishf or some other, in order to receive money for the same, until the bullion can be coined at the Tower of London: And, That a letter be writt to T. Hawkins, to know what quantity of Slaggs are at Neath unsmelted, and if he want men, slag hearths, or any materials for smelting the same.

11 August—
Ordered, That Mr. Waller be instructed that if the Lead at Dovey be cleane and merchantable, then to send 40 tons to Barnestable; but in case it be rich in Silver, then to send the same to Neath, in order to its being refined.

1708—6 October—
Ordered, That the Copper Oar at Dovey ordered to be barrelled up by the Committee at the Mines, be sent to Neath by the first opportunity.

27 October—
Whereas this Court is informed that Mr. Joshua Hayward (a gent. who hath lately been to view the Mines belonging to this Company by instruction of His Grace the Duke of Leeds) is of opinion that he can smelt our hard oars, which are the most chargeable and difficult to be run, much cheaper than they are now smelted, and thereby very considerably advance the interests of the Company. Therefore to the end that the said Mr. Hayward may make a just tryall of the said Oars, and thereby be enabled to make a proposal at what rate he will undertake to smelt the same, it is

* ' A Copper Worker at Neath,' would most probably have come out of the Mines Royal employment ?

1708.
Ordered,—
That Mr. Waller, with all expedition, deliver or cause to be delivered to Mr. Joshua Hayward, on his order, at Bridgnorth in Shropshire, Two Tunns weight of the several sorts of Ore following, viz: Cumsumlock, Goginian, and Cummustwith.

8 December—
Ordered, That 200 Tunns of Lead be delivered to Sir Humphrey Mackworth, or his order, computing the same at £8 the tunn, to pay ready money for the same, and that Sir H. Mackworth bee allowed until the delivery of the said Lead, interest for all such moneys as he shall pay our Officers in the country for carrying on the Works at Neath.

24 December—
Ordered, That the Bullion already refined at Neath be sent by the next Monmouth carrier to London, and consigned to Mr. Dykes there.

It has been generally supposed that the next Copper Works erected in 'The Swansea District' were those at Taibach, for the Governor and Company of Copper Miners, about three quarters of a mile eastward and beyond the Borough of Aberavon. Mr. Talbot was kind enough to look through his leases at Margam Park, and he informed me that the *first* grant of land for works there, was given to Messrs. Newton and Cartwright, in the year 1727. It can therefore be shewn that Swansea *took precedence* of Aberavon in this eventual vast manufacture,* as the Corporation of Swansea gave its formal sanction to the erection of a Copper Works on the site of the old Cambrian Pottery,† just within the Borough boundary, in the year 1720, as the following curious documents in my possession will prove:—

---

* For Dr. Lane had built his works at Landore in 1717, and the Corporation had authorised the Swansea Copper Works as above stated, in 1720. See G. P.'s letter on following pages.

† At present, (1880) the Patent Fuel Works of the French Co., under the management of Messrs. Cory, Yeo & Co.   G. G. F.

"Wee the Portreeve, Aldermen & Burgesses of the Burrough of Swansey in the County of Glamorgan doe hereby certifye all whom it may concerne That Wee doe approue of the erecting of a Copper Worke upon the Bank commonly caled Mr. Ley's, alias Thomas Evans' Coale Bank and wee doe further Declare that it is our unanimous opinion that the carrying on the said Worke will prove very much to the advantage and not in the least prejudicial or hurtful to our said Burrough or the Inhabitants thereof. In Wittnesse whereof Wee have hereunto sett our hands & the Common Seal of the said Burrough this 26th Day of September, A: D: 1720."

"Since ye last Lre ye Portreeve Aldermen (*except* Alderman Ayres *who is Steward to Mr. Popkins*,—Jenkin Jones, whose sonnes in law are imployed in bringing Dr. Lane's Oars & Mr. Da Thos who is p,missed to succeed in ye Dukes affayres) & Burgesses have putt their names and ye Common Seal of the Burrough to an instrumt a Copy whrof is above written.—G.P."

For
    John Burgh, Esq.
       att Troy near Monmouth,   "29th Sept. 1720."
              These.

"Dear Sir. I have been favoured with yors togeather with one inclosed to James Griffith wch I delivered & he has returned an Answear in the same words as the Copy thereof hereinclosed wch will save me the trouble of writeing a great deal of what I thought it my duty to menc'on to you in that affayre. I shall therefore only observe that it must be granted that the Duke by obliedgeing us in a pticular (Taken by others without makeing the least acknowledgemt to his Grace) will gain considerably & if so I hope Mr. Beavans & myselfe will not be thought the worse of encourageing the undertakeing. It may be imagined from the trouble wee take in sollicitng this affayre that our measures are entirely broak if wee are disappointed therein but, if I may creditt our managers, It will not be £10 a yeare losse or advantage to us. They give instances of several workes carryed on without watter but were it absolutely necessary there are other wayes to supply that defect with abt £40 more expence wch were it to fall to my own share I should not value very much but what gives me the greatest uneasinesse is that a cunning crafty pson (I mean Mr. Popkins, for I dare name him tho' he dare not avow his false as wel as sly insinuations now [*sic*: nor?] the 10th pte of his incroachmts upon my Ld Duke & his other neighbours) who has from the beginning opposed my Ld Duke & his interest should prevayle with that family (wch wee have served to the utmost of our power) to Deny us a favor wch tends to his Graces interest. I cannot imagine how he comes to be soe careful of the health of the Inhabitants of Swanzey all of a suddain—he has opposed its welfare all that lay in him & p'ticularly in the contest between us and

H

the out-Burgesses of Loughor for wch reason (among others) wee refused to bring him in Alderman.—Sil: Bevans* and Myselfe are much more concerned for the health of this place, ourselves & family (wch are numerous) live in it & wee are not soe necessitous or soe covetous that we would endanger our healths for any considerations whatsoever. There are several Copper workes† near Neath, several inhabitants abt those workes, & yet we doe not hear the least complaint of any unhealthinesse thereby, nay, I am told there is a Copper worke in ye middle of Southwark—must ours be more unhealthy than those or Doctor Lanes wch is surrounded with inhabitants, verry strange indeed & what wee never heard untill ye last Letter. It was insinuated unto me (who has been at £150 abt my Garden) in order to divert me from this affayre that it would spoyle my Garden—but that I look upon as idle as the least of their ptences. There is but one wind in the 24 & that wch blows ye most seldom vizt N.N.E. that will blow upon any p,te of ye Towne & ye work being three fields distance from ye uppermost house in Towne I am wel satisfyed It will not affect us— But upon ye whole, let ye consequence be what it will, Wee are determined to Goe on & think it very hard that the Inhabitants of this Place should be debarred of seekeing those advantages wch their situation intitles them to without being opposed by Strangers whose Avarice would ingrosse all advantages to themselves!—Had wee the happiness to see you here I should hope to have this affayre terminated in our favor but since that is denyed us I do insist on ye p,mise to visit our friends in Breconshire— Col Vaughan, Major Wms & honest Mr. Will. Aubrey expect you—my house Pennant (wch I desire you will make yrs) is within halfe a mile of Brecon. If you will lett me know ye time—I will be sure to be there to Receive you—I doe not doubt but Ned: Catchmayd & Will: Edwards will attend you."

"I am, worthy S'r
yr most obliedged humble Servant
GAB. POWELL."

To
JOHN BURGH, Esqr.

This "Gabriel Powell" was the then Steward of the Lordship of Gower, and "John Burgh," Trustee of the Duke

* Saw a portrait of him by Zoffany, at the Brighton Exhibition in 1872, lent by Mr. Bevan, his descendant, the Banker of London.

† In the Ministers' Accounts of the Exchequer, of the 17th year of King Edward the 4th, 1479, appears the following entry:—" By the hands of "the Reeve of the aforesaid Town of Swaynsey, for the rent of the "Smelting House, near the Castle there, formerly of Henry Conneway, "which was wont to render 4s. 8d. to the Crown."—*Vide* this, in my letter to *Cambrian*, dated 22nd Sept., 1868, on the next page, as well as in the Evidence of the Case and declaration of Corporation *v.* Lumsden, tried 2nd January, 1832, at Swansea Assizes. G. G. F.

of Beaufort of that time—in those days ruling powers in Swansea. These documents, however, prove to me *that the first Copper Works on the banks of the Tawe near Swansea* were those of Dr. Lane and his relative Mr. Pollard, called

THE LLANGAVELACH WORKS,

erected in that parish a little west and north of the present Tinplate Works* of G. B. Morris & Co., at Landore, and according to a Plan of the fee of Trewyddfa, dated 1761, now before me; they must have stood on the ground partially occupied by the Turnpike Road to Neath, and, as at that date, they are on the plan described "Old Copper Works, Thomas Popkins, Esq.," they were probably disused, if not ruinated. To Dr. Percy I am indebted for a copy of their appearance as shown by a curious old drawing in the Topographical Collection of George the Third, still preserved in the British Museum. When first erected and used I have been unable to discover an authority for, but † the Dr. says they were at work in 1745.

THE SMELTING OF COPPER IN THE SWANSEA DISTRICT
TO THE EDITOR OF "THE CAMBRIAN."

SIR,—My communications in your columns on this subject last year satisfactorily proved the commencement of this important manufacture in our District to have taken place at Neath in July, 1584,‡ but I was at the same time obliged to confess my regret that I had been unable to discover the precise date when the first copper works on the *Tawe* were erected near *Swansea*,§ though they were said to be at work in 1745.

* See the Municipal boundary Map in my Swansea Charters, folio, 1867, p. 119, No. 39 reference.

† They were built in 1717, as described over leaf.

‡ At p. 23 of "History of Swansea," is a note in which it is said "there was no Copper works at Swansea till about 1719, when the first was erected on the site next occupied by the old Cambrian Pottery, but, I believe that a Copper Work was in operation at Neath nearly 20 years before."—L. W. D.

§ *Vide* the orig. work on Copper Smelting, 8vo. 1867, pp. 7 & 8.

G. G. F.

I am now, however, in a position to fix *the* year in which the Copper trade itself began near Swansea, as the following extract from a document still in the Muniment room of our Corporation proves.*

For the purpose of some proceedings at law, on the part of the Burgesses, "a case" was prepared for Counsel, and "the opinion" given thereon is signed N. Fazakerly, 19 April, 1734.* Amongst other matters the Town Clerk of that day set forth was, that "*in the year 1717, Works were first erected upon the river of Swansea for smelting Copper and Lead ores*, which works are scituated above the Town, and about two miles beyond the extent [boundary] of this Corporation. In the year 1720, another work was erected upon Swansea river for smelting of Copper ores,† which is scituated *within* the limits of the Corporation," at Burlaisbrook junction with Tawe.

So that, historically, we now know that the Smelting of Copper at its present several centres in this District was as follows :—

At Neath, by the Mines Royal, in the year		1584
At Swansea, by Dr. Lane and Mr. Pollard	,,	1717-20
At Taibach, by Newton and Cartwright	,,	1727
At Penclawdd, by John Vivian		1800
At Llanelly, by Daniel, Nevill and Others	,,	1805
At Loughor, by Morris and Rees	,,	1809
At Cwmavan, by Vigors & Son	,,	1837
At Pembrey, by Mason and Elkington	,,	1846

I am glad to have thus filled up the only important hiatus in my work, and shall have pleasure in supplying any one who has a copy of the orig. work with this additional information in print, to go in at its page 71, under the sub-head of "Llangavelach works."

I remain, Sir, yours faithfully,

GEO. GRANT-FRANCIS, F.S.A.,
Lt.-Col.

Cae Bailey, 22d Sept., 1868.

Though Dr. Lane had been thus the first to introduce "the great Staple of Swansea" to the banks of the Tawe, it is but bare justice to say, that the perception of its real value to the District and the fixing of the Trade to this Centre, is pre-eminently due to the first Gabriel Powell, and the "Wee, who are determined to go on, let the consequences be what they will," and who thought it "very hard that the Inhabitants of

* For which, let reader examine the 'Miscellaneous Vol.' there for 1545-1844.

† See also, this Vol. earlier, under 'Swansea Works.'

Swanzey should be debarred of seeking those advantages which their situation entitled them to." There was a far-sightedness about this, which was greatly to the credit of the ducal agent of the day, paralleled only by that of the late Mr. F. P. Hooper in the same capacity, when forcing on the Floating accommodation of later years in the Port of Swansea. Though no part of Dr. Lane's Works remain above ground, I am informed that at the present Landore Tin-plate Works,* and in the ground all around, even now, when cutting below the surfaces, the workmen constantly have to drive through large deposits of the well-known "Copper Slag," the out-throw of those old works.

Touching these establishments, Mr. W. Edmond was good enough to hand me the following memorandum, given him by a friend some years since, at Clase, but whence the authority for the dates was obtained by that gentleman he was unable to say:

"Copper Works were erected at Bank-y-Gockus,† at Swansea, in 1719; were removed soon afterwards to Landore; they passed into the hands of Lockwood, Morris & Co., in 1727, and later in the same year were removed up to the then New works at "Forest." In 1747 an assay office was built there, and is still in existence, as well as an underground canal (also still open) through which the coal was brought for use into the Works."

Mr. S. C. Hall, in his "Book of South Wales," copies the following interesting matter, as he states, from an old Swansea Guide Book :—

"It is known that the art of making copper was anciently practised in Great Britain, yet it was certainly from the reign of Queen Elizabeth that it was attempted to be revived by Sir Clement Clark in Cornwall [about

---

* At p. 43 of "Windham's Tour in Wales," 8vo., 1775, that author says :—"Swansea makes a handsome appearance from the approach to it, being built at the mouth of the Tawey, on a semicircular bank above it. The Town is populous and the streets are wide : it carries on a considerable trade in coals, pottery and copper. A large Copper Work is constantly smoking in view of the Town, and another still larger employs many hands a few miles up the river towards Neath." * * * "The plenty of Coal in this neighbourhood and its convenience of export have caused the preference for this locality."

† Bank-y-Gockus, I suspect to have been the spot on which the works of Dr. Lane were built in 1717, or possibly, some place near by, where the first trials and Copper Slags were made.

about [? date], where he built some furnaces;* but finding the price of Coal too high in that country to make copper profitably, he removed his project to the river side Hotwells, near Bristol. Sir Clement soon failed, but having employed Mr. Coster and Mr. Wayne as managers, the latter, in conjunction with Sir Abraham Elton, erected a Copper Works at Screws' Hole near Bristol, where they soon made a profit of £60,000. Mr. Coster, however, erected his Work at Red Brook, in Glostershire, on the side of the river Wye, although by no means a good situation; yet by buying ore in Cornwall at a very low price (it being at that time thrown aside by the miners in working for Tin as good for little or nothing, under the name of *Poder*), he soon also greatly improved his fortune. After his death his sons joined the Brass Wire Company,† of Bristol, (under Messrs. Harford & Co.) considering that to be a better situation than Red Brook; though Mr. Chambers, of London, (now under the name, by charter, of the English Copper Company) thought proper to make erections on the Wye, but which were afterwards removed to Taibach, beyond Neath. About the years 1700 Sir Humphrey Mackworth, with a Company calling themselves "The Mine Adventurers," erected premises for smelting Copper at Mellyn-gry-than, nr. Gnoll, Neath; and about the same time Mr. Pollard, who held considerable Copper Mines upon his estate in Cornwall, in conjunction with his son-in-law, Dr. Lane, erected Works where the old Cambrian Pottery‡ is now carried on near Swansea, and subsequently at Landore; but he having failed, as many others did at the period of the South-Sea bubble, these works were purchased by Richard Lockwood, Edward Gibbon (the grandfather of the great historian), and Robert Morris, Esq., father of the first Sir John Morris, Bart.; by whom and other immediate representatives they were carried on for nearly a century, together with very extensive Collieries, the consequence of which connection very rapidly led to the improvement of Swansea Town and its commerce."

In addition to the foregoing works, I find that one Wm. Wood, a proprietor of Iron and Copper Works, obtained a Patent in 1720, to coin half-pence and farthings for Ireland. The Mint at that time paid 1s. 6d. a lb. for prepared Copper, and the charge for coinage was 4d. a lb.; while the duties and allowances on Copper imported into Ireland were 20 pr. ct. The Copper used by Wood for his beautiful coins was manu-

* Mr. Keates says:—"The Bristol Brass and Copper Co. bought ores "also as Harfords & Co., Harfords and Bristol Brass Co., and also as "Brass Wire Co. Mr. John Bevan of Morriston, was their last smelting "manager."

† In my Report on the Estate of the Corporation, 8vo., 1851, p. 1, an extract from the Cambrian Pottery Lease runs thus:—"The Pottery, being part of the premises formerly called the old Copper Works."—G. G. F.

‡ That this is a mistake has been made pretty clear by the evidence contained in the earlier series of letters in these pages.

factured at the Neath-Abbey Works, until the stupid Irish people urged on by the Drapier's letters, politically written by Swift against the Government of the day, refused in 1724 to accept them in lawful tender, and the unfortunate Patentee was threatened to be "scalded to death in his own melting "Copper and then hanged"!*

Reading my proof of this page and the "Times" of the day (May, 1881), I am horrified to observe that IRELAND is once more resorting to similar political cruelties in roasting no less than three bailiffs alive, under the wretched Land League system of Parnell and Davitt, now actively displacing common sense and its ordinary practices!

There is also an interesting foot-note at p. 339 of Mr. S. C. Hall's work on South Wales, giving an account of the export of copper ores from Ireland to the Swansea centre of manufacture by Col. Hall, that author's father.

For the sake of continuous history however, we must now return to

THE COPPER WORKS AT TAIBACH,

Which I have shown were erected in 1727. But it is not certain when the original builders, Newton & Cartwright, had the first lease of the Collieries at the rear of Taibach, (now held by Mr. Shaw of Cwmavan,† and Messrs. Vivian: it is supposed that they assigned their lease to the English Copper Co. and left Aberavon),‡ but it is not accurately known when "The Governor and Company of Copper Miners in England"§ vacated Redbrook‖ and commenced smelting in Glamorganshire; be

* *Vide* a notice of this in Ch. Knight's "England," vol. vi., pp. 51, 52, where also are to be seen wood-cuts of the 3 coins of Geo. I.

† Whose concern is called "The Gov. and Co. of Copper Miners Successors," Cwmavan.

‡ Oldisworth, says:—"Aberavon is become of more note since the establishment of the great Copper Works, which belong to the Bristol Company, see 1st *Swansea Guide*, 1802, p. 67.

§ More commonly known at present as the "English Copper Company."

‖ A view of these works, as they now exist there, may be seen in Hall's South Wales, p. 105.   G. G. F.

that as it may, when they did arrive they existed and dealt as a Company under the powers of a special Grant from the Crown. To William and Mary they were indebted for a Charter, dated 3rd of August, 1691, the preamble and details of which I shall now give in *abstract* to save both time and space.

THE GOVERNOR & COMPANY OF COPPER MINERS IN ENGLAND,
INCORPORATED BY WILLIAM AND MARY.

Setting out with a Preamble

Of which the recital states That, "Whereas great quantities of Copper ore are found in divers parts of this our kingdom, which, for want of skilful artists to refine and purify the same, is totally neglected and unimproved, to the great loss and detriment of this our kingdom in general, vast sums of money being yearly remitted to foreign parts to pay for the said commodity, and whereas our trusty and well-beloved subjects Sir Joseph Hern, Knight, John Briseve, Francis Tyson, Esquires, Samuel Howard and Richard Munford, of London, Merchants, have set forth that they have formed out several furnaces, engines, and other ways methods and inventions for the more easy and effectual melting down, refining, and purifying the same, that have not hitherto been used or practised in these our Dominions by any other of our subjects. And whereas they have most humbly besought us to incorporate them and divers others hereinafter mentioned to manage and carry on the same by a Joint-Stock."

Now know ye, &c., that, By the name of the Governor and Company of Copper Miners in England they shall be a body Corporate.

To continue for ever and to have perpetual succession by the same name.

May purchase and hold lands not exceeding £6,000 a-year in value; may dispose of any; and may plead and be impleaded in any Court

May have a Common Seal, and alter the same.

A Governor and Deputy-Governor and Assistants to be chosen.

Sir Joseph Hern to be the first Governor.

Power to keep a Court (of management) in London or elsewhere.

Seven or more Assistants with Governor or Deputy-Governor to make a Court.

Power in them to appoint Officers, and make Bye-Laws, and then to alter or annul as they see fit.

Power to inflict penalties, but said penalties to be recovered by action of debt only, and to be for the Company's use.

Power to appoint Sub-Committees, and summon Members to the Court.

Governor, Deputy-Governor and Assistants to be chosen yearly on 29th Sept., or within 14 days.

FROM ORIGINAL DRAWING BY J.M.W. TURNER R.A.
ENGRAVED IN THE NATIONAL GALLERY, LONDON
AND ENTITLED "PICTURESQUE MANUFACTURE"

SKETCH FOR COPPER MANUFACTURE WORKS ACCOMPANY POWELL
IN LANGAFELACH PARISH NEAR SWANSEA.
CIRCA 1750

Decisions to be by plurality of votes.

To continue for a year or until others appointed.

Votes to be sent in writing.

Proportion of Votes to Shares.

The Oaths of the Officers of the Company to be taken within 14 days.

Governor and Company, in Court assembled, have power to remove Officers.

Appointments in case of vacancies.

Persons who subscribe moneys and do not pay within 14 days may be disenfranchised.

The first Governor to take the Oath before the Lord Chief Justice or the Lord Mayor.

Judges, Mayors and public Officers to favour, aid, further, help and assist in all things according to the Charter.

Power to raise a joint-stock of any value, and to increase or reduce the same.

The words of the Charter to be construed to the benefit of the Company.

It should be observed that this Charter gives no power to *imprison* shareholders, as did those of an earlier date.

A month later, a like Charter for Ireland, and two months after, another for New England in America, were granted by the same Sovereigns to the Governor and Company; and several years afterwards, I discovered that a fourth Charter, modifying dates for the election of officers and other working details, was granted by Queen ANNE, but it is quite unnecessary to trouble the reader with their particulars

Mr. John Wright is said to have come from Redbrook, in Gloucestershire, to act as Manager. I have been informed on good authority that while the Taibach Works were being constructed, the English Copper Company rented and used those of Sir H. Mackworth, at Melincrythan, near Neath. This, on the face of it, would appear to be a rather strange proceeding commercially; but I give the statement for what it is worth. From their erection to the present day, however, these works at Taibach have continued to be carried on with success. They are conveniently situated for coal of the right quality, at a moderate cost, with ready carriage to and fro, through the ancient Borough and Port of Aberavon, now more generally known as Port Talbot. After the death of Mr. Wright, the management of the works fell to Mr. Philip Jones, father of Mr. William Jones, which latter gentleman was manager when Messrs. Vivian and Sons purchased the works in 1839, which gentlemen, it is said, revived and enlarged them on a perpetual lease, at a fine certain to the Landowner, Mr. Talbot, and they continue to this day under the personal supervision of one of the acting partners, A. Pendarvis Vivian, Esq., M.P. for Cornwall (West).

Happening to have balance sheets of the Llangavelach works for the years 1743 and 1745, I select those for '45, not only being very full of detail, but as giving interesting particulars relative to the partnership, and the then intended changes therein. "The Swansea Copper Works" are noticed in both these accounts, thus shewing that they were in operation in those years, a fact which I have observed only in them and one of the balance-sheets of the Forest Works, dated 1768.

LANGUVELACK COPPER WORKS, SWANSEA.
"BALLANCE OF THE BOOKS OF THE CONCERNED.
THE 31 DECEMBER, 1745.

"Dr.	£	s.	d.
To James Laroche, of Bristol	846	5	4
,, Voyage to Lisbon per 5 Copper teaches*	59	2	5
,, Consignments from the Works per cargo 28 December, not arrived	934	10	0
,, Voyage to Dublin, unsold 9-16-3-5	1379	16	3
,, Goods in the hands of James Laroche	328	10	4
,, Battered† Copper in London, 15 tons	1960	0	0
,, Silver at the Works, 78oz. 10dwts.	21	11	9
,, Thomas Morris	66	5	0
,, Shares in the Ember Company	226	13	4
,, Stock remaining at the Works	15753	11	8
,, Battery Mills Building Account	4662	0	7

* A technical term for the hollow bottom of a strong copper boiler, formerly much employed when acids came in for use.

† Meaning hammered or beaten out.

IN GLAMORGANSHIRE.

"Dr.	£	s.	d.
To Swansea Copper Works	5	16	7
,, Partners in the Copper Mines at Innerniel	12	10	0
,, Thomas Bennett of Swansea	310	9	2
,, Leasehold house in Salter's Court, London	146	4	7
,, Mark Grey of Swansea	18	0	0
,, Cash	192	15	10
,, Copper smiths, copper warehouse, &c., in company with Thayts*	7911	6	5
,, Copper ore remaining in Cornwall 816 t.	5133	13	5
,, Lead at the Works	53	5	1
,, Lead ore remaining in Cornwall 13 t.	223	17	9
,, Lead in London 60 t.	597	11	1
,, William Johnson	79	6	9
,, Metals in London, pot metal & bell metal	345	15	0
,, Thomas Turner of Birmingham	392	7	8
,, Moses Slade	267	12	1
,, William Thayts*	6134	1	2
,, Battered copper at the Works 11 t.	1430	10	1
,, Battery Mills Working Account	626	16	11
,, Bills remitted us per the Bill on Jos. Gulston, jun.	272	7	11
,, Fine copper in London, 7 tons, 9 cwts., at £112	835	12	0
,, Sir James Creed	408	2	7
,, George Medley of Lisbon	805	4	1
,, Navy Bills	25	18	7
,, Francis Thorne of Dublin	394	5	11
	£50,842	17	7

Cr.	£	s.	d.
By Richard Lockwood, his account current	2042	18	0
,, Edward Elliston Ditto	8087	8	5
,, Hester Gibbon† Ditto	929	0	3
,, The Exors. of Ed. Gibbon† Ditto	1027	13	7
,, The Extrix. of E. Mornington Ditto	258	16	4
,, Robert Morris Ditto	1531	7	1
,, John Lockwood Ditto	985	12	11
,, John Phillips	2006	11	6
,, John Vaughan	21	11	4
,, Account of Discount	2800	0	0
,, The Duke of Beaufort	70	9	0
,, Thomas Popkins	17	1	10

* Mr. Keates suggests that, this should be Thoyts who had a Copper Mill at Merton in Surrey, held afterwards by Messrs. Jas. Shears & Sons.

† Of the great Historian's family.

G. G. F.

"CR.				£	s.	d.
By Charles Du Bois				5592	12	11
,, Richard Lockwood's account of capital per 15·40 Shares				7500	0	0
,, Edward Elliston	Ditto	6	Ditto	5000	0	0
,, Hester Gibbon	Ditto	6	Ditto	5000	0	0
,, Executors of Edward Gibbon	Ditto*	5	Ditto	2500	0	0
,, Executrix of Edward Mornington	Ditto	4	Ditto	2000	0	0
,, Robert Morris	Ditto	2	Ditto	1000	0	0
,, John Lockwood	Ditto	2	Ditto	1000	0	0
,, William Perrin				7	16	3
,, Royal Exchange Assurance Company				338	12	0
,, Stephen Peter Godin				10	9	0
,, Thomas Goldney				16	6	3
,, William Bevan				1924	15	5
,, Robert Morris, our account				320	11	5
,, Bills drawn on us				1928	4	7
,, Phillip Jenkins				43	7	8
,, Thomas Rogers				76	0	0
,, Cutts Maydwell, Esq.				1005	11	9
				£50,842	17	7"

28th May, 1746.

"We do hereby acknowledge to have examined the several accounts from which this balance of our Books is drawn from 31st December, 1744, to 31st December, 1745, and we find there has been a profit of Nine hundred and forty-five pounds, five shillings and ninepence in that year upon our joint capital stock of twenty thousand pounds, which profit is divided according to our respective shares, and carried to the credit of our particular accounts. There are also several debts due and owing to this our partnership which are at present deemed dubious or desperate, of which there is a list annexed, amounting to nine hundred and eighty-six pounds, four shillings and sixpence; and whenever the whole or any part thereof can be recovered and is received, the same is to be divided according to our respective shares; and whereas by Agreement made and signed between us the 18th July, 1744, we did mutually resolve to determine our partnership on the 31st December, 1745; and did also agree that the majority of the partners should have at that time power to sell and transfer our whole Capital to whomsoever they could agree with. Either of the partners interested in this copartnership, or any others with them, at the full amount of our net capital, which being Twenty thousand pounds. And whereas Richard Lockwood, Edward Elliston, John Lockwood, Robert Morris, and Hester Gibbon, have agreed to purchase the same at the sum of Twenty thousand pounds, to be paid to us according to our respective shares and interest therein after the

---

* I would note that, these proportions do not represent equivalents.

G. G. F.

31st December, 1747, and before the 29th September, 1748, and also to pay to us on the 31st December, 1746, two thousand pounds; and on the 31st December, 1747, the like sum of two thousand pounds, being 10 per cent. on our capital for each of these two ensuing years, in lieu of profits and all interest therein. In consideration thereof, we do hereby assign, sell, transfer, and make over our several and joint interests in the Copper and Lead Trade, with all our works and mills for carrying on the same, and also all debts and effects whatsover of which our said net capital of twenty thousand is now composed and consists in, unto the said Richard Lockwood, Edward Elliston, John Lockwood, Robert Morris, and Hester Gibbon, their executors, administrators, and assigns, who are likewise to take upon themselves all debts, engagements, incumbrances whatsoever which our said copartnership now stands liable to and obliged for, and for ever to exonerate and discharge us and our respective heirs, executors, and administrators therefrom."

"The List of Debts referred to in the foregoing Preamble.

John Saunders	10	5	6
John Barley	6	4	10
George Causeway	6	2	1
John Jones	9	8	6
John Hyat	10	12	0
George Lester	6	10	10
William Watkins	22	13	1
William Brokinbrow	5	17	11
John Lord	24	11	9
Richard Matthews	10	8	8
John Mason	233	13	0
Francis Bills	276	1	9
Thomas Badger } John Cowper }	44	5	7
J. Tavarrer } M. De Costa } F. Ferreira }	288	3	10
Longfield Horker	31	3	11
	£986	4	6"

"R. Lockwood for	15-40	Shares.
Edward Elliston for	6-40	,,
Hester Gibbon for*	6-40	,,
As Executor to E. Gibbon, Esq , E. Elliston for*	5-40	,,
As Executrix to Edward Mornington, Esq., Bridget Mornington for*	4-40	,,
R. Morris for	2-40	,,
John Lockwood for	2-40	,, "

* For the celebrated Historian's family.

If we may rely on the statement made by Mr. S. C. Hall, the business of Lockwood, Morris and Co., was moved from the Llangavelach Works up to

The Forest-Copper Works,

situate some half-mile further north on the Swansea river, in the year 1727.

The greater facility of getting in Coal at that point was possibly the reason for this removal, and it has been suggested that the question of "the Copper smoke" had begun to prove troublesome in the previously used local centres.

If it is difficult to fix with anything like precision the date of the opening of the various Works, to ascertain the period of their change or closing is still more so—is indeed, rather to be gathered incidentally than positively; thus, in a previous page I ventured to indicate that the Llangavelach Works were not in operation in 1761, and the balance-sheet of 1768, which will presently be laid before the reader, goes to prove the fact, that the words "old Copper Works on the estate-plan of Mr. Popkins," mentioned further back, may simply mean that they had been there a comparatively long time. The view of the Forest Works taken in 1794, which I have had revived by photography, gives an excellent idea of the arrangement of the furnaces surrounded and connected by a circular wall, which was covered over by one roof, a plan doubtless adopted for the convenience of working (*as well as by* the porch to the doors for the *privacy* which was thereby ensured), and which in the early times of the Trade we have seen was forced on the workmen by the administration of Oaths specially authorized by the Crown Charters!

In one of the many obliging and interesting letters for

which I am indebted to Mr. Wm. Edmond, of Clase, he says:—"In 1747, an assay office was built at Forest, and is still in existence there, and an underground canal, over which was brought the necessary coal direct into the works. The accounts of 1743 shew that they had rolling-mills and hammer-mills ('Battery' Works) on the site now [1867] occupied by the Beaufort Iron-plate Co., built convenient to their Smelting Works at the Forest, and if the 'Llangavelach Works' mean those of Landore, it must have been very inconvenient thus to haul so heavy an article as all their Copper from Landore to Forest. The Forest, or Llangavelach Works are not those now existing at Forest, for in 1834 I was asked to be present at the removal of the last of the old buildings. They were formed of four large *circular* structures; the whole arranged so that the fire-places being on the outside of the circular walls, they* were so placed within them, as to conceal all that was going on in the manufactory. In the centre of these four circular houses stood the 'Refinery' which is still there, and octagonal in its shape. The public road anciently went *under* an arch at the Refinery, and crossed the river at the Hen Bont, or old bridge a little above the late Mr. Hallam's 'Tin-plate Works at Forest.'"

When, precisely, the first firm of Lockwoods† and Morris ceased to be connected with those Works, has not yet been ascertained, but the Rev. J. Evans, in his "Tours in South Wales," of 1803, mentions "Mr. Morris of Clasemont" as one of the then existing eight Copper Smelting firms in the

---

* The Forest Works were bought in 1867, by Mr. H. H. Vivian, M.P., and converted into a Zinc manufactory and so remain to this day.—G. G. F.

† Mr. Lockwood raised a Corps of Rifle Volunteers during the French war, which wore a dark green uniform, mounted in silver lace.—D. R.

Swansea District. In times more within our immediate ken, it is not difficult to remember "Forest" in the hands of Mr Troughton,* a gentleman of some chemical and mechanical skill, who, formerly a Lieut. in the Navy, turned his abilities under a patent, to the more ancient and ill-smelted slags, in the crushing,† mixing, and remelting of which he found ample occupation, if not profit. The next firm which seated themselves there were Messrs. Usborne, Benson, and Co., which shortly mutated into Benson, Logan,‡ and Co., from whom they passed, under a new lease for 21 years, in March, 1845, to the English Copper Company, but the latter having more Works on hand than proved convenient or profitable, they surrendered their lease up to the Duke of Beaufort, as ground landlord, in 18—, and have, I believe, ever since remained idle

To those engaged in Copper Smelting and its details, it would scarcely be possible to supply more interesting matter for comparison than the balance-sheets of the two Works, not merely on account of the particulars which they contain, but as both notice "the Swansea Copper Works," and that in 1768 the Forest Works and Mills accounts were still unclosed, and therefore most probably not at that time completed. As in the previous sheet, so in these following, the names of the partners, with their respective profits, are distinctly set forth.

* Lt. N. Troughton died in 1844, and lies buried with his father and mother, on the N. side of Oystermouth churchyard.

† The crushing down of the old slags for metalliferous purposes caused them to be left in the state of a fine silicious sand; with it and Aberthaw lime, a valuable Cement was formed and largely used, I well remember, in the Thames Tunnel. I am not aware that it was, however, brought into very general use, for with the failure of the crushing, its supply of sand fell off.

‡ Sir W. E. Logan, F.R.S., the eminent geologist in So. Wales and Director of the Government Geological Surveys in Canada.—G. G. F.

Forest-Copper Works, Swansea.
Balances of the Books of the Concerned,
to the 31st December, 1768.

"Dr.   £   s.   d.

To Copper Works, remaining as per inventory 9863 13 3
 „ Coppersmiths' warehouse, old account 304 13 2
 „ Copper ore remaining. p. 2353t. 17c. 2q., in Cornwall... 15886 15 6
 „ Gabriel Powell 9 3 8
 „ Partners in Copper Mines at Inverniel 12 10 3
 „ J. and J. Grey 9 0 0
 „ Swansea Copper Works 4 12 7
 „ Copper Works Building Account 2037 5 9
 „ Penwern Estate 400 0 0
 „ Metals in London 198 19 4
 „ Francis Wainwright 1344 19 3
 „ James Laroche 511 12 1
 „ Voyage to Dublin 1531 15 7
 „ The 'Plenty' Sloop 430 0 0
 „ Cash 115 5 8
 „ William Cole 48 12 0
 „ Goods in hands of J. Laroche, p. 3t. 11c. 1q. 10lbs.
   Rods, and 2t. 0c. 2q. 1lb. Manillas..... .... 617 6 4
 „ David Morgan 82 10 6
 „ Goldney & Co. 59 3 3
 „ The 'Peace' Sloop 430 0 0
 „ Battery Mills Works Account 1189 10 3
 „ Battered Copper in London p. 8t. 19c. 2q. 19lbs. at £122 1095 17 6
 „ David Gwynne 32 15 7
 „ Trial for Coal 4 1 6
 „ East India Co. 9070 0 3
 „ Shruff and Old Plate.. 345 4 4
 „ Consignment to Vaughan & Co., p. 2t. 1c. 3q. 24lbs.
   Rods, and 4t. 12c. 0q. 13lbs. Manillas 618 1 4
 „ Joseph Tealing, Account Current 524 5 5
 „ Joseph Tealing, Mill Account 2268 12 0
 „ Joseph Tealing, Bond Account 1600 0 0
 „ Wm. Thoytes & Son 84 8 9
 „ Fine Copper in London, p. Bowles 12t. 15c. 3q. 8lbs. ;
   Plates, 45t. 5c. 1q. 14lbs. 6287 8 2
                                                                   ─────────
       Carried forward £57,018 3 3

* This was a special production of 1st quality Copper from Sweden, much prized and imitated by English manufacturers; particularly noted in the 1744 drawing of the ' White-Rock ' Wks. as a special Department, and there figured 15. Manillas, in fact, were specially provided for the then Slave Trade of Africa, and consisted of ' Rods ' and ' Manillas,' the former being short pieces of *Copper* Wire 24 to 30 in. long, while the others were cast in *Bronze*, not unlike small horse-shoes, weighing 2 or 3 oz. each. They were exported in large quantities and much used on the Coast as money or by way of barter.

"Dr.

	£	s.	d.
Brought forward	57,018	3	3
To Ember Mills	4000	0	0
,, Executors of Robert Morris	283	15	0
,, Bills remitted us	1346	7	11
,, W. Kinman	35	13	1
,, Coppersmiths' Warehouse, New Account	9411	0	7
,, Battery Mills Building Account	562	0	7
,, Edward Taylor	1036	4	1
,, Arth. Scaife	232	0	0
,, Forest Forge-Iron Account	2096	7	8
,, Copper Hoops	780	0	3
,, J. Bristow	70	19	4
,, J. Chamberlain	35	19	4
	£76,908	11	1 "

"Cr.

			£	s.	d.
By John Lockwood, Account in Company	....		4500	0	0
,, Executors of R. Morris	do.	....	3750	0	0
,, H. Groom	do.	....	2250	0	0
,, C. Maydwell	do.	....	3000	0	0
,, D. Webb	do.	....	3000	0	0
,, J. and T. Lockwood	do.	....	6000	0	0
,, E. Eliot	do.	....	5250	0	0
,, Rev. E. Lockwood	do.	....	1500	0	0
,, E. Gibbon	do.	....	750	0	0
,, John Lockwood, Account Current		....	5195	13	11
,, Executors of R. Morris	do.	....	9894	3	0
,, H. Gibbon	do.	....	158	4	6
,, C. Maydwell	do.	....	2798	5	1
,, D. Webb	do.	....	4499	0	0
,, J. and T. Lockwood	do.	....	557	9	6
,, E. Eliot	do.	....	993	15	2
,, Rev. E. Lockwood	do.	....	105	9	8
,, Edward Gibbon	do.	....	52	14	10
,, Thomas Lockwood			3435	16	8
,, Sir Roger Newdigate & Co. in trust			8106	11	4
,, Desperate Debts			116	4	1
,, Giles Creed			23	10	0
,, Duke of Beaufort			232	17	3
,, John Pidcock			46	4	0
,, Cath. Bevan			3395	13	5
,, Bills drawn on us			4619	13	6
,, Executors of W. Okenden			33	6	8
,, M. Vaughan			18	7	10
,, J. Vaughan			0	10	0
,, M. Lockwood			1050	0	0
,, Cath. Lockwood			1575	0	0

"London, 14th April, 1769.   £76,908 11 1"

"We do hereby acknowledge to have examined the several Accounts from which this Ballance of our Books is drawn from 31st December, 1767, to 1768, and we find there has been a profit of two thousand, one hundred and nine pounds, thirteen shillings and twopence, in that year upon our joint capital stock of Thirty thousand pounds, which is divided according to our respective shares, and carried to the credit of our particular Accounts."

"John Lockwood .... for 6-40 Shares.
As Executors to Robert Morris, Esq.,
   Robert Morris, aud John Morris* .... for 5-40 Shares.
By order of Hester Gibbon, John Lockwood .... for 3-40 Shares.
By order of Cutts Maydwell, John Lockwood......... for 4-40 Shares.
By order of Daniel Webb, John Lockwood............ for 4-40 Shares.
John Lockwood, Thomas Lockwood .... for 8-40 Shares.
Edward Eliot .... for 7-40 Shares.

"Balance Account of Copper Works Partnership, Anno 1768.
   Profit divided £2109 13 2
   Commission charged 677 14 6
                                      £2,787 7 8"

We gradually find ourselves in the nineteenth century, but must nevertheless return to its predecessor; for the success of the early venturers on the western side of the Tawe evidently drew attention to the like suitability of the Foxhole district, at the foot of Kilvey on the eastern bank of the river, enriched as it was from the same Coal field.

In chronological order, then, the establishment which falls next to be described is that called

THE 'WHITE-ROCK' COPPER WORKS.

Mr. Oldisworth, in 1802, in his *Swansea Guide*, says, "North-east of the canal is 'White Rock,' a hill, rendered barren by the sulphurous influence of the neighbouring Copper Works; this place was one of those which felt the shock of the great Earthquake on the 1st Nov., 1755." They were built on lands leased by the last Lord Mansell, in

*The second son of Robert and the *first Baronet* of Clasemont, Glam. (1806.)

1746,* to Thomas Coster and partners, which matter I prefer to give when I come to speak of the 'Middle-Bank' Works, also situated on the banks of the Tawe, above though east of Swansea Town. 'The White Rock' Works eventually passed into the hands of the Messrs. Daniel and others, of Bristol, better known in the Trade as Messrs. Jno. Freeman and Copper Co. They also had Rolling and Battery Mills on the Avon, a few miles above Bristol, at the time when this Firm ceased to exist, Mr. Keates says; a partner of theirs, Mr Stanley Percevall, represented the firm in Liverpool, doubtless a descendant of the original holder named by Mr. Phillips in his dedication of the 'Prospect.' The Works were for a long series of years under the able management of Mr. Elias Jenkins, of Tyrgwl, Kylvey, who, indeed, was the resident partner down to the year 1850. After his death Mr Edward Brown became so till about the year 1853, when they were purchased by their great neighbours of 'Morfa and 'Hafod,' Messrs. Williams and Vivian, who still retain them under a lease from the Earl of Jersey: Messrs. Vivian's portion having since been converted into a Silver-lead Works

Notwithstanding the authorities of 1802 and 7, I am fortunate in being able to produce matter of much original interest, through finding a drawing in Indian ink by an artist of great skill, dated 1744, which I hereto annex for the information of my readers, which having the imprimatur of Mr. Phillips,† may be accepted as most worthy evidence of the form and description that could be obtained of Copper Works of the past century.

* Dr. Malkin, writing in 1807, states that "about the year 1730, or not much sooner, the First Copper Works were erected on the *eastern* side of the river, and it was not till about 1760 anything additional took place."

† "To Messrs. Joseph Percevall and Company, this New Prospect of your Copper Works at 'White-Rock,' (Swansea) is with all due respect inscribed by your obliged Friend and Servant,
RICHARD PHILLIPS."

1. Part of Middle Bank.
2. Mansell's Field.
3. The Mount.
4. An Old Mill.
5. The Pond.
6. The Slag Bank.
7. The Great Coal Road.
8. The Great Calciner.
9. The Four New Smelters.
10. The Four New Calciners.
11. The Great Work House.
12. The Compting House.
13. The Store House.
14. The Quay.
15. The Manilla House & Pay Office
16. The Carpenters' Shop.
17. The Clay Mill and Stamps.
18. The entrance of the Dock.
19. Mansell's Coal Yard.
20. The Quarry.
21. Edward Jones's House.

Fecit, Yr. 1744."

The success of Coster's Works at 'White-Rock' appears to have induced a further outlay in that direction, for Mr. Chauncey Townsend,* who had previously opened and worked large collieries near Gwernllwynwith, took a lease of the Hon. Louisa Barbara Mansell, in 1755, of ground, whereon he built Furnaces and Refineries, then and now known as

THE 'MIDDLE-BANK' COPPER WORKS,

the origin of which is so satisfactorily set forth in a private Act of Parliament, obtained in 1767, that I have pleasure in giving somewhat fully the particulars from

XXII.

An Act for confirming a Lease made by the Honourable Louisa Barbara Mansell, to Chansey Townsend, Esquire, dated 1st September, 1755, and for Granting a new Lease thereof:

---

* "Mr. Chauncey Townsend was an important man in London, and an Alderman of the City. He first leased the Birchgrove collieries of Mrs. Morgan, and shipped coal at 'White Rock,' whither they were conveyed on horses backs in bags. He originated the Coal trade on Kilvey side of Tawe. C. T.'s daughter *m.* Mr. Jno. Smith of the Draper's Hall, Lon., who thus acquired the Gwernllwnwyth leasehold property, which he left to his sons Charles and Henry, jointly, and through them it has descended to the late C. H. Smith, Esq., who was a son of Chas. Smith, and *m.* the *d.* of Sir Geo. Leeds, Bart." Mr. Townsend is stated to have been M.P. for Westbury, in the List of Subscribers to Thos. Richard's Welsh Dictionary, 1 vol, 8vo., 1753.—DD. ROWLAND.

The Act is dated in 1767, the said Louisa Barbara having between 1755 and 1767 married the Hon. George Venables Vernon.*

The Act recites—"That there are Mines of Coal under the Estates in Glamorganshire, belonging to the said Mansell family, and it is of great advantage to the owner of such estates to encourage manufactures for the consumption of such coal, and therefore the said Louisa Barbara Mansell did agree to grant a lease, to Chansey Townsend, for the purpose of building divers Works, for carrying on the business of Smelting, refining, and making Copper Ore into Copper, in the process of which great quantities of coal must necessarily be used and consumed, and in order to promote the same (which the said Louisa Barbara, upon mature consideration and advice, was well satisfied would be of great benefit to the said estates) the said Louisa Barbara agreed to allow, and did pay the sum of six hundred pounds towards the making and erecting such works as aforesaid, and the said Louisa Barbara did, in pursuance of the said agreement, execute a lease as aforesaid, in the words following, that is to say:—

This Indenture, made the 1st of September, 1755, between the Hon Louisa Barbara Mansell and Chansey Townsend, Esquire, witnesseth, &c.

The Act goes on to state that, the said Louisa Barbara had demised and to farm let to the said Chansey Townsend, his exors., admors., and assigns, the parcel of ground known by the name of 'The Middle Bank,' containing about four acres, with some other parcels of land thereunto adjoining, with full authority for the said Chansey Townsend, his exors., admors., and assigns, to build on the said premises any houses, edifices, or buildings, for carrying on the work or business of Smelting and Refining of Copper or other metals, and secures to the said Chansey Townsend certain powers and privileges as shall be necessarily wanted for the purpose, but so as not to interrupt, injure, or incommode the proprietors of certain Copper Works now erected at or near 'White Rock,' held by lease made the 2nd day of March.

* George, second Lord Vernon, who succeeded his father, was born 9th May, 1735, and died 18th June, 1813, having married first (16th July, 1757) Hon. Louisa Barbara, sole daughter and heiress of Bussey, last Lord Mansel: she died without surviving issue, in 1786. — *Lodge's Peerage*, p. 503.

1746, by the late Lord Mansell, to Thomas Coster and others,
It also grants certain other parcels of land, at the yearly rent of 35
shillings, and other lands, containing in the whole about 15 acres, and
other lands containing about 3 acres, with liberty to dig earth and clay
for making bricks for the purpose of making the same new intended
Copper Smelting and refining Houses, the whole for the term of ninety-
nine years, if the said Chansey Townsend, and James Townsend, and
Joseph Townsend, his sons, if any or all of them should so long live,
paying yearly the rent of three pounds five shillings for the same.
The said Chansey Townsend undertakes within four years from the
date of said lease to build one new Smelting House for smelting
and refining of Copper, and expend on such buildings two thousand
pounds at the least, and the said Chansey Townsend doth covenant
that he, his exors., admors., and assigns, at all times during the
continuance of the time hereby demised, burn and use, in the said
intended Copper Works, such coals as shall be raised under the lands
of the said Louisa Barbara Mansell only, and no other coals, so long as
such coals can be raised from the said Louisa Barbara Mansell's lands,
in the parish of Llansamlet, which coals are now raised and worked by
the said Chansey Townsend and his assigns, under a lease bearing the
date 7th Nov., 1750, to him made by the late Lord Mansell, or from
other collieries, in other parishes, from other lands of the said Louisa
Barbara Mansell.

To this gentleman also was granted for the Lord of
Kilvey by Elizth. Duchess of Beaufort, a lease dated 20th
June, 1757, of all brooks, streams, and currents of water
known as Claise and Nant Brane, with full liberty to him to
cut such courses and channels as he should see fit to cut,
make, and dig upon, thro' and over the waste of the said
Duke known as Pen-yr-Rusva, and also through enclosed
lands of the said Duke known as Gwyndy* bach and
Caerwern Vawr, being in the Parish of Llansamlet and the
Manor of Kilvey, for the use and working of any engines the
said Chancey Townsend may erect for draining any waters
hurtful to any Coal works he the said Chancey may set up
for the use of collieries under lands of Geo. Venables Vernon,
Esq., and Mary Morgan, Widow, in the Parish of Llansamlet,
for conveying the said waters for the use of the New Works

* Where the Roman remains were found in the year 1835.—*Vide*
"*Cam.*," 10 Mar., '36.—G.G.F.

lately erected for the smelting and refining of Copper by the said Chancey Townsend and his partners, at a certain place called 'Middle Dock,' or for the use of any works he or they may erect in the said Parish and Manor, for the manufacture of the said Copper, to hold the same for 99 years, at the yearly rent of £21, clear of all deduction, &c., &c.*

One old John Cornelius (living near Foxhole, in June, 1867) said in reference to the 'Middle Bank' Works.

'My Grandfather came there first to work as a smelter in the Lead Works at 'Upper Bank,' from Sir Jno. Morris's Brass-Wire Works in Morriston. He (my G. father) died between 1780-86. The Brass-Wire Works were called John Bevan's Wks., after the name of the manager, at that time.'

'Chansey Townsend and Jno. Smith (who married Miss Townsend) had *Lead* Mines at Pengored, nr. Lechred, in Cardiganshire, and they had an interest in the Lead Works at 'Upper Bank.' This Mr. J. Smith dying at Bath, was brought down to Gwernllwnwyth, and buried at Lansamlet Church on a Lord's Day, abt. the year 1798.'

'There was then a *Spelter Works* where Mr. Grenfell's rolling mill stands at present: one Mr. Brazel was its manager and perhaps part owner too. These works were very compact; they contained 3 conical furnaces, and were commenced before the 'Upper Bank' Works were converted into Copper Works. Some English Workmen came with Mr. Brazel, and many Welshmen, one of them, I remember, was called Smith, and he had sons and daughters who were all employed with him in the Spelter Works. Amongst the Welsh, I recollect David John, Wm. Howell, Thos. Jones, and others. After Mr. Brazel, one Mr. Cox succeeded him, and in the interval the works were suspended, and it fell into a like fate when Mr. Cox left.'

*Ex Gabl. Powell's orig. survey of Gower and Kilvey, folio 1764, in possession of the author, page 134.

'Then came Mr. Catherall, from Flintshire, who made Fire bricks as well as Spelter: Mr. Morgan was the agent of the works in Cox's time, and a Mr. Lewis was afterwards agent in the 'Middle-Bank' Works.'

'My Uncle, Wm. Harris, was his successor in the 'Middle Bank,' and left the employ and the then Master (Doyley) remained to be his own manager at Penclawdd.'

The above I copied from written notes taken down specially for me from John Cornelius himself, by the Rev. E. Thomas, of Kilvey, who says that Cornelius had a very retentive and excellent memory for details.

With the 'Middle-Bank' Works were generally held those called
THE 'UPPER-BANK' COPPER WORKS,
being conveniently placed for joint management. Towards the end of the last century, however, the latter were in possession of Thomas Williams, Esq., M.P., of Anglesey, in connection with whose name I cannot do better than give an account of the then state of the "Copper Trade" as placed by him before a Committee of the House of Commons, on the 20th of April, 1799. He gave evidence that—"It was not until the latter end of the last century that Copper Ore was discovered in Great Britain, and soon after this discovery, in 1691, a Charter was granted to Sir Joseph Herne and others,[*] merchants in London, who were incorporated as a Company for the purpose of refining and purifying Copper, under the Firm and Title of 'The Governor and Company of Copper Miners in England.' In 1694, a copper coinage took place at the Mint, and the Government paid 1s. 6d. per lb. for copper

[*] See the details relating thereto in the earlier pages of this volume, which shew clearly that even Mr. Williams was ignorant of what had been effected by the first settlers in Glamorganshire, at Neath, in the time of Queen Elizabeth, Customer Smythe and his trustworthy manager, Ulrick Frosse.

of fine Swedish produce. In 1717, a further coinage took place of 700 tons of *English* copper, at the price of 15¾d. per lb. In 1702 the first 'Brass Works' at Bristol were erected. So late as 1750, Copper tea-kettles, saucepans, and the like, were imported from Holland. In 1731 the East India Company began exporting Copper *in cakes*, but in 1751 they exported it *manufactured*, paying £135 6s. 8d. per ton. In 1673 new mines had been found in Derbyshire and in Wales, so that the price of Copper through these discoveries gradually fell, in 1781, to £79 per ton for cash. It was in this year also that a great competition took place at the India House between the Cornish copper and the Anglesea copper, the former sacrificing £25,000 to keep the Anglesea copper out of the market!"

In his day, this gentleman (Mr. T. Williams, M.P.) was held to be the leading man in the Trade, and was largely interested in the great Anglesey mines, which made such huge fortunes for their lucky holders. Mr. Williams having joined the Stanley Smelting Company, a new lease was granted by the Earl of Jersey (who had recently succeeded to the Britonferry estates of the Mansells) to Owen Williams, son of Thomas, and Pascoe Grenfell, Esquires, in 1803. So the works continued, until the partnership of Williams and Grenfell ceased, about the year 1825 or 26, the whole merging in the Grenfell family alone; to whom Lord Jersey, in 1828, granted a new lease for 99 years. For many years the conduct of these extensive establishments of 'Upper' and 'Middle Bank,' first built and managed by Mr. J. B. Smith, devolved upon Mr. Pascoe St. L. Grenfell,[*] who, living at Maesteg House, near by, gave all the advan-

[*] Under the Volunteering of the Kingdom, in 1859-60, Mr. Grenfell raised two Companies at their Works, of which he became the Captain-Commandant and eventually Colonel. At first, they wore grey with dark green facings and silver mounts, but afterwards, when consolidated with the Margam and other county Corps, wore scarlet. The Corps itself was enrolled as the 6th Glamorganshire Rifle Volunteers. G. G. F.

tages (especially) to those employed, which ever results from a liberal resident management.

It would be ungracious to pass from these Works without stating that it was here that Mr. Geo. Fred. Muntz, M.P. for Birmingham, completed and carried out his important invention in the manufacture of the brass sheathing and bolts, so well known and extensively used under the name of " Muntz's, or Yellow Metal."*

This Metal having been extensively used by the mercantile marine of the whole world, has lately been adopted by our Admiralty for the Royal Navy: and further, I desire to notice that an effort was made here to benefit the neighbourhood (utterly devastated as had been the western surface of Kilvey) by the promotion of "Gurlt's"† plan for the consumption of the Smoke, and so arrest its exit from the chimneys.

The attempt, I regret to have to say, has utterly failed ; and so we are left to hope for the complete success of Gerstenhöfer's plans at 'the Hafod,' *the only one* at present successfully carried out for the suppression of the ' Copper Smoke Nuisance,' due entirely to the capital and energy of Mr. H. H. Vivian, M.P. for Glamorgan, his co-partners and relatives.

Before stepping into the 19th century, there are several other Works which ought to be noticed as having existed at a prior period, but having failed to ascertain the *exact dates* I must take them at hap-hazard for relative position, leaving it to time and further opportunity to secure precision in these respects.

* Mr. P. St. L. Grenfell told me that in practice he had found that ' best selected Copper' 60, and Zinc 40, made very excellent *Yellow metal*.

† In reply to an enquiry, Mr Grenfell, under date of 10th August, 1868, wrote me word that, "Gurlt's process is a failure. We have tried some little modifications of it, with partial success, but not enough to warrant any great outlay to carry it out."—G. G. F.

The 'Cheadle'-Copper Works.

I have been unable to trace the origin of these Works on the Neath river, further than that they were erected some time in the middle of the last century, through the agency of persons who were at the time interested in similar Works at Cheadle, in Staffordshire.

Mr. John Place, writing from the 'Mines Royal' Works, Neath, on the 8th May, 1797,* says: 'Mr. Weaver, a partner of Roe and Co., of the Cheadle Works, is here.' And, in 1803, I find the Rev. J. Evans, in his 'Welsh Tours,' gives Roe and Co. as a then existing Copper Smelting firm in Wales.

The Neath Abbey Iron Co., who have latterly occupied the old Cheadle premises, on the north of the road to Neath, are unable to say when they were disused for 'Copper smelting,' though they do say that, it was prior to the commencement of their own works, which as such were started in 1824 or 5.

Mr. D. Howell Morgan, lately Mayor of Neath, informs me that "Mr. Keates, now of ' St. Helen's ' Copper Wks., Lanc., succeeded a Dr. Plumb in the management of the 'Neath Cheadle' Works, and remained there until the bottoms of the furnaces were broken up and sold," which is confirmed by Mr. Keates himself, who writes, "that all remnants not suitable for removal to Cheadle, were sold to Vivian and Sons in the year 1821."†

In 1812, a penny Token in copper was issued and made payable at "London, Cheadle, and Neath" by "The Cheadle Copper and Brass Company" (*vide* Appendix 35), which must rather tend to upset the notion of the Abbey Works Co. that the Cheadle were not *then* at work on the banks of Neath river.

* See p. 55, *ante*.
† Mr. Keates tells me it is within his memory that the Cheadle Works occupied them from 1809 to 1821.

G. G. F.

THE 'CROWN'-COPPER WORKS,

also on the Neath, were certainly in use within the last century, and were erected by a Birmingham firm for which a copper Token of one Penny was also struck. It had the device of a Crown Royal in the field, and was dated 1811, issued by the 'Crown Copper Company,' and made payable at 'Birmingham and Neath' (*vide* Appendix, No. 25).

For many years these works had been in the hands of Messrs. Williams, Foster and Co. under a lease from Lord Dynevor, but which in 1866 passed into the hands of Messrs. Moore, Thomas and others, who after reducing some 20 tons of ore to metal and holding possession for a few weeks, abandoned their taking, when the works again reverted to the landowner, Lord Dynevor, who subsequently leased them to a Company styling themselves the Laxey Neath Co., who converted part of the Works into Zinc Works. The whole since came to be taken up by Mr. Humby, of Bath (who now also holds the Rhondda Neath Coke Works), who, however, has never worked them.

In Lord Dynevor's Estate Act, 1837, I find that there appears in the Schedule :—" Crown Copper Works, comprising several quantities of pasture land and garden ground ; Crown Copper Co., 45a. 1r. 6p., £55 os. od."

THE 'PENCLAWDD' COPPER WORKS.

'I believe,' writes Mr. Keates, 'that the Copper Works at "Penclawdd" were commenced by John Vivian, in conjunction with the Company,' and, in Mar., 1869, he further wrote to me saying that, "I was quite a boy when the Cheadle Co. and old Mr. John Vivian gave up Copper Smelting at Penclawdd. I am sorry that I never ascertained from my Father when they *began*, or what was the exact nature of the connexion between the two parties. My impression however, is, that Mr. Vivian bought ores in Cornwall, for the Cheadle Co.'s account, but I have a notion also, that he was ultimately interested in the *Smelting* of them likewise. *I know* that the Cheadle Co. were buyers of Ores in Cornwall *for Penclawdd*, previous to the year 1798, but do not know *how long* before that date.'

Some Penclawdd people assure me that the place was called the Park-House, and that one Mr. Doyley had the 'Penclawdd original works' prior to the arrival of Mr. John Vivian; he, Doyley, is said by old Cornelius to have gone to them from 'Middle Bank' Copper Works, where he remembered him in full swing.

Those on the south side of the river Loughor in Gower, were originally known as the 'Kent-house' Lead Works, and they were converted from Lead to Copper-smelting under the auspices of the first of the Vivian family who came from Truro, it is said, somewhere about 1800 to represent the 'Associated Miners of Cornwall,' who had an idea that the value of their ores was not paid to them by the smelters (a view by the way, which has prevailed from that day to this), and who therefore opened the Penclawdd Copper Works on their joint account, charging a commission for smelting according, as they averred, to the real outlay. Be that as it may, it was soon found not to answer on general account; but the managing partner, Mr. John Vivian, had proved to his own satisfaction that Copper Smelting was a worthy and profitable occupation, and, astute man as he was, he sent his second son, John Henry, to the Mining Schools of Germany to fit him for the work, and having found a suitable site for new works, with an ample supply of Coal of the proper quality and price, at 'Hafod' on the Swansea river, land was there taken of the Duke of Beaufort and Lord Jersey, in 1810, in the names of Richard Hussey and John Henry Vivian, Esqrs., and those works were constructed, which have since obtained such a deserved world-wide reputation—of them, however, by and bye.

Between Hafod and Forest, on the western side of Swansea or Tawe river, and at the foot of the sloping ground towards Morriston, within gunshot of each other, will be found 'The Landore,' 'The Rose,' and 'The Birmingham' Copper Works, which were certainly all established and in work at the end of the last, and the beginning of the present century. I have, however, been completely baffled in my efforts so far, to discover the exact period of their individual erection.

Commencing then with

'THE BIRMINGHAM' COPPER WORKS,

Which appear to have been built for a Company calling itself "the Birmingham Mining and Copper Company," and from Halfpenny Tokens which it issued in 1791 and '92, "payable at Birmingham, Redruth and Swansea," it may be inferred that miners and smelters were acting harmoniously together— the device on the coins assists the idea, for a placid female is seated on a rock holding a fasces in her hand —types of strength and union: but, as another like token was issued in 1793, without being payable at Swansea,* I fear the presumed amity was not of long standing: the works,† however, were continued till 1831 or thereabouts, when they were closed, and so remained, until purchased by the Williams's and Vivians, which latter firm eventually obtained sole possession and converted them some years ago into Spelter Works for the reduction of zinc ores, to which use they are still devoted by the firm of Vivian & Sons.

* The reverse of all these Coins has the field occupied by a Heron or Liver standing on a cornua full of flowers—the heraldic device of Liverpool City.   G. G. F.

† At the beginning of this century, Timothy Smith and Jno. Dickenson of Birmingham, were chief proprietors of the Birmingham Copper Works.
       D. ROWLAND.

The 'Rose' Copper Works*

which were in the hands of a Birmingham firm in 1803, (and in 1812 issued a Token for one penny, *vide* Appendix No. 38) are to us chiefly interesting as being the scene of the first smelting operations of the now important firm of Williams, Foster and Co., which commenced its Manufacturing career at the 'Rose'† about the year 1830, first as, Grenfell Williams and Fox,‡ then Grenfell withdrew and Foster came in, and lastly Fox retired and the partners came to be, as just stated, the well-known firm of Williams, Foster and Co., for whom, perhaps, I cannot do better than shew the appreciation of the public, by quoting the final departure of one of their leading Members as given by the *Cambrian*, of 1st April, 1870 :—

THE LATE SIR W. WILLIAMS, BART.,
OF TREGULLOW, CORNWALL.

The funeral of this gentleman took place in March, 1870, and excited great interest among the mining population of Cornwall, who lose in him a long-tried and generous friend. The late Baronet was the last surviving son of Mr. John Williams, who by energy and perseverance had risen from a station little above that of a practical miner to be a large owner both of mines and land throughout the County. The sons inherited all the father's industry, and, starting of course where he left off, realised enormous fortunes, and have taken for many years a very leading part in Cornish affairs. Sir William's brother, Mr. Michael Williams, of Trevince and Caerhayes Castle, was M.P. for West Cornwall from 1853 to his death in 1858, and during that time a principal authority in the House of Commons upon mining affairs. Sir William himself, who was created a Baronet in 1866, was, according to the *Western Morning News*—

High-sheriff of Cornwall in 1851, and at the time of his death was deputy-lieutenant and magistrate for Cornwall, a deputy-warden of the

---

* As we have already shewn at p. 77, these works, so far as a name can shew it, were probably in existence as early as 1795. Unless, indeed, we may take this smelting for the Company, as rather indicating that *the ante Works* were not then built or ready for use.

† Early in the 19th century, Mr. Thos. Bigg (a quaker gentleman) was manager at the Rose Works.—D. ROWLAND.

‡ Mr. Keates writes, 'Williams, Foster and Company commenced smelting in 1823, and not in 1830.' *I* however got the date 1830, from their agent at Morfa. G. G. F.

Stannaries, and chairman of the East Kirrier Highway Board. About seven years since he retired from partnership in the well-known Copper Company of Williams, Foster, and Co. He was the senior partner in the firms of Williams, Harvey, and Co., tin smelters, Truro; Williams's Portreath Co., coal merchants; Williams's Perran Co., timber and guano merchants; and Williams's Perran Foundry Co., founders. He was also a partner in the Cornish Bank at Truro, Redruth, Falmouth, and Penryn; and in the firm of Williams and Sons, Tregullow Office, Scorrier. As a mining adventurer he was justly celebrated, having large interests in the Tirony and Cloncbanc sulphur mines in Wicklow; Nanthwyn lead mines, Wales; in the mines in the Gwennap district, Cornwall; and holding moreover three-fourths of the Clifford Amalgamated Mines, with the greater portion of Dolcoath. He also held a large portion of the Cook's Kitchen, Carn Brea, South Crofty, and West Basset interests.

During the distress in the Copper trade, a few years since, Sir William was one of the greatest friends to *the Miners*, and sacrificed large sums of money to keep concerns going through any period of *temporary* depression. His charities were also very large in North Devon, where he owned very considerable landed property. The deceased Baronet is succeeded by his eldest son, now Sir Frederick Martin Williams, who is the Conservative M.P. for Truro (1870). Another son is also in the House of Commons as M.P. for Barnstaple, Devon.

In connection with the Rose Works various tokens were issued; in 1811, pence and halfpence in copper were struck and inscribed 'Rose Copper Company, Birmingham and Swansea.' In the following year a penny only was issued, with a rose in the field; while on the *obverse* side a lion rampant exhibits a shield with the same sweet emblem; but why this device or name was adopted no one seems well able to explain; it certainly did not typify 'the *locale*,' but it *may* have the *color of the metal*—if it did, it was I think a rather far-fetched idea for any such English metal.

THE 'LANDORE' COPPER WORKS.

It is not clear, from Evans, what Company in 1803 were possessed of these premises: from Wood, in 1811, we learn, however, that they were worked by "The British Copper Company,"* and this is confirmed by three very fine penny

---

* May, 1869. Passing up the Thames, I noticed that a sign over the offices of Messrs. Williams, Foster & Co., was headed, in gilt letters, "British Copper Company."   G. G. F.

Copper Tokens dated 1812 and 1813. (See Appendix No. 39.) There is also a half-penny with 1813 in the *exergue*, a lion of precisely the same type in the field, and on the *reverse* within an oak-wreath, Britannia seated, all evidently betokening the word 'British' in the title of the Company. About 1825 or 26, these works were in the hands of Mr. Henry Bath, senr., and Mr. R. J. Nevill, with the name of 'Henry Bath and Co.,' and so continued with the management of Mr. J. Penrose and Mr. Letcher down to 1834. The Works were eventually purchased in 18— by Messrs. Williams, Foster and Co., and still remain in their hands, conveniently situated for their Rolling mills and offices at 'Morfa,' near by. They have all on the *obverse* the device of a lion passant, in the field; that of the 1812 issue has the face nearly full, while the other two types are three-quarter, and surrounded by the sentence 'Rolling Mills at Walthamstow.' The *reverses* are all alike enriched with a wreath of oak encircling the words 'British Copper Company,' surrounded by 'Smelting Works at Landore.'

The great output of Slag at the several works, which from its semi-metallic lustre and great density had given an idea of riches yet to be won from it, induced much chemical research and the erection of

THE 'NANT RYD Y VILAIS' WORKS,

at Landore, on the brook of its name, to the north of the Tin-plate Works of the late G. B. Morris and Co. They were air furnaces of an exceptional character, neither for Copper nor Iron, and yet for both. They were established by the Bevans, of Morriston, about 1814, in the hope of extracting some copper from the slags which it was supposed had not been smelted with sufficient care, and for getting out the iron which was *known* to form a proportion of at least 50 per cent. of the slag itself.

The result was a *scientific* success, but though a little

copper was reclaimed, and bar *iron* was rolled out at the mills, it was found impossible to "weld" it, and so, the article being unmarketable, the proprietors came to grief, the works were closed, and the question 'How to extract a *marketable Iron* from the millions of tons of ore in the form of slag in the Swansea District' has yet to be accomplished! Does NATURE really not afford a material which when scientifically compounded, shall expel the obnoxious, and produce the requisite *facile* of chemical coincidence to a useful and practical result?

This Company of Nantrydyvilais issued a penny Copper Token in 1813, No. 42 in Appendix, and so its name will be perpetuated as having existed at that date, and as having been ready to exchange its local coin either in "Morriston or Swansea," where the chief partners resided.

I have been lately informed that in 1816 this firm were founders of brass and iron, and were also makers of the edge tools and shovels, at that time largely sold in the District.

The Rev. J. Evans, in his "Tours in South Wales," written 1803, and published the following year, says at p. 165: "There are eight large Copper Houses in the vicinity of Swansea,* the

    1st—The Brass Wire Works of Harford and Co.
    2nd—Those belonging to the Birmingham Mining Co.
    3rd—To the Birmingham Rose Co.
    4th—To Mr. R. Morris of Clasemont.
    5th—To Williams and Hughes.
    6th—To Freeman and Co.
    7th—To Mr. Williams, and the
    8th—To Roe and Co."

I do not see my way exactly to the proper appropriation of these eight establishments. The 1st were at 'Forest,' for Wood says so, and as may be seen a little further on; the 2nd

---

* See page 78, *ante*, for the Smelters in 1798.

is that still known as the 'Birmingham'; the 3rd as the 'Rose' Works; the 4th, if taken as they lie on the river bank, should be the 'Landore,' but I was not previously aware that Mr. Morris had these in work; the 5th was evidently the Anglesea firm, the Williams (either Owen or Thomas) spoken of in connection with 'Middle and Upper' Bank at p. 86, *ante*, but then I can give them no works, for Freeman and Co. (No. 6) had the 'White Rock,' and this would leave 7 as the last to be appropriated to doubtless the 'Middle and Upper' Bank; while Roe and Co., No. 8, never were at Swansea, but at Neath: it is very possible, therefore, that Mr. Evans made up his list from a Ticketing paper at Swansea, and there no doubt they all appeared as buyers for their several Co.'s or Works.

Wood, in his "Rivers of Wales,"* written in 1811, and published in 1813, at p. 93 of the 1st volume, writing of Morriston, states, that it 'was begun by Mr. Morris, from whom it takes its name, about the year 1768, and is now of considerable extent and population. It has a Church and some dissenting meeting houses. There are large Copper Works at 'Forest,' belonging to Messrs. Harfords & Co., with adjoining Rolling Mills, where a great deal of Copper has been utilised for the use of the Navy. A little lower is a work belonging to the 'Birmingham Mining' Company, and near that, another worked by the 'Rose' Company. At Landwr, is another worked by the 'British' Copper Company, and below that a large one lately built by Messrs. Vivian & Co., at 'Hafod,' in the construction of which a laudable attention has been paid to the comfort and convenience of the workmen by a different arrangement of the furnaces. On the Eastern side of the river, are the 'Upper and Middle Bank' Copper

* The book is enriched with several views of the Tawe, and the then existing Copper Works on its banks, which are very interesting for reference.

Works, belonging to Messrs. O. Williams, P. Grenfell and Co.; and lower down, on the same side of the river, is a larger work carried on by The 'Bristol' Company. This "Bristol Company," I presume, meant Messrs. Daniels, of that city and of The 'White Rock' Works, *vide* p. 82, *ante.* I have two Tokens, penny and halfpenny, both dated 1811, with the arms, crest, and motto of the City of Bristol; on the *reverse* " B. B. and Copper Co." in the field, surrounded by the words " Penny (or Halfpenny) payable at Bristol,* Swansea, and London." I am told these coins do not relate to the White Rock Works, but to " The Bristol Brass and Copper Co.," who were not *smelters* at Swansea, but buyers only of metallic copper, which they rolled and manufactured at Bristol. If so, it is not clear to me why "Swansea" was inserted, unless, indeed, the House may have had an office and agency here.

We are, at length, fairly in the Nineteenth century, and find ourselves once more able to deal with authenticated dates.

At the beginning of this century there was evidently a great disposition to construct works and invest capital in connection with Copper Smelting. There was about the trade itself something magnificent; the quantity of ores produced from the Cornish and the Anglesey mines, the latter in particular, was so large, the profit so ample, the rise of modest men into nobles (as examplified in the case of Hughes, Lord Dinorben), and the increase of wealth, by those who were the fortunate holders of a comparatively few acres of copper ore, so vast, that it produced the natural result—"a rush into the Copper trade"—and hence the erection of many Works at this period near those Coal districts which it was supposed would best supply the proper

* Vide Appendix, Tokens, 28, 29.

fuel for smelting at fair and reasonable charges, with certainty of continuity of supply.

In the year 1805 a step was taken to the *westward*. At Llanelly, in Carmarthenshire, on the banks of the river Burry, Messrs. Daniel, of Cornwall, Savill of London, Guest of Birmingham, and Nevill of Swansea and Birmingham, selected a site and erected the works called

THE 'LLANELLY' COPPER WORKS,*

which have been successfully carried on by some of the original folk or their representatives from that time to the present day; Mr. Charles W. Nevill remaining the able and respected managing partner there.†

The example set on the west, by Llanelly, of leaving the immediate neighbourhood of Swansea, seems to have been followed on the extreme *East* of the South Wales Coal-Field; for the only Copper Works ever attempted in Monmouthshire, were those erected in 1807, by the "Union Company," ‡ and called

THE 'RISCA' COPPER WORKS,

from the village of that name, near the town of Newport. Mr. O. Morgan, M.P., says "that the copper trade being much depressed in 1817, the smelters determined to reduce the number of works, and they accordingly drew lots to decide which works should be given up! The lot fell upon the Risca, which were consequently abandoned, and have since been converted and used as Chemical Works."

I suspect an unintentional error here as regards the *original* Company, for coins in my cabinet § shew that a penny token

* Of which I have an admirable drawing, by Baxter, in my Swansea Topographic Collection, giving their appearance in 1811.

† His father and predecessor, Mr. R. J. Nevill, appears 4th in the Magnates in this volume.

‡ *Vide* Percy's Metallurgy, Vol. I., page 293.

§ Since presented by the Author to Royal Institution Museum, Swansea. G. G. F.

was issued in 1811 by "The Birmingham and Risca Copper Company," with the device of a pair of clasped hands in the centre over the date. On the *reverse* is impressed "One Penny Token, payable in Birmingham." Another Penny I have, issued in the *same year*, with a *like reverse*, but the device on the *obverse* changed from the united hands to a Copper Works with eight smoking Furnaces, the date as before, being 1811, but the inscription changed to "Risca Union Copper Company." In 1812 another penny Token was issued by "The Union Copper Company, Birmingham," those words surrounding the first device of the united hands—the *reverse* stating that this "One penny Token" was "payable in Cash-notes." What Cash-notes meant I am at a loss to know, unless it was a modest idea of the Company that *their notes* were as good as *cash*. Of one thing we may be quite certain—"the Union" *succeeded* "the Birmingham" Company, and that in the year 1811. Its ignoble deposition, we have already stated, took effect in 1817, and thus the County of Monmouth lost its solitary Copper Manufactory.

Mr. Keates tells me, "The Union Company built the Works at Risca and issued the Tokens as you say, but the words Birmingham and Risca on the coins denoted which were intended to circulate in the respective Districts. The fate of the Risca may have been determined by lot, but Mr. Betts, the late Silver refiner (and a Shareholder) of Birmingham, told me that the business was given up, because those Shareholders who were consumers of Copper, found that they could buy it cheaper from others than they could produce it themselves," a sufficiently cogent reason commercially certainly.

About A.D. 1809, another site on the banks of the Loughor river, opposite the Borough of that name, was selected on a point, or spit of sandy ground, part of the adjoining

Llangennech estate, in Carmarthenshire, and there Messrs. Morris and Rees* erected

The 'Spitty' Copper Works.

The latter gentleman had for some time been manager at Penclawdd, under the first Mr. Vivian, the other had been land agent to Mr. Tunno, at Llangennech Park, not far off.

Subsequently the Works were carried on by Messrs. Mary W. Shears and Son, with Mr. Keates (now of St. Helen's, Lancashire) as manager: † after whom Mr. Schneider, M.P., now of Furness Abbey, and Sir William Foster, of Norwich, with the late Mr. Champion Jones for manager; together with Messrs. Napier and Cameron for chemists, here carried out some interesting patented experiments to prove whether the extracting of Copper more by chemical combinations than direct smelting, could not be successfully accomplished; but, after a few years, we must assume a non success, for the works were closed, and in 1858 the firms of Williams and Vivians purchased the lease, broke up the furnace bottoms, and to the great loss of the immediate neighbourhood they have remained idle as to Copper ever since.

The year 1810 saw the commencement of the now celebrated

'Hafod' Copper Works,

at Swansea, on the lands of the name, belonging to the Duke of Beaufort and the Earl of Jersey, granted by lease in that year, to Messrs. Richard Hussey and John Henry Vivian.‡ Their father, John Vivian, Esq. (whose family name in connection with metallurgic manufactures has now obtained a world-wide reputation), I have already stated, first

* This Mr. W. Rees, when he left Spitty, was employed at the Aberavan Works, and thence went to Amlwch Copper Works, where he died.

† See a note as to this Gentleman at page 125.

‡ Full particulars of this letting may be gathered from the Act of 1st Vict., cap. 25, 3rd July, 1837.   G. G. F.

VIEW OF THE HAFOD COPPER WORKS.
ON THE SWANSEA RIVER, TAWE.
CONSTRUCTED BY MESSRS VIVIAN & SONS.

A.D. 1810.

came over to Wales from Truro, in Cornwall, on behalf of himself and other mine owners.*

The prosperous state of the trade, and the consequent great increase of furnaces along the banks of the Tawe, created such volumes of sulphurous acid gas (the so-called Copper Smoke) that at length the neighbouring Landowners began to complain of the mischief to their land, stock and crops, and legal proceedings being threatened, it was at these works that (with the stimulus of £1,000 reward for the cure of the nuisance) Professors Faraday and Phillips conducted the first series of experiments, under the immediate supervision of the then managing partner, Mr. John Henry Vivian, in the year 1812. No effort was wanting, no expense spared, but alas! success was *not then* to crown their efforts.†

As in the course of events the chief direction of these great works fell to the share of Mr. H. Hussey Vivian, M.P., so the Copper Smoke now is by that gentleman likely not merely to be abated, but converted into a means of profitable use for the manufacture of super-phosphate manures—a kind of chemical retribution little dreamt of a few years ago! for many particulars connected with which, I would refer the reader to the Appendix of this volume.

The late Mr. J. H. Vivian informed me that the first practical trials to that end, worthy of note, were made at 'Hafod' in May, 1820, and that Sir Humphrey Davy took a lively and personal interest in the subject down to the year 1822; that further experiments were continued at 'Hafod,' and improvements to the same end were publicly notified so late as 1832 and '33.

* *Vide* account of the Penclawdd Works, page 125-26, *ante*.

† A pamphlet was printed in 1823 giving full details of all the experiments and trials, and their results, as made at Hafod, a copy of which is to be found in Jermyn-street, the British Museum, and Royal Institution, Swansea. G. G. F.

Of the original partners and brothers, the elder entered the army, and having greatly distinguished himself in the Peninsular War, was created a Baronet for his eminent services, and eventually, on retiring from his military command in Ireland, created a Peer, by the title of Lord Vivian of Glyn. The junior, Mr. John Henry Vivian, devoted himself to commercial pursuits, and turning his natural abilities and early scientific training* to account, became managing partner of the 'Hafod' Works, and the admitted head of the Copper Trade in this country. Mr. J. H. Vivian was elected F.R.S. for his 'paper on Copper Smelting,' as printed in the Royal Society's transactions. He was also one of the earlier members of the Geological Society; and in 1832 was returned to represent SWANSEA, Neath, Aberavan, &c., in the first reformed Parliament, the which he continued to do in six successive Parliaments, until his death, in 1855; and, having greatly endeared himself to his constituents and friends, a Bronze Statue to his memory was erected in the Guildhall square, Swansea; On its solid pedestal of grey Cornish granite is inscribed—

JOHN HENRY VIVIAN, ESQ., F.R.S., F.G.S., M.P.,
WHO REPRESENTED THIS BOROUGH AND ITS CONTRIBUTORIES
IN SIX SUCCESSIVE PARLIAMENTS;
ERECTED BY HIS CONSTITUENTS AND FRIENDS,
A.D. MDCCCLVII.

BORN AT TRURO,
MDCCLXXIX.,
HE DIED AT SINGLETON,
MDCCCLV,
UNIVERSALLY LAMENTED.

* This training it was, no doubt, which induced the appointment of a regularly educated German Chemist (Mr. G. B. Herrmann) as part of the staff at 'Hafod' long before a like arrangement was attempted at either of the neighbouring works.—G. G. F.

To 'Hafod,' foreigners now resort when desiring to see its great staple in process of manufacture; to 'Hafod,' the cadet classes of Woolwich annually repair for instruction in metallurgy; and great as was its progress under the late Mr. J. H. Vivian, it still retains its pre-eminence under the management of Mr. Hussey Vivian, whose father's mantle has fallen on shoulders fully equal to the position.

'Hafod' is now the centre of a busy population, surrounded by several of the Works which I have attempted to describe, denuded of every vestige of verdure: what it was in days when nature had her sway (150 years ago) may be gathered from the following interesting lines penned evidently by one who fully appreciated the scene, and very happily expressed what he saw and felt:—

ON HAVOD, NEAR SWANSEA, 1737.

Delightful *Hafod*, most serene abode!
Thou sweet retreat, fit mansion for a god!
Dame Nature, lavish of her gifts we see,
And Paradise again restored in thee.
Unrivall'd thou beneath the radiant sun;
*Sketty and **Forest* own themselves outdone.
Thy verdant fields, which wide extended lie,
For ever please, for ever charm the eye:
Thy shady groves afford a safe retreat
From falling show'rs, and summer's scorching heat:
Thy stately oaks to heaven aspiring rise,
And with their utmost tops salute the skies;
While lowlier shrubs amidst thy lawns are seen,
All clad in liv'ries of the loveliest green:
From every bush the feather'd tribe we hear,
Who ravish with their warbling notes the ear.

But what compleats the beauty of the whole,
And has with raptures often filled my soul;
Here *Swansea* virgins every morn repair,
To range the fields and breathe in purer air;
And soon as *Phœbus* ushers in the day,
Regale themselves with salutary whey.
Here lovely *Morris* charming nymph is seen,
Fair as an angel, graceful as a queen.

*Pleasant places near Swansea.

Here *Helen*, too, the flow'ry pasture treads,
Whom none in beauty, none in wit exceeds :
Here *R——s* comes, for ever brisk and gay,
Who steals insensibly our hearts away ;
Her killing eyes a frozen priest would move,
The youth who sees her cannot chuse but love.
Here *Rosalinda* does uncensured go,
To meet her swain, and cares not who shall know ;
For what ill-natur'd tongue will dare to say
She came to meet him, when she came for whey ?
S——s, W——r, W——s hither all resort,
Nymphs that would grace the greatest monarch's court ;
So sweet, so charming, so divinely fair,
You'd swear a train of goddesses were there.
Here oft they pass their blissful hours away
In pleasant chat, or else in sportive play ;
Or sometimes in harmonious concert sing,
While neighbouring groves with sweetest echoes ring :
The birds are hushed, and all amazed appear, .
Sounds more melodious than their own to hear :
Hard by old *Taway** gently glides along,
And stays his stream to listen to their song ;
While t'other side a distant brook we hear,
Run murm'ring, 'cause he can't approach the fair.
  Oh happy place ! the world I'd freely give,
That I might always at my *Havod* live :
My *Havod* should in deathless pages shine,
Were I, like *Pope*, a fav'rite of the nine :
Or on †*Kilvay*, or *Kevenbrin* they dwell,
Or in ‡ *Cwmboorla's* unfrequented vale :
Would they propitious but inspire my lays,
The world should ring with charming *Havod's* praise.
  But Oh ! the muses deign not to inspire,
My bosom burns not with poetick fire ;
I then must cease and lay aside my quill,
Lest I eclipse thy fame by praising ill.

It has been suggested that these lines may have been penned by the poet Savage, but the date (1737) precludes that assumption, for this most unfortunate of men did not come to reside at Swansea, we know, till the year 1741.

* The river *Tawe*, of Swansea, running along *Hafod*, towards Breconshire.
  † Hills not far from Swansea.
  ‡ A vale joining the Tawe, near Swansea.

There is also too much topographical and individual detail for a stranger to have mastered during the short period Savage resided here.

The 'Morfa' Copper Works

lie next adjacent to the Hafod; a portion of the lands for Morfa were leased by the Duke of Beaufort to Messrs. John Williams the younger, of Burncoose, Michael Williams of Trevinse, William Williams of Scorrier House, all in Cornwall, merchants; and also Sampson Foster, of Bromley, Middlesex, merchant; Joseph Talwin Foster, of Upper Clapton, Middlesex, merchant; Francis Hearle Rodd, of Trewortha Hall, Cornwall, esquire; Samuel Stephens, of Tregarron Castle, Cornwall, esquire; Collan Harvey, of St. Day, Cornwall, merchant; and John Sampson, of Plymouth, Devon, gentleman. The land granted was fifteen acres, and the lease dated 5 Dec., 1831, and on this taking the Copper Works proper were first built in 1834, near the river, while the Rolling Mills (built in 1828) and the Silver Works, (constructed in 1840) with the large Stone Chimney near the Canal are on lands once belonging to Mr. Bennett, of Laleston, at the sale of whose estates the freehold of this was, I am told, bought up by Messrs. Williams.

Some of the foregoing details, with much that relates to the 'Hafod' Works, may be found in the interesting recitals, schedules, &c., contained in the confirming Act, cap. 25 of the 1st of Victoria.

The offices abutting on the canal, near the entrance to the 'Morfa' Works, are also built on lands of the Duke; indeed, the mixed character of the properties hereabouts can scarcely be properly understood without a plan; so inconvenient was it found at 'Hafod,' that Lord Jersey exchanged lands with His Grace, to enable the latter to complete the lease to the Messrs. Vivians under one ground landlord.

THE 'CAMBRIAN' COPPER WORKS,
at Llanelly, were erected by Messrs. Mary Glascott and Sons, in the year 1830. Copper smelting did not turn out successful with the firm, and about the year 1838 to 1840 they undertook smelting on commission for the Grenfells, the Mines Royal, and the Governor and Company of Copper Miners, but this, too, after a year's trial, was also given up, and the works closed. The 'English' Copper Company then took to them with the assistance of Mr. John Williams, of Swansea, as manager. The ground landlord, Mr. Pemberton, insisting that the coals used should come from certain collieries at a price named in the lease, which being higher than they could be purchased for elsewhere, and this being looked upon as a hardship, the Company abandoned their lease and declined to go on. So the works lay idle till Messrs. Nevill and Co. purchased them as convenient to their other premises at Llanelly, and converted them to Lead and Silver smelting, in 1847. I understand that they hold and continue them in those branches of metallurgy to the present time.

In the little valley of the Afan, above the Town which lies not far from its junction with the sea, on the East of Swansea Bay, is to be found the great establishment known as

THE

'CWM-AFAN' COPPER AND METALLIFEROUS WORKS,
remarkable in the surrounding district for its enormous chimney, carried up tunnelwise to the top of the adjacent hill, and rising to a height of 1,200 feet above the works, giving the mountain an Etna-like effect by the volumes of smoke, which at a distance, and from the Bay, appear to issue from it as though from a natural crater. While erected at great cost in the hope of remedying the admitted evils of Copper Smoke, it was said, unhappily, to

have produced a mischievous effect upon the lands within its range. Indeed, Mr. N. E. Vaughan, as the owner of some farms lying to the south-west, brought an action against the 'English Copper Company,' at the Summer Assizes of 1866 at Swansea, but the cause became a *remanet*, and so remains untried, and the question unsettled.*

Neath, 31 *Aug*, 1839.
Mr. C. Tennant, when writing to Lord Jersey, as agent, said:—

"The English Copper Company were a wealthy Copper Body, and have lately sold their extensive works at Taibach, Margam to Mr. Vivian in disgust and despair, as is supposed, of the new Port Talbot Works." Their Cornish Agent, in answer to C. T., says "I shall myself recommend *Neath* in preference to any other place hereabouts for Copper Works."

These works, however, were built on lands of Earl Jersey, on a lease granted to Messrs. Vigors and Co., in 1837. Three years afterwards, in 1840, they were bought by the 'Governor and Company of Copper Miners in England,' who continued to hold them, having in addition to Copper, introduced the manufacture of Iron bars and rails, Tin-plates and Chemicals, the whole having been under the active superintendence of the late †Mr. W. P. Struvé, C.E., as resident agent, and manager, after whose time they passed under various managers, until the Company went into liquidation, and were bought up by a syndicate, composed of Messrs. Spence, Dixon (of Cleopatra Needle renown) and Shaw, the two first-named gentlemen subsequently sold out, leaving Mr. Shaw the present proprietor. The Tin-plate Works were sold off, and the remainder conducted under the style and title of "The Successors of the Gov. and Com. of Cop. Miners in England." The concern has quite recently

---

* See however agreement between them at p. 110, in appendix, post.

† Mr. Struvé, like his neighbours at the great works of the District, raised a corps of Volunteer Rifles in 1840, and was appointed their Captain Commandant; they wore grey at first, and then red, with silver mounts.

G. G. F.

been transformed into "The Cwmavon Estate and Works Company."

THE 'PEMBREY' COPPER WORKS.

This manufactory is the most western in the District, built on the margin of the Burry, near the village of Pembrey, in Carmarthenshire, on the estate of Lord Ashburnham, and near extensive mines of suitable coal. These works were constructed for the eminent firm of Mason & Elkington, of Birmingham and London.

The great stack, or chimney, which rises from the flat moor, thence to a height of some 250 feet, has the date of its erection in dark bricks on its northern face—1847—and from its top may be seen issuing the long stream of thin white gas wandering over the country where the wind listeth.

THE 'RED-JACKET' COPPER WORKS

were erected near the mouth of the river Neath, by the Messrs. Bankart and Sons, in the year 1849, between the canal and the river, in a locality possessing great facilities for the carriage of coal, ores, &c. The name is derived from a small public-house on its bank, used by the frequenters of the adjoining passage to Briton Ferry.

THE 'PORT-TENNANT' COPPER WORKS

were built by Mr. Charles Lambert, an extensive mine owner and smelter of Chili, who having large business connections in that country, was nevertheless anxious to have a settlement in the true Copper manufacturing District of Great Britain, and accordingly in 1852 took lands for the purpose, near the East pier, and immediate entrance of Swansea Harbour, from the Duke of Beaufort and Earl Jersey, and thereon erected the extensive works, as often subsequently known by his personal name as by the locality where they are situated. They are now under the direct supervision of Mr. Lambert's son-in-law, Mr. Edward Bath.

About a mile to the north-west of Swansea, in Cwmbwrlais, a small Works for the reduction of Copper dross and old metal, was erected in 1852, by Mr. James Stephens, and eventually some furnaces for the smelting of ores were added, and the whole called

THE 'BLACK-VALE' COPPER WORKS,

I imagine from its neighbourhood being covered with heaps of old colliery debris.

THE 'BRITON-FERRY' COPPER WORKS,

were constructed in 1853, by a junior member of the firm of Bankart & Co., of 'Red Jacket' Copper Works, in conjunction with the firm of Sweetland, Tuttle & Co., and they naturally enjoy the like facilities for trade, being very conveniently placed for coal, which can there be had in abundance at a moderate price. When Mr. Bankart retired from this firm he was replaced by Mr. Barclay, who, ultimately becoming sole proprietor, sold the works to the 'Cape Copper Mining Company' for the reduction of their own ores from the Cape of Good Hope, a curious revival of the condition of things existing in the early years of the present century, as previously related.

THE 'DANYGRAIG' COPPER WORKS

were also erected on Earl Jersey's estate by Mr. Jennings, who came from the Clyne-Wood Works, in 1860. Copper-smelting is here, nevertheless, but a secondary consideration, the ores purchased being selected on account of their containing Arsenic and Sulphur, the which having been extracted, the remainder is run down for such Copper as can be got out.

Messrs. Williams, Foster and Co. bought up Mr. Jennings' interest in the firm, but Mr. J. M. Williams complaining of a

L

clause in the lease requiring an extra £10 per annum for every Copper furnace erected, the agreement for sale was cancelled, and so Mr. Hadland became and remains the sole proprietor and manager.

In 1862, a return was once more made to the old Copper-Works District, on the banks of the Tawe, by the conversion of a pottery premises not long previously built by Mr. Calland, a little to the north of the South Wales Railway Viaduct. This conversion was effected by "The Landore Arsenic and Copper Company," and their place of business is known as

THE 'LITTLE LANDORE' COPPER WORKS,

to distinguish them from their near neighbour the old 'Landore' Works of Messrs. Williams, Foster, and Co. These works stand on what no doubt was the eastern portion of the premises leased to the first Llangavelach Copper Works, of 1744, previously described, for it appears that, whenever the surface is broken through, *old* copper slags immediately show themselves in abundance.

THE 'LLANSAMLET' WORKS,

with like objects to those at Danygraig, were in 1866-7 in course of construction by the same Mr. Jennings, between Smith's Canal and the Swansea Vale Railway above the old Copper Works on the eastern side of the River Tawe, also on lands of Lord Jersey, in the parish from which they take their name.

In addition to what may be considered the regular manufactories, there have been from time to time works so small as to consist of only a furnace or two; these small beginnings have always been looked upon with great jealousy and suspicion, and they have generally had to succumb to a pressure which was too great for them to resist. Thus, I recollect near the Pipe-house, at the head of the Canal wharfs, a single furnace erected by Mr. Edw. Merry;

another below the South Wales Railway on the Strand, belonging, I believe, to Mr. R. G. Thompson, and there may possibly be others in 'The District." A like concern *may* have existed at Bank-y-Gockus, as mentioned in previous pages; and I have a strong suspicion that some such furnace once existed within the precincts of Swansea Castle, for on opening the ground in Worcester-place some years since for town drainage, north of the Post-office, we came upon quantities of regularly tipped ill-smelted copper slag, very green in parts from the copper it carelessly contained. It is not impossible that this may have been from a trial furnace permitted to be put up by Gabriel Powell, when the Duke's Agent at Swansea, early in the last century. I have myself seen quantities of roughly smelted lead ore from the floor of the then chandler's premises in the N.E. corner of the Castle at Swansea, proving that it was at the time looked upon as pretty nearly waste ground there.

Brought at length near the end of my labours, I cannot help noting that while in the earlier age of Copper Smelting, Lead was nearly always a concomitant manufacture*—now, that chemistry has become the handmaid of art, the nobler metals, Gold and Silver, in connection with Copper, as well as other metals, have, for several years been largely extracted at Swansea; and so long as this was done secretly by the few, it gave them a handsome return for the science they employed beyond the less informed buyers of argentiferous or auriferous ores, as the case might be; and thus also by the extension of scientific knowledge, the Arsenic and the Sulphur are now specially

---

* As a curious illustration of this, I notice that the old Docket of Town and Quay dues ordered to be issued for Swansea Borough in 1808, contains no other ores than those of "Copper or Lead," which were charged 2d. a ton. In the tariff of Swansea, in the time of the 1st Mary, there is no notice of ores at all, and one could hardly expect there would be. G. G. F.

sought for and utilized, instead of being dissipated into noxious gases. Long may these progressive steps continue, and the ores brought hither from each division of the globe yield fruit after their kind for the use of man ; and let us say with old Mr. Gabriel Powell—

"Wee are determined to goe on, and think it very hard if"
"wee should be debarred of seeking those advantages which"
"the situation [of Swansea] entitles us to."

My readers who have had the patience to follow up the information which I have gathered and utilized for their knowledge, have, perhaps, scarcely brought their minds to bear on the gigantic results which have flowed from the localization of the Copper trade by Customer Smyth and Ulricke Frosse, at Neath, (A.D. 1586) Elizabeth's reign, when one "John Bwaple, of Wales, had delyvered into his Bark at St. Ives, a frayght of Copp'r Owre of 15 tonnes and 8 hundreds waight in seven daies." In the place of these scanty supplies from Cornwall, we have now a magnificent fleet of first-class ships constantly trading to the port of Swansea from all parts of the world, whose tonnage amounts to an aggregate for the year of upwards of 200,000 tons of Copper, Silver, Gold Lead, Zinc, Nickel, Cobalt and Bismuth Ores.* When, again, we reflect on the number of persons engaged, not simply in navigating the ships for this tonnage, but the thousands of hands employed at the various Copper and other adjacent Works, and the numerous Collieries from which their daily supply of fuel is extracted (to say nothing of the trades which indirectly supply their numerous wants) we must, indeed, be struck with the mighty success which has followed the original planting of "Copper Smelting in the Swansea District."

* Though recently large Works have been erected at Llansamlet, under leases from Lord Jersey for the treatment of complex Ores.

May this Trade exist and long continue to flourish, and while it immediately benefits those who carry it on, may it, by the wise aids of science and skilled labour, be deprived of all noxiousness, so that "One and All" may alike rejoice, and with earnest voice, cry

"GOD SPEED THE COPPER TRADE."

MEMORANDUM :—*January*, 1869.

"God Speed the Copper Trade."— It would indeed be somewhat remarkable if it should turn out that, while I was expressing so ardent a wish, this gigantic manufacture was then on the eve of a great change! In fact, shortly afterwards it was gravely stated at Swansea, "the days of the Copper Trade are numbered, and Swansea has seen its grand climacteric!" *I*, for one, boldly doubted the latter assertion, for I argued—even supposing that the 'Copper Trade' had unfortunately reached its climax, and was about to change its policy and localities,—there was still *for Swansea* a great Trade to be done in Silver and Gold, Iron and Steel, Zinc and Tin-plates, Nickel and Cobalt, Alkalis and Chemicals, which *might and ought to* nestle on the banks of Tawe, between and around the hills of my native place, finding there the material element of *Coals of every description suitable* to their several necessities.

GEO. GRANT-FRANCIS, F.S.A., Col.

APPENDIX.

It having been urged on me that I have scarcely done justice, at pp. 190-192, to the subject of "Copper Smoke," in my 1st Edition, I append my letter to the *Cambrian* at the end of 1865, to shew that *I*, at least, have not overlooked or underrated its vast importance.

IMPROVEMENT OF SWANSEA.

SUPPRESSION OF COPPER SMOKE.

To the Editor of "THE CAMBRIAN."

SIR,—Copper Smoke and Swansea are with great numbers of persons interchangeable terms. The latter flourishes alongside an admitted evil! Under cover of it, other noxious vapours have successfully nestled, so that those who suffer in mind, body, or estate, are quietly but firmly informed that the creation of Smoke, *in this District* has now become a Prescriptive right. To open the question at all requires some boldness, from a fear which generally exists that, it is better to leave things as they are, than risk the chance of injury to a great local trade. The sufferers, though their name be *legion*, have now for some years lain dormant, chiefly, I believe, in the hope that Chemistry and Legislation were marching forward simultaneously for the benefit of the Public health and the abatement of acknowledged nuisances.

Dr. Percy, in his "Metallurgy," published in 1861, at p. 339, says:—"The proprietor of the Patent Swansea Fuel Works has been compelled, at great expense, to construct a long flue and chimney to the top of Kilvey hill, in order to carry further away some dark-coloured, foul-smelling smoke, which is intolerable to the inhabitants of a Town which can submit without a murmur to the sulphurous and choking exhalations of the Copper Works. Nay, it has, I understand, even been gravely maintained by some persons that Copper Smoke is beneficial, if not agreeable rather than otherwise. The smoke is an unmistakeable nuisance; and the man who pretends that it is not, must either have a peculiar constitution, or lie under some strange delusion."

This is the opinion of a competent scientific and perfectly independent witness; how many will endorse it locally, I leave to your readers to consider and determine, if so inclined.

The late Mr. J. H. Vivian had the honesty to declare that "the suppression of the Smoke would be advantageous to the Town and its neighbourhood."

So much for the disagreeable part of the question, and I will now enter on the "sunny side" of it by stating *That a Remedy has been discovered, has been tested, found practicable and profitable, and is now being carried out at the 'Hafod' and their other Works!*

The questions which not unnaturally arise are, May we hope to see the Valley again compare with our lovely Bay?—Can Nature again recover her lost position? Can our hills once more be with verdure clad? It will, I feel assured, be admitted that these are most interesting questions to us as Swansea folk. If our atmosphere could be pure, if our naked hills could be clothed with grass and our cattle once more graze and fatten thereon, who could complain? and if this "consummation devoutly to be wished," could not only be brought about, but, at the same time, bring *profit* to the Copper Smelters, then should we indeed have cause for common congratulation and rejoicing!

PORTRAIT OF H. H. VIVIAN Esq.
F.G.S. J.P. & M.P FOR GLAMORGANSHIRE.
WHO FIRST ESTABLISHED THE GERSTENHÖFER SYSTEM
AT HAFOD AND TAIBACH.
IN THE YEAR 1868

It being well-known that I have taken an active interest in this question for many years, a copy of the annexed letter has been sent to me by the personal kindness of Mr. Nash Vaughan. The prospective advantages to the Swansea District are so great, that I lost no time in laying it before the public :—

5, Upper Belgrave Street, London,

20th June, 1865.

DEAR VAUGHAN,—I am in receipt of your letter of to-day's date.

It is quite true that we have purchased Mr. Moritz Gerstenhöfer's Patent, and are carrying it out energetically. We have had two calciners at work for some months and are now building twenty-six between our Hafod and Taibach Works.

As far as I can form an opinion, it is a perfect success, and will put an end to all vapours arising from our calcining and roasting furnaces. I believe that when this furnace is universally adopted the only vapours arising from the Copper Works will be those of the *melting* furnaces. At a rough guess, probably upwards of two-thirds will be condensed and turned to profitable account. The outlay involved is, however, considerable, and much time will be necessary to reconstruct such large works without bringing them to a stand. Although, as you are aware, no pressure has been put upon us for many years, still I have never lost sight of the subject, and when the 'Landore' Alkali Works came into the market about eighteen months ago, we took them chiefly with a view to work out this problem. We were about to enter into a course of experiments when Mr. Gerstenhöfer's novel and beautiful invention was brought under my notice by our chemist, Mr. B. S. Herrmann. We at once made arrangements for its use, and ultimately for its purchase. If it turns out, when in extensive use, to be as successful as I at present believe it to be, it will be a subject of great gratification to us to have been instrumental in introducing an improvement so important and beneficial.

You are at liberty to make any use you please of this letter.

Believe me,

Yours very truly,

H. HUSSEY VIVIAN.

NASH E. VAUGHAN, Esq.,
Rheola, Neath.

1st January, 1868.

Having gone up to-day to Hafod to swear in special constables, as one of the two County Justices so deputed, in *re* "Fenianism;" after we had finished, Mr. Hussey Vivian asked me to go through the Works and see the changes which the adoption of the Gerstenhöfer furnaces had made, and also to see the conversion of the "smoke" into sulphuric acid. I went with pleasure and found only *four* of the old calciners remaining out of 35. Many of them had been removed and replaced, others were in course of demolition, and others blown out, but still warm; so that really the year of 1865 saw the expiry of the old system of Copper calcining at Hafod.

The new Furnaces may be termed perpendicular—the old ones horizontal, and this change of form has necessitated the raising of the side walls and roofs of the buildings, but this change though costly to the owners is a benefit to the workmen in light and air. Thence we proceeded to the old slag banks which had been levelled at top and now afford an extensive flat area on which had been erected immense wooden structures whose internal sides and tops have been covered with sheet lead, and into which large culverts convey the gases driven off from the calciners and up to themselves, and when the necessary introduction of nitrous acid and steam converts the fumes of Copper smoke into sulphuric acid, which being condensed into proper receivers, its strength is tested and it is stored for use or sale. At this great elevation it is readily conveyed by pipes to Mr. Vivian's alkali works on one side, or to the phosphate works,* on the other, by which means a great saving of carriage and loss

---

* At the gates entrance of the works I had noticed the following important intimation which I saw at once meant *business* :—

"Messrs. Vivian and Sons, Hafod Phosphate Works, Swansea, are in want of Agents for the sale of their super-phosphate and other manures in districts where they are not already represented. A liberal commission will be given to competent and energetic salesmen."   G. G. F.

by waste is effected. The very great size of these chambers may be gathered when I say they are upwards of 100 feet high, 30 feet long and 25 feet wide. We then got up on the flat tops or roofs, and thence were able *to see* the material difference between the chimneys of the calcining furnaces at Hafod and the neighbouring works where Gerstenhöfer's plans are not carried out, and although its proprietor said all was not yet effected at 'Hafod' that he hoped to carry out, yet the difference was very marked. Seeing is, indeed here, believing!

Before parting, Mr. Vivian told me that he had recently bought the "Old Forest" Copper Works, and was then converting them into zinc or spelter works, and that he expected thirty *German* workmen with his manager, Mr. Daehne, there to-morrow, and the works to be in operation next week—further, that he anticipates manufacturing 20,000 tons of zinc ores on the banks of Swansea River. That the ores he was using were chiefly carbonates, but that a good deal of blende or sulphuret of zinc would be used by and bye, and if so, he should pass it all through Gerstenhöfer's furnaces and so save the *sulphur*, and, I beg to add, the necessary additional nuisance.*

* HAFOD COPPER WORKS, SWANSEA,
June 28*th*, 1881.

DEAR SIR,—The dimensions of our Acid Chambers, which you saw at "Hafod," were as follows:—

3 Chambers, each 40 × 30 × 20 = 72,000 c. ft.
,,   ,,   40 × 30 × 24¼ = 87,300 ,,
,,   ,,   120 × 30 × 25 = 90,000 ,,
,,   ,,   150 × 30 × 25 = 112,500 ,,
,,   ,,   115 × 30 × 25 = 86,250 ,,
,,   ,,   117¼ × 30 × 25 = 88,000 ,,
                                    ———
                                    536,050 ,,

I cannot obtain the exact date when the Works ("Forest") were given up to the Duke of Beaufort, but know that they have not been used as "Copper Works." You are aware that they now form part of our "Morriston Spelter Works."

Yours very truly, WM. MORGAN.

Col. G. GRANT-FRANCIS, F.S.A.,
    New Athenæum Club,
        London.

I cannot conclude this notice on my visit without expressing the pleasure there is to be derived from visiting so busy a scene with the active spirit of him who has not only the will but sees the way to carry into effect such gigantic measures as I have endeavoured here to describe. Mr. Vivian has my heartiest good wishes for his entire success in a manufacture, bearing, as he does, the estimable character which his Father did before him of "doing the right thing at the right time," and to which I hope my neighbours will cordially respond.—AMEN.

G. G. F.

Cae Bailey, Swansea,

New Year's Day, 1868.

I have the pleasure of knowing Herr Gerstenhöfer personally, and he has assured me that not only is this mode of treating sulphurous ores a proved success in Germany, but he has little doubt but that it will be a key whereby to fetter many other gaseous nuisances. It is a curious fact, that the Germans were our instructors in copper smelting nearly three centuries ago, and that now one of the greatest improvements in the *modus operandi* of that important manufacture should emanate from the same source.

A brief description of so valuable an invention may here be pardoned—

The ores of Copper are oxides, carbonates, and sulphurets —little or no mischief arises from the smelting of the two first named, but the sulphur contained in the latter is readily driven off by heat, and appears at the top of the chimney and through the region over which it passes as white and tenaceous gaseous clouds, too well known locally as "Copper Smoke," which gases are created by roasting the ores with coal fires in the calcining furnaces.

The object of the new mode is, by a properly constructed furnace, so to divide the ore as it passes from the regulated hoppers at the top, that it shall fall on a triangular bar, and then on to similar bars below each other, and thus expose the ore to continued subdivision till it reaches the bottom and is freed from the sulphur. The heat has converted it into sulphurous acid, the which is constantly passing off through side chambers into condensers, and becoming a marketable article, is retained and prevented from escaping into the atmosphere and becoming a common mischief.

A most important item in the invention is, that no fuel is required, for the sulphur catching fire at the upper bars, the heat evolved within the furnace suffices to keep the falling ore in a state of ignition. Simplicity is indeed here coupled with economy.

Mr. Vivian is emphatic in his declaration as to the value of the discovery, and proves his belief in its success by the erection of no less than 28 new furnaces at Swansea and Taibach, Glamorgan. When it is recollected "that 46,000 tons of sulphur are volatilized into 92,000 tons of sulphurous acid, that in the works near Swansea 65,900 cubic meters of this acid are projected into the atmosphere, and that Le Play estimates the value of the sulphur thus dissipated daily at £200,000 yearly"! we may readily appreciate the importance of the commercial side of the question, and rest satisfied that the Smelters elsewhere will have an equal interest with Mr. Vivian in availing themselves of Moritz Gerstenhöfer's admirable invention.

I remain, Sir,

Yours faithfully,

GEO. GRANT FRANCIS, F.S.A.

Cae Bailey, Swansea,

8th Aug., 1865.

———

The process and practical working of this valuable invention will be best shewn by a speech of Mr. Vivian, to the West Glamorgan Agricultural Association, in December, 1866. This gentleman having touched on various subjects, continued :—

"His (Mr. Vivian's) experience in managing affairs—which was considerable—had shown him how very much depended upon the power of choosing men; and he was quite convinced that if Bonaparte had not known how to choose good generals, he would never have been Bonaparte. (Hear, hear, and laughter.) As far as he individually was concerned, his chief thought and occupation in life, as they all knew, was to keep in activity those gentlemen whom they saw in such numbers smoking their pipes about a mile to the north of this town. (Laughter.) He believed some people considered that the peculiar 'tobacco' smoke which issued from those pipes was not of a high agricultural value. Of course he differed from that opinion. (Laughter.) No one had ever yet been able to convince him that it was not of very considerable agricultural value; and he believed he was now in a position to prove that the opinions that he had always entertained on the point were correct. He could assure them that he had given a great deal of time and thought of late to bottling that smoke, and his conviction was that when it was bottled it would be of great agricultural value. In fact he firmly believed that this District was destined to become the fertiliser of a very large portion of England. A short time ago, when partridges were in season, he was walking through a very fine field of turnips, near Llangafelach—in a part where he believed no turnips had ever grown before. He turned round to the man in charge and asked 'What do you put on those fields?' He replied, 'Deed I don't know—five hundred weight of stuff which Mr. Taylor did send me.' 'Oh,' said he (Mr. Vivian) 'then two and a half hundred weight of it is copper smoke!' (Hear, hear, and laughter.) And this was the fact; half of the manure which was put on that land was copper smoke, and judging from the crop there was no doubt at all that copper smoke agreed very well with turnips. He had, as he had said, given great attention to the subject lately, and was putting up a little works which were now covered with those rose coloured roofs which they might have observed about half-way between this and Landore; and he thought the result of the experiment would be that they would produce manure enough for something like 40,000 acres of turnips every year. (Hear, hear.) He looked upon it merely as an experiment—as just a little feeler— and if it answered, as he hoped and believed it would, he thought, as he had said, that this district would turn out to be the chief fertilizer of a large portion of England, because that on which they were now experimenting represented but a very small portion of that beautiful white smoke—(laughter)—which they saw rolling away in such abundance over Kilvey hill, and of which he hoped a large portion would evidently be condensed and transformed into Superphosphates. As he had once before taken occasion to say in that room, his opinion was, that this was a green country—a country peculiarly adapted for the growth of green crops—and he thought therefore that they would act wisely in giving their attention especially to this department. He could not take to himself credit as an agriculturalist but he could have a sincere desire to assist the agriculturalists, and to obtain what he believed would prove a very valuable fertilizing agent from a substance which most people had hitherto said though he had never believed it—(laughter)—was quite the reverse. He had every confidence of success in the undertaking, and if so he thought he might at any rate claim credit for having found out a mode *ex fumo dare cerem*—out of smoke to produce rich corn. And if he did this, he thought he should be quite prepared to show his face at any Agricultural Society in the kingdom. (Hear, hear.)"

Having, at p. 143, made reference to the action commenced against the 'English Copper Company' at Cwm-Avan, for damage caused by their smoke, I have much pleasure in annexing the details, handed to me by Mr. Vaughan, of the terms of the negociations which have been so far brought to a satisfactory conclusion. It is impossible to exaggerate the importance of this Case in the District.   G. G. F.

"VAUGHAN v. CWM-AVAN COPPER CO."

TERMS AGREED UPON.

1.—That the Company shall at once use all reasonable means, consistent with the smelting processes of Copper, to abate and do away any deleterious effects which may arise from their works; and that if, at the expiration of two years from this date, Mr. Vaughan, or his Tenants should be of opinion that all necessary steps have not been taken to effect the above object, then that the question whether they have used all such reasonable means or not, shall be referred to a person to be named by the Board of Trade, whose decision on the question in dispute shall be final.

2.—That in the event of his deciding that sufficient steps have not been taken, a verdict to be entered in the Action for Ten Pounds damages, each party paying his own costs.

N. EDWARDS VAUGHAN.

For the Governor & Co. of
Copper Miners in England } WILLIAM P. STRUVE.

MEMORANDUM.

That the Actions by my Tenants shall be withdrawn—no Costs either side.

N. E. VAUGHAN.*

WILLIAM P. STRUVE."

February, 1867.

---

* "Mr. Vaughan, of Rheola, died at Inchbar, Rosshire, N.B., on 5th September, at the age of 57 years," *vide Cambrian* of 11th September, 1868.   G. G. F.

Tokens.

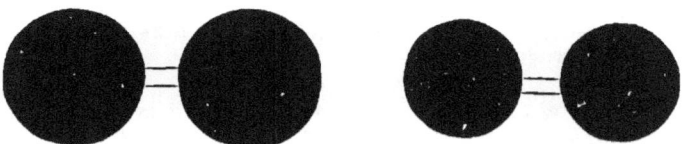

BRASS, COPPER, AND SILVER TRADE TOKENS current in "*The Swansea District*" between the years 1666 and 1813, described from the originals in the Cabinet of Col. Grant-Francis, F.S.A., 1867:—

TO THE EDITOR OF THE "CAMBRIAN."

The value of Coins and Medals in the elucidation of History has too often been dwelt upon and admitted to need enlargement from me: how useful they have proved in connection with the subject which has occupied our attention recently in these columns must have been noticed by all who have perused my letters. Before, therefore, entirely concluding my communications on "Copper Smelting" I am anxious to ascertain whether any other *Tokens* are to be found in the neighbourhood which may assist in throwing a further light upon that interesting subject, and with this view I beg now to send a descriptive list of the series in my Cabinet, and I shall esteem it a particular favour if any one having a coin of a different type or date will send a description of it either to your columns or to me direct.

I have since presented the entire series to the Museum of the Royal Institution of South Wales, where I am glad to find they are careful preserved, and much thought of by the Visitors.

Cae Bailey. G. G. F.

1.

1666. Halfpenny in brass. *Obverse.* In the field a shield bearing the bust of the Virgin. Between a cinquefoil mintmark and two stars, "Matthew Davies, in." *Reverse*, "Swanzey. Mercer. 1666. His Halfe Peny."

2.

1666. Farthing in brass. *Obv.* "Isaac After." I. A., between two roses. *Rev.* "In Swansea. I. A."

3.

1666. Fartning in brass. *Obv.* "Thomas Love," in the field, the arms of the Mercer's Co., as No. 1. *Rev.* "Of Neath. Mercer." "T. B. L." in the field.

M

4.

1656. Brass farthing *Obv*. "William Burten," W.S.B. in the field *Rev*. "At Swansea, 1656." W.S.B. as on the obverse. This Token was sent to me by Mr. Boyne as possibly belonging to Swansea; but I rather doubt it.

5.

1787. Penny in copper. *Obv.* A Druid's Bust, surrounded by a closely woven wreath of oak leaves. *Rev.* "P. M. Co." in Italian text capitals, surmounted by the date, 1787, and inscribed, "We promise to pay the bearer one penny." On the edge, "On demand in London, Liverpool, or Anglesey."

6.

1788. Halfpenny and Farthing in Copper. *Obv.* Similar device to foregoing, but the wreath is more open in its arrangement, and acorns are freely interspersed. *Rev.* and *edge* same as foregoing, but dated one year later, and inscribed "Anglesea Mines Halfpenny." The farthing is not called by that name, but "Half halfpenny," and its *edge* milled. The initials on these fine coins stand, of course, for "Parys Mining Company."

7.

1789. Halfpenny in copper. *Obv.* The bust of a Bishop mitred, a crosier in the field (some types are without the crosier). Inscribed "Cronebane Halfpenny." *Rev.* The arms and crest of the "Associated Irish Mine Company," in the field 1789. Another type has a female figure seated and leaning on a harp, inscribed "Hibernia."

8.

1791. Halfpenny in copper. *Obv.* Devices as on the previous three coins, but more boldly executed; the artist has added R. D. under the bust, the design for which was evidently taken from the figure of a "Chief Druid" engraved on the title page of Powell's History of Wales, 1774 edition. *Rev.* "Cornish copper. Half an ounce. 1791," the field charged with arms of the Duchy of Cornwall, surmounted by a ducal coronet.

9.

1791. Halfpenny in copper. *Obv.* Portrait bust, surrounded by "Charles Roe established the copper works 1758." *Rev.* A female seated with emblems of machinery, with the date underneath, 1791, and inscribed "Macclesfield Halfpenny." On the *edge*, "Payable at Macclesfield, Liverpool, and Congleton."

10.

1792. Farthing in copper. *Obv.* and *Rev.* precisely the same designs as No. 9, but inscribed "Macclesfield Half Halfpenny, 1792."

IN GLAMORGANSHIRE.

11.

1791. Halfpenny in copper. *Obv.* In the field a female in flowing drapery seated, and resting her right hand on a rock, supporting with her left a bound fasces, which is resting on her left knee: inscribed, "Birmingham Mining and Copper Company, 1791." *Rev.* In the field a Stork, Heron, or Liver standing on a cornua full of flowers, with "Halfpenny payable at (on the *edge*) Birmingham, Redruth, and Swansea."

12.

1792 and 1793. Halfpence in copper, with exactly the same devices as the foregoing, but that the dates are altered, and the last, I am told, in some instances, has Swansea omitted from the *edge*.

13.

1793. Halfpenny in copper. *Obv.* same as in the year 1787, but of very inferior execution. *Rev.* The Field occupied by "R. N. G." in travesty apparently of its prototype, with the date at the top, 1793. Inscribed "North Wales halfpenny;" and on the *edge*, "Payable at John Fincham's, Suffolk."! *

14.

1793. Farthing in brass. *Obv.* A rudely executed male bust, inscribed "South Wales Farthing." *Rev.* The Prince's Plume in a shield, surrounded by "Pro bono Publico. 1793," and a wreath.†

15.

1793. Halfpenny in copper. *Obv.* A Druid's bust within a wreath of oak, two sprigs of which are brought out on the field near the centre. *Rev.* A Welsh harp within a wreath of oak, date above, 1793, and inscribed "North Wales Halfpenny." This coin is of very poor execution.

It may be well here to mention that there are a number of types with this Druid's Head on *Obv.* It was probably a favourite, not only on account of its Welsh design, but the 1787 type was the *first Token* issued in the Kingdom in the 18th Century.

16.

1795. Halfpenny in copper. *Obv.* A fine quasi portrait bust, inscribed, "Jestyn-ap-Gwrgan, Tywysog Morganwg, 1091," round the neck, from a chain, is suspended a shield *sable* bearing a cross *or*. *Rev.* A draped Britannia seated on a globe, shield and spear in her left hand, while with her right she points to the distance; in front is a ship, and behind her a pillar supporting a crown, up towards which a laurel is growing; inscription, "Y Brenhin ar Gyfraith, 1795." On the *edge* "Glamorgan Halfpenny."

---

* This puzzles me greatly. How came North Wales and Suffolk to be thus coupled together? The coin was current in the former, doubtless, owing to its connections with the Copper trade.

† Some are in Copper and inscribed "Medallion of St. David."

17.

1795. Halfpenny in copper. *Obv.* An ugly, ill executed bust of a female, inscribed "Princess of Wales." *Rev.* A Portcullis (the device of the Borough of Swansea), surmounted by the crest of the Duke of Beaufort and at present the device, etc., the Welsh plumes, inscribed, Halfpenny 1795." The *edge* has no inscription, but is diagonally milled.

17a.

1795. I have *seen* a Halfpenny with the bust of George Washington and a shield with the stars and stripes, and an inscription "Liberty and Security." Inscribed on *edge*, "Payable at *Swansea*, London, and Birmingham," but as yet do not possess it. G. G. F.

18.

1795. Halfpenny in copper. *Obv.* and *Rev.* similar designs to Nos. 11 and 12, but inscribed "The Birmingham Metal and Copper Co. 1795. Payable at Birmingham, Redruth, and Swansea."

19.

1796. Halfpenny in copper. *Obv.* and *Rev.* like to the foregoing No. 18, but inscribed "Birmingham Coining and Copper Co. 1796. Payable at Birmingham, Redruth and Swansea."

20.

1796. Halfpenny in copper. *Obv.* View of Swansea Castle, inscribed and dated, "Swansea Halfpenny, 1795." *Rev.* A key suspended from a knotted ribbon, with words, John Voss, draper, &c." On the *edge*, "Payable on Demand."*

21.

1811. Shilling in Silver. *Obv.* Swansea Castle, inscribed "Swansea Token for XII. pence. MDCCCXI." *Rev.* The suspended key as on the foregoing, but inscribed " Payable by John Voss, Draper, &c. ;" the *edge* being milled.

22.

1811 Shilling in silver. *Obv.* as the last but no inscription or date; this latter, however, I learnt from Mr. Padley himself, was 1811. *Rev.* A wreath of laurel surrounds the words, "Payable at S. Padley's and J. Andrews's."† The inscription near the rim is "Swansea Silver Token for 12 pence."

* This token almost rivals in execution the celebrated series issued for Coventry, and was evidently the type from which the two following in silver were executed; but, like most copies, they do not equal the beauty of the original.

† Padley and Andrews were traders and brothers-in-law residing at Swansea, the former being Portreeve of that Borough in the year 1833.

23.

1811. Shilling in silver. *Obv.* The field occupied by the arms of the Borough of Neath, inscribed " Payable at H. Rees and D. Morgan." *Rev.* " Neath. Silver token." The field filled with the words " 12 pence. 1811."

24.

1811. Sixpence in silver. Precisely the same as on the last mentioned shilling, except that the date is omitted and a wreath of laurels surrounds the word " Sixpence " on the *Rev.*

25.

1811. Penny in copper. *Obv.* An imperial crown in the field, surrounded by " Birmingham and Neath, 1811." *Rev.* " Crown Copper Company. One penny."

26.

1811. Penny in copper. *Obv.* A Cornish pumping engine and a whim, dated underneath, " 1811," inscribed, " Cornish penny." *Rev.* In the field, a fish haurient between four cakes of copper and three blocks of tin, inscribed, " Payable in cash notes at Scorrier House."

27.

1811. Penny in copper. *Obv.* " Tavistock penny Token," the field occupied with the Prince's plume. *Rev.* A mining engine in the plain, backed by hills, and inscribed " Devon Mines, 1811."

28.

1811. Penny in Copper. *Obv.* Within a buckled garter, the arms of the City of Bristol, surrounded by its motto and crest with the date " 1811" underneath. *Rev.* " One Penny Token. Bristol and South Wales," surrounded by the Welsh Plume of Feathers in the field.

29.

1811. Penny and halfpenny in copper. *Obv.* Arms and crest of the City of Bristol, encircled by its motto " Virtute et Industria. 1811." *Rev.* The field occupied by italic capitals " B. B. and Copper Co." (Bristol Brass and Copper Company), and inscribed " One Penny Payable at Bristol, Swansea and London."

30.

1811. Penny and halfpenny in copper. *Obv.* " Rose Copper Company," and in the field, " Token 1811." *Rev.* " Birmingham and Swansea. One penny.'

31.

1811. Penny, Halfpenny and Farthing in copper. *Obv* The field occupied by a ship under sail, but the artist, being no sailor, has made a sad mess of the design on *the farthing* by placing the sails the wrong side of the mast. All are inscribed "Patent Sheathing Nail Manufactory, Bristol." *Rev.* "Penny (Halfpenny or Farthing) Token. 1811. Payable at Bristol and London."

32.

1811. Penny in copper. *Obv.* In the field above the date "1811" a pair of clasped hands frilled at the wrists, inscribed "Birmingham and Risca Copper Company." *Rev.* "Payable in Birmingham. One Penny Token."

33.

1811. Penny in copper. *Obv.* Three copper smelting houses with eight smoking chimnies; underneath is the date "1811," and around "Risca Union Copper Company." *Rev.* "Payable in Birmingham. One Penny Token."

34.

1812. Penny in copper. *Obv.* As No. 31, but more boldly engraved, dated "1812," and inscribed "Union Copper Company, Birmingham." *Rev.* "Payable in cash notes. One Penny Token."

35.

1812. Penny in copper. *Obv.* "Cheadle Copper and Brass Company. Token. 1812." *Rev.* "Payable in London, Cheadle, and Neath. One Penny."

36.

1812. Penny in copper. *Obv.* The entire surface occupied by the arms, supporters, motto, and coronet of Lord De Dunstanville. *Rev.* Inscribed "Success to the Cornish Mines. 1812. Penny piece."

37.

1812. Penny in copper. *Obv.* In the field a Plume of Feathers, inscribed, "Birmingham and South Wales. 1812." *Rev.* A Horse trippant. Around, "Copper Token. One Penny."

38.

1812. Penny in Copper. *Obv.* In the field a lion rampant regardant sustaining between its three paws an oval shield enriched with a rose branch: the whole inscribed "Birmingham and Swansea. 1812." The *Rev.* is occupied with a sprig bearing a rose full blown, and the words "Copper Token, One penny," round it near the rim,

39.

1811. Pennies in copper. *Obv.* In the field a lion passant (in one of the types the face is three-quarter, in the other affronté or full,) underneath "One penny. 1813," and circling the whole are the words "Rolling Mills at Walthamstow." *Rev.* Within an oak wreath, "British Copper Company," and without the wreath "Smelting Works at Landore."

40.

1812. Halfpenny in copper. *Obv.* A female figure seated on a bale of merchandise, holding a branch in her right hand, and a caduceous in her left. Above are the words, "Trade and Navigation," and below the date, " 1812." *Rev.* Halfpenny Token. " Pure Copper preferred to paper"—a quiet hit, I suppose, at " Cash Notes." *Vide* Nos. 26 and 33.

41.

1813. Penny in copper. *Obv.* "One Penny Token." "Swansea and South Wales, 1813." *Rev.* "Payable at the Cambrian Pottery, Swansea, by L W. Dillwyn, T. Bevington, and J. Bevington."

42.

1813. Penny in copper. "One Penny. *Obv.* Nantrhydyvilas Air Furnace Co." *Rev.* "Payable at Swansea and Morriston. 1813."

43.

1813. Penny in copper. *Obv.* In the field a shield containing the arms of Carmarthen, and inscribed "Carmarthen Penny." *Rev.* "Payable by William Moss, Carmarthen, Swansea, and at Jacob and Halse, London, 1813," encircled by a wreath of laurel.

44.

1813. Halfpenny in copper. *Obv.* Within a wreath of laurel, Britannia seated. *Rev.* A Lion passant, three quarter face, inscribed " Halfpenny, 1813."*

45.

No date. Shilling in Silver.† *Obv.* Four dexter hands coupled at the wrists, finished with bands; surrounded by the words "London, York, Swansea, and Leeds." *Rev.* In centre "One Shilling Token." Surrounding the *edge*, "To Facilitate Trade."

---

* This is evidently the halfpenny to match No. 38, the Lion (three-quarter) being *exactly* the same, and the *Obv.*, properly represented the name of the Co.—*British* Copper Company.

† The above is extremely rare, if not unique. It is unknown to all the collectors to whom I have shewn it, and there is no impression of it in the British Museum, or my own collection.

46.

ANOTHER TOKEN CONNECTED WITH SWANSEA.

TO THE EDITOR OF "THE CAMBRIAN."

SIR,—Some few months ago you were good enough to give insertion to a list of Tokens issued from or connected with Swansea. A silver shilling has recently come into my possession of an entirely unknown type. The device is, *Obv.* Four right hands cuffed at the wrist, conjoined; inscribed "London, York, *Swansea* and Leeds." *Rev.* In the field, "One Shilling Token," and around it, "To Facilitate Trade." As this coin is unknown at the British Museum, and not given in Boynes's work, it must be extremely rare. Can any of your readers give any account of it, or any reason for the assumed connection between the four towns inscribed on it?

Yours faithfully,

GEO. GRANT-FRANCIS, F.S.A., Col.

Langland Bay,
20th Nov., 1868.

NOTE.—It is, of course, well known to Collectors that no Tokens were issued after 1814, as they were suppressed by proclamation. In "The Swansea District," however, I well recollect their remaining *in currency*, the best evidence being that the foregoing were selected and put away out of my own pocket money up to so late a date as 1825. Since 1830 another Trade convenience has been created by the issue of little Copper, Brass, and Gilt Tokens, or Medallets termed "cheques:" they are of the halfpenny and farthing size (chiefly the latter) and represent their nominal value, 1½d., 2d., and 3d., and are used nearly always at small taverns, where games are played, to enable the customer, as I am informed, to call in at any subsequent time and have his refreshment to the value indicated. I possess more than twenty different types, dating from 1832 to 1865 inclusive, but they are scarcely worthy of a detailed description on this occasion. When a new tenant comes in he often counter-marks the cheques so as to be answerable only for those issued in his time.—G. G. F.

A Series of Interesting Statistics
ON
Sales of Copper at Swansea

From the Books preserved in the MINING RECORD *Office, at Jermyn Street, London.*

COPPER ORES SOLD AT TICKETINGS.

1804.—14th May, Sold at Swansea	...	...	...	52 Tons.
1806.—12th June, ,, ,,	...	...	...	62 ,,
20th Oct., ,, ,,	...	...	...	41 ,,
1809.—23rd May, ,, ,,	...	...	...	770 ,,
1810.— ,, ,,	...	...	...	1,003 ,,

AGGREGATE PRODUCTIONS FROM THE COPPER MINES OF THE UNITED KINGDOM.

	Ore.			Copper.
1875	... ... 71,528 Tons.	...	...	4,323 Tons.
1876	... ... 79,252 ,,	...	...	4,694 ,,
1877	... ... 73,141 ,,	...	...	4,486 ,,
1878	... ... 56,094 ,,	...	...	3,952 ,,
1879	... ... 51,032 ,,	...	...	3,462 ,,
1880	... ... 52,128 ,,	...	...	3,662 ,,

COPPERY PYRITES IMPORTED AND TREATED AND PRECIPITATE OBTAINED.

	Ore.		Copper.
1874.—Colonial and Foreign,	27,500 Tons.	...	8,750 Tons.
Pyrites treated here	450,000 ,,	...	9,000 ,,
1875.—Colonial and Foreign,	70,212 ,,	...	16,140 ,,
Pyrites treated here	480,000 ,,	...	9,600 ,,
1876.—Colonial and Foreign,	57,959 ,,	...	15,792 ,,
Pyrites treated here	379,269 ,,	...	15,000 ,,
1877.—Colonial and Foreign,	109,950 ,,	...	30,750 ,,
Pyrites treated here	425,000 ,,	...	17,000 ,,
1878.—Colonial and Foreign,	104,803 ,,	...	27,914 ,,
Pyrites treated here	577,719 ,,	...	14,443 ,,
1879.—Colonial and Foreign,	481,392 ,,		—
Pyrites treated here	385,874 ,,	...	14,158 ,,
1880.—Colonial and Foreign,	658,047 ,,	...	—
Pyrites treated here	415,567 ,,	...	15,000 ,.

We learn that the "Widnes Metal Company" have, this year (1881), commenced Smelting their own Copper Precipitate, and we believe some other Works contemplate doing the same.

We find that in 1880 the "Rio Tinto Company" sent of Spanish Pyrites into the Mersey 138,567 tons, the total import amounting to 280,326 tons.

ROBERT HUNT, F.R.S.

LONDON, *October*, 1881.

AN INTERESTING SPECIMEN OF DETAILS IN COPPER TRADING by the Aristocracy in time of Geo. 1st.

LONDON, August 20, 1722.

At a General Court of the Welch Copper Company, held on Thursday last at Sadler's-Hall, (where was a numerous Appearance) his Grace the Duke of Richmond address'd himself to the Proprietors in the following Speech:

Gentlemen,

BY the Minutes of the last General Court, you may observe your Court of Assistants and Committee had purchased several considerable Mines of Copper, Lead, Tin, and other Minerals; as also convenient Work-houses for Smelting the Ores that should be raised or bought, for which your Court of Assistants contracted to pay 14,000*l*. And in order to raise a Sum to comply with such Payments as were then necessary, the said General Court agreed to a Call of One Pound *per* Share.

Your Court of Assistants being willing to contribute every Thing that might tend to the Ease and Service of the Proprietors, thought it would be more agreeable to them to pay the said Call in two Payments, and therefore resolved to receive at that Time only 10*s*. *per* Share in Money, and three Months after the remaining 10*s*. in Money or Shares, at 30*s*. *per* Share, hoping the Call being made so easy, every Proprietor would chearfully have comply'd therewith.

But contrary to Expectation, and very much to the Prejudice of the Company, there has been no more receiv'd upon the Call than 4736*l*., there has been paid 3359*l*. in Part of the Purchase of the Mines, and now remains due 10,641*l*., which your Court of Assistants are not at present in a Condition to pay.

The Proceedings on the *Scire Facias*, and the Calamity of the Times, have proved very detrimental to your Affairs, and may have discouraged a great many from paying their Calls: But as the Vigilance and Care of your Assistants have preserved their Charter inviolable, and have removed that heavy and expensive Prosecution, by His Majesty's most gracious Favour in granting a *Nolle Profequi*, publish'd in the Gazette the 10th of July last; it is hoped those, who have not complyed with what might justly have been expected from them, will now (all Objections being removed) readily make their Payments, and agree to such Resolutions as may be thought proper for the Interest of the Company.

By Advices from the Country, and returns of the Money already expended, the Mines which the Company are concerned in, are capable to employ a considerable Number of Men to great Profit, and may be made very extensive, so as to produce such Quantities of Copper, Tin, Lead and Silver, as may make constant Annual Dividends, when a sufficient Sum is raised to carry them on to the best Advantage, which your Court of Assistants and Committee have good Reason to believe they shall easily effect by the following Method:

I. That a Call be made of 20*s*. *per* Share, to be paid in a Month, with a Discount of 12*d*.

London, August 20, 1722.

At a General Court of the Welch Copper Company, held on Thursday last at Sadler's Hall, (where a numerous Appearance) his Grace the Duke of Richmond address'd himself to the Proprietors in the following Speech:

Gentlemen,

BY the Minutes of the last General Court, you may observe your Court of Assistants and Committee had purchased several considerable Mines of Copper, Lead, Tin, and other Minerals; as also convenient Work-houses for Smelting the Ores that should be raised or bought, for which your Court of Assistants contracted to pay 19000 *l.* And in order to raise a Sum to comply with such Payments as were then necessary, the said General Court agreed to a Call of One Pound *per* Share.

Your Court of Assistants being willing to contribute every Thing that might tend to the Ease and Service of the Proprietors, thought it would be more agreeable to them to pay the said Call in two Payments, and therefore resolved to receive at that Time only 10 *s. per* Share in Money, and three Months after the remaining 10 *s.* in Money or Shares, at 30 *l. per* Share, hoping the Call being made so easy, every Proprietor would chearfully have comply'd therewith.

But contrary to Expectation, and very much to the Prejudice of the Company, there has been no more receiv'd upon the Call than 4736 *l.* there has been paid 3359 *l.* in Part of the Purchase of the Mines, and now remains due 10,641 *l.* which your Court of Assistants are not at present in a Condition to pay.

The Proceedings on the *Scire Facias*, and the Calamity of the Times, have proved very detrimental to your Affairs, and may have discouraged a great many from paying their Calls: But as the Vigilance and Care of your Assistants have preserved their Charter inviolable, and have removed that heavy and expensive Prosecution, by His Majesty's most gracious Favour in granting a *Nolle Prosequi*, publish'd in the Gazette the 10th of July last; it is hoped those, who have not complyed with what might justly have been expected from them, will now (all Objections being removed) readily make their Payments, and agree to such Resolutions as may be thought proper for the Interest of the Company.

By Advices from the Country, and returns of the Money already expended, the Mines which the Company are concerned in, are capable to employ a considerable Number of Men to great Profit, and may be made very extensive, so as to produce such Quantities of Copper, Tin, Lead and Silver, as may make constant Annual Dividends, when a sufficient Sum is raised to carry them on to the best Advantage, which your Court of Assistants and Committee have good Reason to believe they shall easily effect by the following Method:

1. That a Call be made of 20 *s. per* Share, to be paid in a Month, with a Discount of 12 *d. per* Share to such Proprietors as pay the said Call in 15 Days.

II. That such Proprietors who do not comply with this and the former Call within a Month, be Mulct 1 *s.* for each Call in Arrear; and in case they should not pay the said Calls and Mulcts, that the Court of Assistants be directed and impower'd by this General Court to file a Bill in the Court of Chancery or Exchequer, to oblige such Defaulters either to pay up their Calls, or relinquish their Shares to the Company.

III. And whereas the former Calls have not hitherto been complyed with, it is further proposed, that the Court of Assistants be impower'd to dispose of any Number of new Shares, (not exceeding 5000) in such Manner and to such Persons as they shall think fit; but not at less than 40 *s. per* Share, to be free from this new and former Calls, with the Allowance of 12 *d. per* Share for prompt Payment.

This is the best Method your Court of Assistants could think of to put all the present Adventurers as near as possible upon an equal footing; for as it would be unreasonable to expect a Profit without paying the Calls, so it would be equally unjust for any Person to continue an Adventurer at the Expence and Hazard of another.

If any Proprietor should be excluded for not paying the Calls, their Shares will be sunk to the Benefit of those who comply with the same.

Your Court of Directors think it Needless to use any Arguments to shew the Necessity of an Unanimous Concurrence in the Method proposed, without which, or some other effectual Means to raise Money, all that is already advanced will be in Danger of being lost; and the well-wishers to the Company who have paid their Calls, can have no Benefit, but an intire Disappointment, occasion'd by those, who tho' they appear desirous to be Adventurers, yet omit paying what is Incumbent on them, to the great Prejudice of the other Proprietors.

The Money that comes in upon the past and present Call, as also by the 10,000 *l.* to be raised by the Sale of 5000 new Shares added to the Stock, will be such an effectual Fund, to work the Mines, and Manufacture the Produce thereof, that the Company can't avoid being establish'd upon a certain, solid and profitable Foundation, without making future Calls, or uniting with any other Society or Corporation.

An Objection was made against the Call, but was fully removed by the Duke of Richmond, Earl of Clarendon, Sir R. Knipe, Sir Fisher Tench, Mr Ward and others; and then the General Court agreed to empower the Court of Assistants to call in One Pound *per* Share, and to sell 5000 new Shares, as proposed by them for raising an immediate Sum to carry on the Company's Affairs to the best Advantage.

It was remarkable, that when the Question was put by the Governor, there was but one Hand held up against it.

per Share to such Proprietors as pay the said Call in 15 Days.

II. That such Proprietors who do not comply with this and the former Call within a Month, be Mulct 2*s*. for each Call in Arrear; and in case they should not pay the said Calls and Mulcts, that the Court of Assistants be directed and impower'd by this General Court to file a Bill in the Court of Chancery or Exchequer, to oblige such Defaulters either to pay up their Calls, or relinquish their Shares to the Company.

III. And whereas the former Calls have not hitherto been complied with, it is further proposed, that the Court of Assistants be impower'd to dispose of any Number of new Shares, (not exceeding 5000) in such Manner and to such Persons as they shall think fit, but not at less than 40*s*. *per* Share, to be free from this new and former Calls, with the Allowance of 12*d*. *per* Share for prompt Payment.

This is the best Method your Court of Assistants could think of to put all the present Adventurers as near as possible upon an equal footing; for as it would be unreasonable to expect a Profit without paying the Calls, so it would be equally unjust for any Person to continue an Adventurer at the Expence and Hazard of another.

If any Proprietor should be excluded for not paying the Calls, their Shares will be sunk to the Benefit of those who comply with the same.

Your Court of Directors think it Needless to use any Arguments to show the Necessity of an Unanimous Concurrence in the Method proposed, without which, or some other effectual Means to raise Money, all that is already advanced will be in Danger of being lost; and the well-wishers to the Company who have paid their Calls, can have no Benefit, but an entire Disappointment, occasion'd by those, who tho' they appear desirous to be Adventurers, yet omit paying what is Incumbent on them, to the great Prejudice of the other Proprietors.

The Money that comes in upon the past and present Call, as also by the 10,000*l*. to be raised by the sale of 5000 new Shares added to the Stock, will be such an effectual Fund, to work the Mines, and Manufacture the Produce thereof, that the Company can't avoid being establish'd upon a certain, solid and profitable Foundation, without making future Calls, or uniting with any other Society or Corporation.

An Objection was made against the Call, but was fully removed by the Duke of Richmond, Earl of Clarendon, Sir R. Knipe, Sir Fisher Tench, Mr. Ward and others; and then the General Court agreed to empower the Court of Assistants to call in One Pound *per* Share, and to sell 5000 new Shares, as proposed by them for raising an immediate Sum to carry on the Company's Affairs to the best Advantage.

It was remarkable, that when the Question was put by the Governor from the Chair, there was but one Hand held up against it.

THE OLD COPPER WORKS, SWANSEA, SHEWING THE CIRCULAR ARRANGEMENT OF COPPER FURNACES.
FROM AN ENGRAVING FROM THE ORIGINAL IN POSSESSION OF COL GRANT FRANCIS, F.S.A.

Swansea Harbour.

IT is in a great degree due to the FACILITIES FOR SHIPPING in Swansea that the COPPER TRADE has established itself there; these facilities have from time to time been greatly improved upon, otherwise, in all probability, or as may be said to be the rule, the trade would have taken to itself wings and have established itself elsewhere. The necessity for *Docks* in Swansea has always been unquestionable, but the port seems to have enjoyed in times past the sometimes questionable advantage of being the subject of numerous consultations; at the same time the want of the gift of clear prevision, as shewn by the Swansea Harbour Trustees, has caused Bristol to lose its chance and its position among the great ports of the COUNTRY; and on the opposite coast the time was when Bideford was the largest western port in England, in the days of the Armada sending more ships to fight the Spaniards than any other in Her Majesty's dominions.

The first gentleman consulted was Captain Huddart, F.R.S., whose name is very familiar to practical engineers of the present day, though living in the beginning of the present century, and it seems his opinion was often sought by Harbour Authorities and was said to attend to these things principally for amusement, never making a charge. The Swansea Harbour Trustees composed, as far as we can gather, of the following gentlemen of the Town, viz.:

SURVIVING REPRESENTATIVE TRUSTEES.

Richard Row.	William Padley.
William Jeffreys.	Richard Phillips.
Wm. Grove.	David Rowland.
C. R. Jones.	Charles Collins.
Rob. Prance.	Thomas Lott.
Griff. Jenkins.	Griffith Hitchings.

George Haynes.

Lord Vernon, Representative Trustee.

thereupon Resolved that "if it would appear that Captain Huddart had made surveys for the improvement of harbours, and that work has been done in consequence of them, he should be offered fifty guineas beyond his expenses."

One of the first things Captain Huddart mentions in the Report consequent upon this Resolution was that "Dispatch is the life of Trade, and is the general principal next to safety that gives one port an advantage over another, provided the internal situation is much the same, *dispatch in the end*, finds its own account, as all detention ultimately falls upon the freight." From the situation of Swansea in the Bristol Channel, and the large mineral manufacturing district with which it is connected, it must at all times command a very large portion of the Trade of South Wales, which admits of almost unlimited extension. It has been remarked that she possesses advantages which are denied to other ports, and it rests with those to whose hands her interests are committed to turn them *to proper account*.

Prior to this, the first Trustees of Swansea Harbour, appointed so far back as 1791, promptly erected a *doubled*

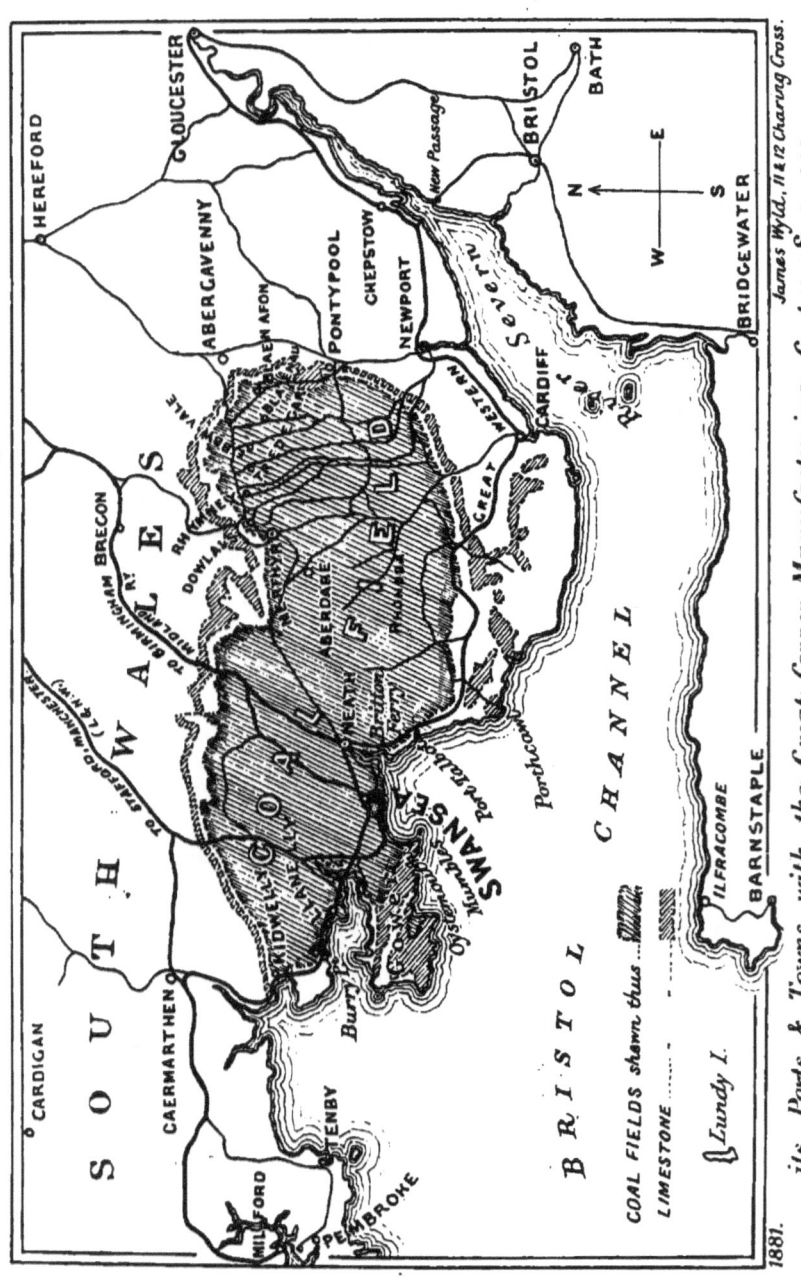

THIS REDUCED COPY OF AN ORIGINAL DRAWING IN THE POSSESSION OF THE HARBOUR TRUSTEES SHOWING THE EXIT OF THE RIVER TAWE ITS DOCK & RAILWAY APPROACHES.

beacon on the Mumbles Head, which marked out Swansea and the direction of the Harbour. From that time down to the present day it has always been stated, in the first instance, by the Admiralty Surveyors as *an important fact* that Swansea Harbour is always *accessible to strangers* that may arrive in the Bay when blowing *too strong for pilots* to get off.

Under the fostering care of the Swansea Harbour Trustees the Port has grown to its present magnitude and in connection with which there is no beneficial interest whatever to the twenty-six Trustees, the Swansea Harbour Trust being governed much upon the same principle as the Mersey Dock and Harbour Board except that in the case of the latter there is no one responsible head to whom all can refer or confer with, hence it is not surprising that Liverpool has found, and is finding every day, that there is strong competition from South Wales, for this Officer can act promptly where the exigencies of the trade or the working of the Harbour require immediate decision. Every exertion has been made to improve the present capability of the Port by deepening the entrance of the channel, and by providing a new dock which may be entered by the largest ships upon any tide of the year. The central stone of the lock of this New Dock was laid with great public rejoicing by H. Hussey Vivian, Esq., M.P., on the 31st of March, 1880, and in his speech at the public banquet afterwards he made the following interesting statement:—" The geographical position of Swansea is manifestly as good as it possibly can be. The distance from Lundy Island to the pier head at Swansea is but 40 miles east, while to the Bute Docks it is 60, and 75 to Newport. Taking into consideration the time of the tide flowing, and presuming a vessel to sustain a speed of 10 knots from Lundy Island, one third of the vessels passing up the channel would save a tide by coming to Swansea only. A vessel coming into Swansea would leave Swansea seven hours sooner than Cardiff and be that much further on her way. He hoped soon we should have an improved light at the Mumbles. When that is done there will be very few nights in the year when a ship would not be able to make the Port of Swansea without anchoring at all." Another fact sometimes lost sight of is, that bad weather prevails more at full and change of the moon than at spring tides and at neap tides. It naturally follows favourable opportunities of beating to sea are often lost for want of water at the neaps; another fact is that the range of tide at Swansea *not being so great* as it is at Cardiff and Newport, the fall of the tides at the latter place for example being nearly half as fast again as at Swansea, presents an element of danger of no mean character; more time *is necessarily at command at Swansea* on tide for the working of the Harbour, and vessels *are not detained in the roadstead* until they receive official permission to enter the Dock *as is the case at Cardiff*. The "Economist' Newspaper last year draws special attention to the rapid growth of the Port of Swansea, which the New Dock is designed to continue, and notwithstanding the great depression, it gives the figures of the great increase in the shipping trade, remarking that in 1850 the capacity of ships entering Swansea but little exceeded a quarter of a million tons, while in 1876 it reached a million tons, and the "Economist" was of opinion that Swansea appeared destined to rise yet higher in the scale of our home shipping ports, though not in the slightest degree depreciating the characteristics or local utility of other ports in the Bristol Channel. It is obvious that in these days of complete railway communication the port lying nearest to the sea commanding at its entrance sufficient depth of water, possesses special advantages which only require energy and the well directed expenditure of capital to turn to the proper account, a well constructed harbour being something more than a mere speculative undertaking, for it is almost certain to bring vast wealth, power, and influence to the city with which it is connected. The Trustees now desire by economy and good management to *draw a trade to the port* and not drive it away by heavy taxation; they have repeatedly reduced materially their rates on shipping and goods, and it may be asserted they would never have been so liberal towards the public if they were not themselves, as a body, in affluent circumstances. The public, never a very thoughtful body, view with jealousy the prosperity of any such body and impute it to their (the public) patronage, but the truth is, it is more generally *due to good and careful management*, and *especially to economy* in their capital expenditure.

Swansea has been referred to by the London Press of late as "a very Fortunate Town," and it will be a matter of surprise if it does not secure a share, and perhaps the larger share, of the Bristol Channel Trade; the "Coal and Iron Trade Review" remarking that Swansea has, in some quarters, long been credited with taking but a secondary part, as an Export, of one of the largest manufacturing districts of the kingdom, will, from the near date of the opening of new East Dock, prove to do so no longer, for these are days when merchants and ship owners will seek and secure facilities for the prosecution of their business regardless of all local and inferior considerations.

There is no other harbour in the Kingdom where such an amount of work is *done on a given space* as at SWANSEA.

The County of Glamorgan contains nearly one-third of the whole *population* of Wales.

The *acreage* of the County is *one-eighth* of the whole.

Its gross *rental* is *one-half* of the entire Principality.

And the *population* of Swansea is one-fifth of that of the County of Glamorgan. Important proportions to remember, and, if correct, to base calculations upon.

The rates levied on Shipping are the same as they were 25 *years ago*, on the average 6d. per ton nett register all round, whilst at Liverpool during the same period they have increased to over 11d.

This brief notice may be concluded by adding a list of the Trustees in office at the three great epochs in the History of the Harbour, 1851, 1859, and 1872, beyond those already embodied as holding office on the 24th June, 1791, described as the Surviving Representative Trustees at p. 174.

NORTH DOCK, OPENED JANUARY 1st, 1851.

The DUKE OF BEAUFORT, K.G.   MARQUIS OF WORCESTER.
F. P. HOOPER.   FRANCIS PRICE.
J. G. JEFFREYS.   C. COLLINS.
A. MURRAY.

Proprietary—

RICHARD AUBREY.	THOS. S. BENSON.
HENRY BATH.	STARLING BENSON.
L. W. DILLWYN.	L. L. DILLWYN.
DAVID FRANCIS.	R. D. GOUGH.
P. S. GRENFELL.	CHRISTOPHER JAMES.
C. R. JONES.	W. MARTIN.
J. W. JAMES.	G. B. MORRIS.
JAS. POOLEY.	JOHN RICHARDSON.
C. H. SMITH.	JOHN J. STRICK.
H. H. VIVIAN.	J. H. VIVIAN.
W. WALTERS.	THOS. WALTERS.

MICHAEL WILLIAMS.

Corporation—

S. BENSON.	JOHN GLASBROOK.
G. G. BIRD.	T. GLOVER.
W. K. EATON.	W. HALLAM.
T. B. ESSERY.	J. W. JAMES.
G. GRANT-FRANCIS.	M. J. MICHAEL.
JOHN OAKSHOT.	C. H. SMITH.
THOS. OWEN.	W. H. SMITH.
E. M. RICHARDS.	T. E. THOMAS.

OWEN G. WILLIAMS.

Of the above there are present Members of the Trust—

H. H. VIVIAN.   L. L. DILLWYN.
JOHN GLASBROOK.   FRANCIS PRICE.

Living, but not now Members of the Trust—

OWEN G. WILLIAMS.   G. GRANT-FRANCIS.

SOUTH DOCK OPENED SEPTEMBER 23rd, 1859.

Trustees—

STARLING BENSON.   JOHN W. JAMES.
F. P. HOOPER.   CHAS. COLLINS.
RICHARD HALL.   FRANCIS PRICE.
JOHN GASKOIN.   JAMES P. BUDD.
H. H. VIVIAN.   JOHN JOSE STRICK.
C. H. SMITH.   SYDNEY HALL.
D. FRANCIS.   THOS. ELFORD.
P. S. GRENFELL.   HY. J. BATH.
                L. L. DILLWYN.

Corporation—

T. E. THOMAS.   J. TREV. JENKIN.
E. M. RICHARDS.   J. ROLLEY TRIPP.
JOHN HOARE.   J. C. RICHARDSON.
JOHN GLASBROOK.   GEO. B. STRICK.
                JOHN OAKSHOT.

Of the above there are now Trustees—

FRANCIS PRICE.   JOHN GASKOIN.
H. H. VIVIAN.   L. L. DILLWYN.
JOHN GLASBROOK.   J. C. RICHARDSON.
            GEORGE B. STRICK.

Now living but not now Trustees—

J. TREV. JENKIN.   JAS. P. BUDD.

The oldest Trustee is L. L. Dillwyn, 1840.

The next oldest, H. H. Vivian, 1848.

TRUSTEES, 1872.

Ex-Officio.

CHARLES BAKER.	EDW. STRICK.
R. HALL.	FRANCIS PRICE.

JOHN GASKOIN.

Proprietary—

STARLING BENSON.	J. P. BUDD.
H. H. VIVIAN.	C. H. SMITH.
W. H. FRANCIS.	J. GLASBROOK.
SYDNEY HALL.	G. B. STRICK.
P. S. GRENFELL.	ALFRED STERRY.
HY. J. BATH.	L. L. DILLWYN.

Corporation—

W. H. BROWN.	E. R. DANIEL.
THOMAS DAVIES.	THOMAS FORD.
J. JONES JENKINS.	J. LIVINGSTON.
M. MOXHAM.	T. PHILLIPS.

FRANK ASH YEO.

Of these, the following are still Trustees—

Ex-Officio—

C. BAKER.	ED. STRICK.
F. PRICE.	JOHN GASKOIN.

Proprietary—

H. H. VIVIAN.	W. H. FRANCIS.
JOHN GLASBROOK.	G. B. STRICK.

L. L. DILLWYN.

Corporation—

E. R. DANIEL.	T. DAVIES.
T. FORD.	J. JONES JENKINS.

F. A. YEO.

Living, but no longer Trustees—

J. P. BUDD.	W. H. BROWN.
J. LIVINGSTON.	M. MOXHAM.

T. PHILLIPS.

TRUSTEES, 1881.

Ex-Officio—

THE EARL OF JERSEY, J.P. CHARLES BAKER.
EDWARD STRICK. FRANCIS PRICE, J.P.
JOHN GASKOIN.

Proprietary—

CHARLES BATH, J.P. THOMAS FORD, J.P., Alderman.
JNO. RICHARDSON FRANCIS, J.P.
FRANK ASH YEO, J.P., Alderman. HY. HUSSEY VIVIAN, M.P., J.P.
JNO. JONES JENKINS, J.P., Alderman, MAYOR.
THOMAS CORY, J.P. LEWIS LLEWELYN DILLWYN, M.P., J.P.
WM. HARRIES FRANCIS. JOHN GLASBROOK, J.P.
JNO. CROW RICHARDSON, J.P., HIGH SHERIFF.
GEO. BURDEN STRICK, J.P.

Corporation—

EDWARD BATH. ED. HENRY BATH.
ROBT. DICKSON BURNIE. EDW. RICE DANIEL, J.P., Alderman.
THOMAS DAVIES, Alderman. WM. FRED. RICHARDS, J.P.
JOHN CADY. WM. ROBINSON SMITH.
WM. THOMAS, J.P., Alderman.

OFFICERS, &c.

ROBERT CAPPER, Assoc. Inst. C.E.,
*General Superintendent of the Docks, Railways, and Estate;
Royal Commissioner on Tonnage.*

Clerk and Solicitor—
FRANCIS JAMES.

Treasurers.
THE GLAMORGANSHIRE BANKING COMPANY.

Engineer-in-Chief—
JAMES ABERNETHY, F.R.S.E., Pres. Inst C.E.,
4, Delahay Street, Westminster.

Resident Engineer—
AUGUSTUS JAMES SCHENK.

Cashier—	*Accountant—*
JAMES CHARLES COKE.	WILLIAM HOSKINS.
Collector—	*Auditor—*
ROBERT JOHN MURPHY.	GEORGE ALLEN.

Harbour Master—
ROBERT CAPPER, F.R.G.S.

Deputy Harbour Master—
JOHN ROSSER.

Harbour Master's Assistants—

GEORGE ROSSER.	SAMUEL HARMAN.
JOHN BEVAN.	JOHN WOODMAN.
Foreman of Works—	*Keeper of Pier Light—*
ALEXANDER RITCHIE.	JAMES W. TURPIE.

Keeper of Mumbles Light—
ABRAHAM ACE.

Index.

A.

	PAGE.
Aberavon Copper Works	96, 103
Aberthaw Lime	112
Acid Chambers at Hafod	155
Acts of Parliament	117, 141
Action against English Copper Company	143, 159
Admiralty, adoption of Muntz's Metal by	123
Adventurers. *See* Fortunate Adventurers.	
Alexandra (H.R.H. the Princess), Armorials of	172
Alum, an evil humour in Copper, &c.	33, 60
Amlwch Copper Works	136
Anglesea Copper Mines	78, 122, 133
Anne, Queen	v., 84, 90—92, 105
Antimony, an evil humour in Copper	32
Appendix	151
Argentiferous Ores and Early Smelters	13
Aristocracy, Copper Trading by	170
Arms, Heraldic, of Companies, &c.	[79, 89, 130, 131
—— of Wales (H.R.H. the Prince's), iii., 89	
Arsenic, an evil humour in Copper	31
——, utilization of	147
Arsenic and Copper Company	146
Ashburnham, Lord	144
Assay of Copper and Silver	13
Assay Master (Wm. Humphrey), grant to	58
"Assays" of Lazarus Ecker	70, 72
Associated Miners of Cornwall	126

B.

	PAGE.
Bacon, Sir Nicholas	70
Bankart and Sons	144, 145
Bank-y-Gockus Copper Works	101, 147
Barclay, Mr.	145
Barnz, Alderman	35
Bath, E.	144
Bath and Company	130
"Battery," meaning of	57
See Mineral and Battery Works.	
Beaufort, Duchess of	119
Beaufort, Duke of, 87, 99, 112, 126, [136, 141, 144, 155	
Beaufort Iron Plate Company	111
Bedford, Duke of	70
Bedfordshire, Mine in	73
Betts, Mr.	135
Bevan, Messrs.	98, 120, 130
Bigg, T.	128
Birmingham Copper Company	127, 131
—— Rose Copper Company	131
—— and Risca Copper Company	135
Black Copper	20, 27, 33
Black-lead Pencils	73
"Black Raven," Southwark	87
Black Stone, an evil humour in Copper	33
Black Vale Copper Works	145
Boards and Directors	86
Bokellye, in Cornwall	4
Bond, Sir W.	64
Bone Ashes, sent from London	73
Box, G., of Liége	73

INDEX.

	PAGE.
Brass (or Latten)	39, 57, 74
—— Battery Company	79
—— Melters	94
—— Trade Tokens	161
—— Wire Works	102, 131
—— Works	74, 122
Breton, Mr.	91
Brewer, Mackworth v.	81
Bridgewater, coals sent to	84
Bristol, lead from	85, 90
Bristol Brass and Copper Co.	102, 133
—— Brass Wire Company	102
—— Brass Works	122
—— Channel Trade	177
—— Copper Works	102
British Copper Company	129
British Museum, Documents, &c., in	74, 81, 99
Briton Ferry Copper Works	145
Bullion sent from Neath to London	96
Burd, W.	35
Burgh, J.	87, 98
Burleigh, Lord	35, 37
Bushel, Mr.	73
Bwaple, J.	17, 148

C.

Cabinet of Coins and Medals (the Author's)	161
Cadoxtan j. Neath	68
Cæsar, Sir Julius	63
Calamine	57, 58, 74
Calbeck Mines	25, 28, 29
"Calcator," an evil humour in Copper, &c.	32, 72
"Cambrian," letters to	99, 151
Cambrian Copper Works	142
—— Pottery Works	96, 99, 102

	PAGE.
Cape Copper Mining Company	145
Cape of Good Hope Copper Ores	145
Cardiganshire, Lead Mines, &c., in	73, 84
Carew, the Cornish Historian	vii., 1
Carmac and Company	78
Carnesew, J.	18
Carnsewe, W.	1, 6, 9—25
Cash Notes	135
Cecil, Mr. Secretary	25
——, Robert Lord	63
Centres of Copper Smelting	100
Chadwick's "De Foe" quoted	81
Chambers, T.	82
—— and Company	78
Charcoal	20, 67
Charles II., "Mines Royal" in reign of	37
Charters, Royal. *See under* Names of Sovereigns.	
Cheadle Copper Works	36, 78, 124
Children, education of poor	85
Chimneys, great	142, 144
Chauncy, Mr.	87
Clarendon, Earl of	171
Clark, Sir C.	101
Clyne Wood Copper Works	145
Coal, in connection with a lease	142
—— of Neath, &c., 42, 82, 85, 91, 117, [133, 149	
"Coal and Iron Trade Review," quoted	177
Coins and Medals, 73, 89, 102, 121, 161 *See* Copper Coinage.	
Common Seals of Companies	80
Cooper, Lord Ashley	69
Copies of this Work, presented	ix.
Copper	34, 57, 78
Copper Cakes	122
—— Coinage	102, 121

INDEX.

	PAGE.
Copper Companies	57, 78
—— Furnaces	75
—— Houses	131
—— Miners' Company, 82, 104, 105, 142, [143	
—— Mines	29, 169
—— Ores 10, 24, 33, 74, 83, 121, 169	
—— Pyrites	169
—— Refiner, &c.	20, 24
—— Roste	20, 27, 33
—— Sales	169
—— Slags	81, 130
—— Smelting ... vii., 1, 27, 78, 99, 133	
"Copper Smelting," by J. H. Vivian	138
—— Smoke, 75, 110, 123, 137, 142, 151, [153, 157—160	
—— Stone	27
—— Tokens ... 79, 124—135, 161	
—— Trade ... 35, 121, 148, 149, 173	
—— Trading, by the Aristocracy ...	170
Copper Works :—	
Aberavon	96, 103
Amlwch	136
Anglesea	78, 122, 133
Bank-y-Gockus	101, 147
Birmingham ...	127, 131, 135
Black Vale	145
Bristol	102, 133
British	129
Briton Ferry	145
Cambrian	142
Cheadle	36, 78, 124
Clyne Wood	145
Crown	125
Cwmavan 100, 142, 144	
Cwmbwrlais	145
Danygraig	145, 146
English 78, 81, 102, 142, 143, 159	

	PAGE.
Copper Works—continued.	
Entral	75
Forest	110, 113
Fortunate Adventurers	86
Governor and Company ...	75, 81
Gnoll 75, 77, 86, 102	
Hafod ... 126, 127, 136, 153—155	
Harfords'	78, 132
Hayle	75
Keswick	29, 72
Lamberts'	144
Landore, 96, 101, 102, 127, 129, 146	
Lane's	96, 100, 101
Laxey Neath	125
Little Landore	146
Liverpool	78
Llanelly	100, 134
Llangavelach, 99, 106, 110, 111, 146	
Llansamlet	146, 148
Loughor	100, 136
Mackworths', 76, 77, 80—96, 102, 105	
Margam	96
Mason and Elkington's	144
Melincrethyn	75, 102
Merry's	146
Middle Bank 117, 120, 121, 126	
Mine Adventurers 80—82, 102	
Mineral and Battery, 14, 37, 40, [57, 58, 80	
Mines Royal, 6, 27, 35, 37, 40, [57, 68—79, 142	
Monmouthshire ... 74, 134, 135	
Morfa	141
Nant-ryd-y-vilais	130
Neath. *See* Neath.	
Newlyn	74
Old Forest	155
Pattens'	35—73

O

	PAGE.
Copper Works —*continued*.	
Pembrey	100, 144
Penclawdd	100, 125, 136, 137
Port Talbot	143
Port Tenant	144
Redbrook	74, 81, 82, 102
Red Jacket	144, 145
Rio Tinto	169
Risca Union	134, 135
Rose	77, 78, 127, 128
Saint Helen's	124
Screw's Hole	102
Spitty	136
Swansea. *See* Swansea.	
Taibach	75, 82, 96, 100—105, 153
Tawe River	146
Thompson's	147
Union	134, 135
Upper Bank	120, 121
White Rock	115, 132, 133
Yorkshire	78
Copperas	27, 60
Corisumlock Mine	73
Cornelius, J.	120, 121
Cornwall, Copper Ores, &c., of,	24, 102, 122, 126, 133, 148
Corporation of Neath and Companies	94
Coster, T.	116—119
Coventry Tokens	164
Criminals, as Workmen in Mines	88
Crown Copper Works	125
Culverwell	35
Cumberland Copper Ores	26
Customer Smythe. *See* Smythe.	
Cwmavan Copper Works	100, 142, 144
Cwmbwrlais Copper Works	145

D.

	PAGE.
Daehne, Mr.	155
Daniel, Mr. (probably Daniel Hoechstetter). *See* Hoechstetter.	
——, Nevill, and Company	100
Daniell, Mr.	28—36
Daniels, Messrs.	133, 134
Danygraig Copper Works	145, 146
Davies, J.	93
Davy, Sir Humphry, on copper smoke	137
De Foe, on extracting silver from lead	81
Deldon, Van	42
Demetrius	42, 73, 74
Denham, Mr.	7, 8, 15—23
Dickenson, J.	127
Dillwyn, Mr. L. L.	179
Dinorben, Lord	133
Dovey, ore from	85, 95
Doyley, Mr.	126
"Drapier's Letters" quoted	103
Ducket, Alderman	35
——, Ant.	35
——, G.	35
Duckett, Sir L.	6
Dudley, J.	35
Dues of Swansea Borough	147
Dutch (or German) Miners	vi, 3, 24
Dynevor, Lord	68, 125

E.

Eaglebush Family	83
East India Company, exportation of copper by	122
"Economist" quoted	176
Edgecom, Mr.	5
Edmond, W.	69, 78, 101, 111
Edmondson's "Complete Body of Heraldry" quoted	79
Edward IV.	70, 98
Elizabeth, Queen	v., vi., viii., 23, 24, 38, 58, 69—72, 101, 121, 148

INDEX.

	PAGE.
Elkington, Mr.	100
Elton, Sir A.	102
English Copper Company	78, 81, 102, [142, 143, 159
Entral Copper Works	75
Ercker, Lazarus, the metallurgist,	70—72
Esher, wire works at	73
Evans, D.	83
Evans, Sir H.	83, 85
Evans's "Tours in South Wales" quoted	111, 124, 131

F.

Faraday, Prof., on copper smoke	137
Fazakerly, N.	100
Feeld, M.	35
Fire Bricks	121
Fleet Prison, Pettus imprisoned in	71
Forest, T.	94, 127, 131
Forest Copper Works	110, 113
—— Tin-Plate Works	111
—— Zinc Manufactory	111
Fortunate Adventurers, committee of	86
Foster, Sir W.	136
Freeman and Company	78, 131
Frosse, Ulricke	2—24, 69, 121, 148
Fuel (Patent) Works	151
Furnaces	90, 146

G.

Gamage, Alderman	35
——, W.	42
Gaunse, Jochim	24—34
George I.	170
German Miners. *See* Dutch Miners.	
Germans, in relation to Metallurgy, vi., 24, [74, 94, 138, 155, 156	
Gerstenhöfer's Patent	75, 154—158

	PAGE.
Gibbon, Edward (ancestor of the Historian)	102, 107, 108
Glamorganshire, population, &c., of	177
——, smelting furnaces in	84
Glascott and Sons	142
Glasmount Works (view of)	104
Gloucestershire, lapis calaminaris, &c., in	73, 74
Gnoll Castle, papers at	86, 88
—— Copper Works, &c.	75, 77, 86, 102
Gode's Gifte Myne	25
Gold, in connection with Copper	147
——, tenth part of, to the Queen	39
—— Mines in Bedfordshire and Gloucestershire	73
Goldsmith's Mark on Neath Maces	93
Governor and Company of Copper Miners	75, 81
Grenfell, Messrs.	75, 122, 123, 128, 142
Grose's "Tour" quoted	74
Guardians and Governors of Mines for Edward IV. and Henry VII.	70
Guest, Mr.	134
Gurlt's Smoke Process	123
Gwyn, F.	89

H.

Hadland, Mr.	146
Hafod Copper Works	126, 127, 136, [153—155
—— Phosphate Works	154
Halifax, Marquis of	69, 70
Hall, Colonel	103
Hall's "Book of South Wales" quoted	101, 103, 110
Hallam, Mr.	111
Hanbury, Mr.	77
Harfords and Company	78, 132

	PAGE.
Hawkins' "Silver Coins of England" quoted	89
Hawkins, T.	87, 95
Hayle, copper furnaces at	75
Hayward, J.	95, 96
Henry VII.	70
Herald's College. *See* Arms.	
Hering, H.	8, 9, 16
Hermann, B. S.	153
Herne, Sir J.	104, 121
Herrmann, G. B.	138
Hoechstetter (Hechstetter, or Hogstetter), Messrs.	25, 36, 38, 40, 42, 60
Holland, copper kettles, &c., from	122
Hooper, F. P.	101
Hopkins, L.	93
House of Commons' Committee on Copper Trade	121
Huddart, Captain	173
Humby, Mr.	125
Humphrey, W.	39, 58—64
Hunt, Mr. Robert	32, 169
Hussey, R.	136

I.

Illustrations, List of	x.
Imprison, power of companies to	66
Ireland, coinage for	102
——, copper ores from	103
——, cruelties in	103
Iron, an evil humour in copper	33
——, making of, with pit coal	94
—— Bars and Rails	143
—— Wire Mills	73

J.

James I.	14, 38—40, 57
Jennings, Mr.	145, 146
Jersey, Earl of	87, 116, 122, 126, [136, 141—145, 148

	PAGE.
Jochim, Mr. *See* Gaunse, Jochim.	
John Bevan's Works	120
Jones, C.	136
——, P.	106
Juries, exemption of officers of mining company from serving on	66
Justices of the Peace, complaints against	82—85

K.

Karwethers, H.	18
Keates, Mr.	36, 77, 78, 102, 107, [116, 124, 125, 128, 135, 136
Kebulls of Copper Ore	25
Kent House Lead Works	126
Keswick Copper Mines	29, 72
Kilvey Manor	119
Knight's "England" quoted	103
Knipe, Sir R.	171

L.

Lambert, C.	144
Lancaster, Sir J.	64
Landore Alkali Works	153
—— Arsenic and Copper Company	146
—— Copper Works	96, 101, 102, [127, 129
—— Tin-plate Works	99, 101
Lane, Dr.	96, 100, 101
Langfforde, W.	15
Lapis Calaminaris	39
Latten	39, 43, 57, 58
Laxey Neath Company	125
Lead, extracting silver from	81
——, refining of	91
—— at Dovey	95
——, in connection with Copper Smelting	147
—— and Silver Smelting Works	84, 142

INDEX.

	PAGE.
Lead Mines	72, 73, 84, 120
—— Ore, smelting of...	83
Ledes, R.	25
Leeds, Duke of	81, 88
Leicester, Earl of	35
Leigh, Capel	76
Le Play...	157
Litharge	83, 87
Little Landore Copper Works	146
Little Taunton (Gloucestershire), gold mine at	73
Liverpool, Copper Works near	78
—— City, heraldic device of...	127
Llanelly Copper Works	100, 134
Llangavelach Copper Works	99, 106, 110, [111, 146
Llangennech Estate	136
Llansamlet Copper Works	146, 148
Lockwood Messrs.	102, 115
——, Morris, and Company	78, 101 [110, 111
Logan Copper Mine	10, 14
Logan, Sir W. E.	11
Loughor Copper Works	100, 136
—— River	126

M.

Maces and Seal of Neath	93
Mackworth Family,	76, 77, 80—96, 102, [105
—— v. Brewer...	81
Malkin, Dr.	116
"Manillas" for African Slave Trade	113
Manlove, R.	71
Mansell Family	83, 87, 115, 117, 122
——, Lord	115
Margam Park Leases	96
Martin, Mr.	17, 20, 22

	PAGE.
Mason and Elkington...	100, 144
Medallets or Cheques...	168
Medals. *See* Coins.	
Melincrethyn Copper Works...	75, 102
——, Mine Adventurers at	80
Memorandum on the Copper Trade...	149
Men prest at Neath	92
Merry, E.	146
Metalliferous Manufactures, early history of	vii.
Middle Bank Copper Works,	117, 120, [121, 126
Middle Dock	120
Miers, Mr.	77
Mine Adventurers' Company	80—82, 102
Mineral and Battery Works Society	14 [37, 40, 57, 58, 80
Mines, early guardians of	70
Mines Royal,	v., 6, 27, 35, 37, 40, 57, 68— [79, 142
—— —— Book, extracts from	75—78
—— —— Sailing Vessel	78
Mining Localities, in Ercker's book	72
"Mining Master"	14
Mining Record Office, statistics from	169
Mining Works, early	68
Ministers' Accounts of Exchequer	98
Mint, copper coinage at	121
—— at Shrewsbury	73
Mohun, Mr.	5
Monineca	73
Monmouthshire Copper Works,	74, 134, 135
Morfa Copper Works...	141
—— Silver Works	141
Morgan, Mr. D. H. (Mayor of Neath).	124
——, Mr. O.	134
——, Mr. W.	155
Morris, Sir J.	120

	PAGE.
Morris, Mr. R....	102, 111, 131
—— and Company	99
—— and Rees...	100, 136
Morriston Spelter Works	155
Mountjoy, Lord	27, 35
Muntz's Metal...	123

N.

Nant-ryd-y-vilais Works	130
Napier and Cameron...	136
Napyan, Mr. ...	18
Neath, earliest Copper-smelting in	vii., 99
——, Coal at ...	42, 92
——, Letters posted to	91
——, Ore of, sent to Cardiganshire ...	91
"Neath and its Abbey," quoted,	vii., 92, 94
Neath Abbey Iron Company...	124
—— Canal	77
—— Cheadle Works ...	124
—— Copper Trade	148
—— Copper Works,	1, 22—26, 75, 80—[82, 88, 90, 100
—— Corporation, seal, &c., for	93
—— Lead Works	84
—— Melting House ...	9
—— Red Lead Mills...	90
—— River	68, 124
—— Silver Mills	90
Needham (or Nedham), G.	25, 29, 34, 35
——, F....	42
Nevill, C. W. ...	134
—— and Company	75, 142
Newlyn Copper Works	74
Newton, N. ...	89
—— and Cartwright ...	100
Northumberland, Earl of	70, 72
Nottinghamshire, lapis calaminaris in	74
Nuisance from Copper Smoke. *See* Copper Smoke	

O.

	PAGE.
Oaths taken by Officers of Company,	92, [105
Old Forest Copper Works .. *See* Forest Copper Works.	155
Oldisworth, Mr.	115
Ores, Metalliferous, reserved to the Crown	36
—— of Copper. *See* Copper Ores.	
Otes, J....	16, 18

P.

Padley and Andrews ...	164
Parsons, R. ...	78
Patent Fuel	151
Patents from the Crown,	25, 38, 40, 57, [58, 91, 104, 105, 151, 153
Patten Family...	35—37
Peat used in Smelting	26
Pemberton, Sir J.	64
Pembrey Copper Works	100, 144
Pembroke, Earl of	35, 42, 63, 69
Penclawdd Copper Works,	100, 125, 136, [137
Pengored Lead Mines	120
Percy, Dr., "Metallurgy" of, &c.,	vii., 23, [36, 99, 134, 151
Perrin Sands Mineral Works,	5, 8—11, 22
Pettus, Sir John	69—71
Phillips, Prof., on Copper Smoke	137
——, R.	116
Philosopher's Stone ...	71
Pipe House	146
Pirates, as Workmen in Mines	88
Place, J.	77, 124
——, R.	74, 75
"Poder"	102
Poem on Havod	139

INDEX.

	PAGE.
Pollard, Mr.	99, 100
Popkins, Mr.	97
Port Talbot Copper Works ...	143
Port Tennant Copper Works	144
Post Office, complaint against	91, 92
Potters' Ore delivered at Neath	90
Pottery Works. *See* Cambrian Pottery Works.	
Powell, Gabriel, 87, 98, 100, 120, 147, 148	
Precipitate of Copper...	169
Pressing men at Neath	92
Prince of Wales, arms of ...	89
Pryce's "Mineralogia Cornubiensis" quoted	75
Pryse, Sir Carbery	84
Pullox Hill (Bedfordshire), Gold mine at	73

Q.

Quicksilver, tenth part of, to the Queen	39

R.

Record Office	vi.
Redbrook Copper Works, 74, 81, 82, 102	
Red Jacket Copper Works ...	144, 145
Red Lead Mills ... ...83—85, 90	
Rees, W.	136
Refining Processes, secresy as to ...	91
Regulus	27
Rent of Smelting Mills, &c., at Neath	90
Revet, T.	35
Rhondda Neath Coke Works ...	125
Richmond, Duke of, on Copper Trading	[170
Rigby, A.	17
Rio Tinto Company	169
Risca Union Copper Company	134, 135
Roberts, T.	17
"Rods" for African Slave Trade ...	113

	PAGE.
Roe and Company 78, 124, 131	
Rolling Mills at Walthamstow ...	130
Roman Mines in Wales	73
—— Remains at Gwyndy-bach ...	119
Rose Copper Company, 77, 78, 127, 128	
Rowland, D.	85, 127
Royal Institution of South Wales, Coins presented to ...	v., 161
Royalty, early patronage of Mining Companies by	69
Rupert, Prince	69, 70

S.

Sadlers' Hall	170
Saint Anne's Copper Mine	10
Saint Helen's Copper Works ...	124
Saint Ives, Ore of 16, 17, 21	
Saint Just, Ore of 16, 17, 21	
Sales of Copper at Swansea	169
Savage, poem on Hafod attributed to	140
Savill, Mr.	134
Savoy, Master of	38
Schneider, Mr.	136
Schutz, C. ... 14, 39, 58—64, 73	
Screw's Hall Copper Works... ...	102
Sea Coals	20
Shareholders in Mines Royal Society	35
Shears and Son	136
Shrewsbury, Mint at	73
Silver in copper ... 13, 28, 73, 147	
——, tenth part of, for the Queen ...	39
—— in Wales	73
——, extracting from lead	81
—— Bullion, coining of, with Arms of Wales	89
—— Coinage	73
—— Mills at Neath	90
—— Trade Tokens	161

INDEX.

	PAGE.
Sites for Furnaces	42
Slags	95, 112, 130
Slave Trade	113
Smiles's "Huguenots" quoted	73
Smith, J.	120
——, Sir J.	46
——, T.	127
Smoke Nuisance. *See* Copper Smoke.	
Smythe, Customer, vi., 4—12, 23, 35, 37, [69, 121, 148	
Soames, Colonel	92
Somersetshire, lapis calaminaris in	74
South Kensington Museum, portrait of Queen Elizabeth in	69
Southwark, refining furnace at	87
Spar, an evil humour in Copper	34
Spence, Dixon, and Shaw	143
Spinola	35
Spitty Copper Works	136
Springham, Alderman	35
Stanley Smelting Company	122
Statistics of Swansea Copper Sales	169
Statue to Mr. J. H. Vivian	138
Stembarger, Mr.	24—31
Stephens, J.	145
Stone, J.	12, 18
Stourbridge Bricks	90
Street, Mr., engraver	93
Struvé, W. P.	143, 160
Swaine, S.	74, 75
Sulphur, an evil humour in Copper	31
——, utilization of	75, 147
Surrey Brass Works	74
Swansea and the Copper Trade, vii., 23, [36, 75, 78, 96, 99, 100, 148, 149	
——, new furnaces at	157
—— Castle, furnace in precincts of	147
—— Charters	99

	PAGE.
Swansea Copper Smoke	151
—— District, tokens current in	161—168
—— Harbour and Docks	173—182
—— Patent Fuel Works	151
—— River	126, 127, 155
—— Sales of Copper	169
—— Topographic Collection	134
Swedish Copper	113
Sweetland, Tuttle, and Company	145
Swift's "Drapier's Letters" quoted	103

T.

Taibach, new furnaces at	157
—— Copper Works, 75, 82, 96, 100—[105, 153	
Talbot, Mr.	96
Talibont Mine	73
Tamworth	35
Taverns, meeting of Mining Company at	93
Tawe River, 99—101, 115, 127, 137, 140, 149	
—— —— —— Copper Works	146
Tax on Workhouse at Neath	93
Tench, Sir F.	171
Tennant, C.	143
Thames Tunnel	112
Thomas, Rev. E.	121
——, Mr. J	39
Thompson, R. G.	147
Thurland	25, 35, 38, 40, 60
Tickettings	132, 169
Tin Plates	143
Tintern, iron wire mills at	73
Tokens (*See* Copper Tokens) v., 161, 168	
Tower, the, silver bullion taken to, 89, 95	
Townsend, Chauncey	117
Trade Tokens	161, 168
See Copper Tokens.	
Trevinian, Mr.	21
Trewoorth Mineral Works	8, 13, 14

INDEX.

	PAGE.
Troughton, Mr.	112
Trustees of Swansea Docks	175
Tunno, Mr.	136

U.

Union Copper Company	134, 135
Upper Bank Copper Works	120, 121
Usborne, Benson, and Company	112

V.

Vaughan v. Cwm-Avan Company	160
——, Messrs.	143, 153, 159, 160
Vernon, Lord	118, 174
Vessels for carrying metals from Neath to London	92
Vigors and Company	100, 143
"Visitation of Cornwall"	2
Vitriol, an evil humour in Copper, &c.	32, 34
Vivian, Mr. A. P.	106
——, Mr. H. Hussey, 75, 123, 126, 136, [137, 153, 154, 175, 179	
——, Mr. John	100, 125, 126, 136
——, Mr. J. H.	126, 136—138, 152
——, Lord	136—138
——, Messrs., 75, 105, 106, 124, 127, 136, [141, 154—158	
—— (Vyvyan), Mr. R.	1
Volunteers, Rifle	122, 143
Vos, Cornelius de, mining of Alum and Copperas by	60

W.

Wales (H.R.H. the Prince of), Armorials of	iii., 89
—— (H.R.H. the Princess of), Armorials of	172
——, Coinage and Arms of	89
——, principality of	60, 73, 122
——, Roman mines in	73
——, silver in	73
—— (South), copper smelting in	1
——, ——, coalfield of	134
Waller, Mr.	89—93, 96
Walsingham, Mr. Secretary, vi., 24, 25, 35, 37	
Walthamstow Rolling Mills	130

	PAGE.
Ward, Mr.	92, 171
Warden of the Fleet	71
Warwick, Earl of	70
"Weigh" of Coal	83
Welch Copper Company	171
Westmoreland Copper Ores	26
Weston, Mr.	3—14, 22
White Rock Copper Works, Swansea, [115, 132, 133	
White Stone, an evil humour in Copper	34
Widnes Metal Company	169
William and Mary, charters of, &c., 72, 80, 88, 104	
Williams, Messrs. 85, 121, 131, 141, 142	
——, Sir W.	128
——, Foster, and Company, 80, 125, 128, [129, 145, 140	
——, Grenfell, and Company	122, 133
—— and Hughes	131
—— and Vivian	116, 136
Windham's "Tour in Wales" quoted, 101	
Windsor Castle, Pettus imprisoned in	71
Wind-way, foot-rid, or waggon-way	84
Winter, Sir W.	6
Wire Mills	73
Wood, W., his patent for Copper Coinage	102
Wooden Railway for Coal	84
Woods for Fuel	3
Wood's "Rivers of Wales" quoted	132
Woolwich Cadets, visits of, to Hafod	139
"Work Master"	14
Wright, J.	105
Wynsor, P.	19
Wynter, W.	35

Y.

Yellow Metal. *See* Muntz's Metal.	
Yorkshire Copper Company	78

Z.

Zinc	39, 57, 58, 67, 74
Zoffany, portrait of Bevans by	98
Zucchero, portrait of Qn. Elizabeth by	69

www.ingramcontent.com/pod-product-compliance
Lightning Source LLC
Chambersburg PA
CBHW021837230426
43669CB00008B/1002